Volume XXXVI, Nos. 3 & 4   Fall/Winter 2010

CONTENTS

Introduction

Ian Boyd

Some years ago when George W. Bush visited China, he spoke about the religious character of America in words borrowed from Chesterton. America, the President said, was a nation with the soul of a Church. It was eighty years ago that Chesterton made the second of his two American visits, the country which had welcomed him so warmly. First in the early nineteen-twenties at a time shortly before he was received into full communion with the Catholic Church and now again some ten years later, when he returned to it as a Catholic and as the guest of two well-known Catholic universities. The articles that discuss these visits were first read as papers a few months ago at Notre Dame and Holy Cross College the institutions that were his hosts during the second of his American tours, and were now celebrating the anniversary of that memorable visit. Our issue also includes various pieces that Chesterton himself wrote about America.

In the "Articles Section" there are pieces that discuss such topics as Pope Benedict's recent visit to the U.K.; Chesterton and Science; Chesterton and Belloc as solvers of the vexing problems of the contemporary world; Britain's place in the new Europe; and the social and political thought of Pope Benedict. The "Book Review Section" examines books about the Father Brown stories, about the key writings of Belloc, about Chesterton and Tolkien as theologians, and about Shakespeare and Catholicism. Among the "News and Comments" items, special attention is given to the death of Joseph Sobran, a distinguished journalist and a dear friend of the Review. The "Programme Notes" begin with a report about a Christmas event in New York City co-sponsored by Communion and Liberation and the Chesterton Institute, an event

A small section of Llyn Brianne just showing nestled between the hills that celebrated Chesterton as the poet of Christmas. The section also includes a report about an art exhibit on a Chestertonian theme held at Seton Hall University and sponsored by the Chesterton Institute. There are also accounts of Institute events held at the United States—College of the Holy Cross in Worcester, Massachusetts, the Russell Kirk Center in Mecosta Michigan and at Notre Dame University. But when one looks back at our work over the last year, it is clear that its most striking feature is the way in which it has become international. Institute conferences were held in Paris, San Sebastian, Pamplona and Madrid in Spain, Rio de Janeiro, Brazil and Santiago, Valparaiso and Puerto Varas in Chile. *The Chesterton Review* continues to add other language editions. In 2010 the Review was published not only in English, Spanish and Portuguese but also in French.

Calbuco Volcano from All Saints Lake, Chile

American Notes

G. K. Chesterton

The following is Chesterton's Introduction to an edition of the Dickens book American Notes and Pictures from Italy *published in London by J. M. Dent and Co. and in New York, 1907, by E. P. Dutton & Co.*

American Notes was written soon after Dickens had returned from his first visit to America. That visit had, of course, been a great epoch in his life; but how much of an epoch men did not truly realise until, some time after, in the middle of a quiet story about Rochester and a ridiculous architect, his feelings flamed out and flared up to the stars in "Martin Chuzzlewit." The "American Notes" are, however, interesting, because in them he betrays his feelings when he does not know that he is betraying them. Dickens's first visit to America was, from his own point of view, and at the beginning, a happy and festive experiment. It is very characteristic of him that he went among them, enjoyed them, even admired them, and then had a quarrel with them. Nothing was ever so unmistakable as his goodwill, except his illwill; and they were never far apart. And this was not, as some bloodless moderns have sneeringly insinuated, a mere repetition of the proximity between the benevolent stage and the quarrelsome stage of drink. It was a piece of pure optimism; he believed so readily that men were going to be good to him that an injury to him was something more than an injury: it was a shock. What was the exact nature of the American shock must, however, be more carefully stated.

The famous quarrel between Dickens and America, which finds its most elaborate expression in "American Notes," though its most brilliant expression in "Martin Chuzzlewit," is an incident which has been

---

Aerial view of Tiber River in Rome

much discussed and about which, nevertheless, a great deal remains to be said. But the thing which most specially remains to be said is this. This old Anglo-American quarrel was much more fundamentally friendly than most Anglo-American alliances. In Dickens's day each nation understood the other enough to argue. In our time neither nation understands itself even enough to quarrel. There was an English tradition, from Fox and eighteenth-century England; there was an American tradition from Franklin and eighteenth-century America; and they were still close enough together to discuss their differences with acrimony, perhaps, but with certain fundamental understandings. The eighteenth-century belief in a liberal civilisation was still a dogma; for dogma is the only thing that makes argument or reasoning possible. America, under all its swagger, did still really believe that Europe was its fountain and its mother, because Europe was more fully civilised. Dickens, under all his disgust, did still believe that America was in advance of Europe, because it was more democratic. It was an age, in short, in which the word "progress" could still be used reasonably; because the whole world looked to one way of escape and there was only one kind of progress under discussion. Now, of course, "progress" is a useless word; for progress takes for granted an already defined direction; and it is exactly about the direction that we disagree. Do not let us therefore be misled into any mistaken optimism or special self-congratulation upon what many people would call the improved relations between England and America. The relations are improved because America has finally become a foreign country. And with foreign countries all sane men take care to exchange a certain consideration and courtesy. But even as late as the time of Dickens's first visit to the United States, we still felt America as a colony; an insolent, offensive; and even unintelligible colony sometimes, but still a colony; a part of our civilisation, a limb of our life. And America itself, as I have said, under all its bounce and independence, really regarded us as a mother country. This being the case it was possible for us to quarrel, like kinsmen. Now we only bow and smile, like strangers.

This tone, as a sort of family responsibility, can be felt quite specially all through the satires or suggestions of these "American Notes." Dickens is cross with America because he is worried about America; as if he were its father. He explores its industrial, legal, and educational arrangements like a mother looking at the housekeeping of a married son;

he makes suggestions with a certain acidity; he takes a strange pleasure in being pessimistic. He advises them to take note of how much better certain things are done in England. All this is very different from Dickens's characteristic way of dealing with a foreign country. In countries really foreign, such as France, Switzerland, and Italy, he had two attitudes, neither of them in the least worried or paternal. When he found a thing in Europe which he did not understand, such as the Roman Catholic Church, he simply called it an old world superstition, and sat looking at it like a moonlit ruin. When he found something that he did understand, such as luncheon baskets, he burst into carols of praise over the superior sense from our civilisation and good management of Continental methods. An example of the first attitude may be found in one of his letters, in which he describes the backwardness and idleness of Catholics who would not build a Birmingham in Italy. He seems quite unconscious of the obvious truth, that the backwardness of Catholics was simply the refusal of Bob Cratchit to enter the house of Gradgrind. An example of the second attitude can be found in the purple patches of fun in "Mugby Junction"; in which the English waitress denounces the profligate French habits of providing new bread and clean food for people travelling by rail. The point is, however, that in neither case has he the air of one suggesting improvements or sharing a problem with the people engaged on it. He does not go carefully with a notebook through Jesuit schools nor offer friendly suggestions to the governors of Parisian prisons. Or if he does, it is in a different spirit; it is in the spirit of an ordinary tourist being shown over the Coliseum or the Pyramids. But he visited America in the spirit of a Government inspector dealing with something it was his duty to inspect. This is never felt either in his praise or blame of Continental countries. When he did not leave a foreign country to decay like a dead dog, he merely watched it at play like a kitten. France he mistook for a kitten. Italy he mistook for a dead dog.

But with America he could feel—and fear. There he could hate, because he could love. There he could feel not the past alone nor the present, but the future also and, like all brave men, when he saw the future he was a little afraid of it. For of all tests by which the good citizen and strong reformer can be distinguished from the vague faddist or the inhuman sceptic, I know no better test than this—that the unreal reformer sees in front of him one certain future, the future of his fad; while the real reformer sees before him ten or twenty futures among which his country must choose, and may, in some dreadful hour, choose the wrong one. The true patriot is always doubtful of victory; because he knows that he is dealing with a living thing; a thing with free will. To be certain of free will is to be uncertain of success.

The subject matter of the real difference of opinion between Dickens and the public of America can only be understood if it is thus treated as a dispute between brothers about the destiny of a common heritage. The point at issue might be stated like this. Dickens, on his side, did not in his heart doubt for a moment that England would eventually follow America along the road towards real political equality and purely republican institutions. He lived, it must be remembered, before the revival of aristocracy, which has since overwhelmed us—the revival of aristocracy worked through popular science and commercial dictatorship, and which has nowhere been more manifest than in America itself. He knew nothing of this; in his heart he conceded to the Yankees that not only was their revolution right but would ultimately be completed everywhere. But on the other hand, his whole point against the American experiment was this—that if it ignored certain ancient English contributions it would go to pieces for lack of them. Of these the first was good manners and the second individual liberty—liberty, that is, to speak and write against the trend of the majority. In these things he was much more serious and much more sensible than it is the fashion to think he was; he was indeed one of the most serious and sensible critics England ever had of current and present problems, though his criticism is useless to the point of nonentity about all things remote from him in style of civilisation or in time. His point about good manners is really important. All his grumblings through this book of "American Notes," all his shrieking satire in "Martin Chuzzlewit" are expressions of a grave and reasonable fear he had touching the future of democracy. And remember again what has been already remarked—instinctively he paid America the compliment of looking at her as the future of democracy.

The mistake which he attacked still exists. I cannot imagine why it is that social equality is somehow supposed to mean social familiarity. Why should equality mean that all men are equally rude? Should it not rather mean that all men are equally polite? Might it not quite reasonably mean that all men should be equally ceremonious and stately and pontifical? What is there specially Equalitarian, for instance, in calling your political friends and even your political enemies by their Christian name in public? There is something very futile in the way in which certain Socialist leaders call each other Tom, Dick and Harry; especially when Tom is accusing Harry of having basely imposed upon the well-known imbecility of Dick. There is something quite undemocratic in all men calling each other by the special and affectionate term "comrade"; especially when they say it with a sneer and smart inquiry about the funds. Democracy would be quite satisfied if every man called every other man "sir." Democracy would have no conceivable reason to complain if every man called every other man "your excellency" or "your holiness" or "brother of the sun and moon." The only democratic essential is that it should be a term of dignity and that it should be given to all. To abolish all terms of dignity is no more specially democratic than the Roman emperor's wish to cut off everybody's head at once was specially democratic. It involved equality certainly, but it was lacking in respect.

Dickens saw America as markedly the seat of this danger. He saw that there was a perilous possibility that republican ideals might be allied to a social anarchy good neither for them nor for any other ideals. Republican simplicity, which is difficult, might be quickly turned into Bohemian brutality, which is easy. Cincinnatus, instead of putting his hand to the plough, might put his feet on the tablecloth, and an impression prevail that it was all a part of the same rugged equality and freedom. Insolence might become a tradition. Bad manners might have all the sanctity of good manners. "There you are!" cries Martin Chuzzlewit indignantly, when the American has befouled the butter. "A man deliberately makes a hog of himself, and *that* is an Institution." But the thread of thought which we must always keep in hand in this matter is, that he would not thus have worried about the degradation of republican simplicity into general rudeness if he had not from first to last instinctively felt that America held human democracy in her hand, to exalt it or to let it fall. In one of his gloomier moments he wrote down his fear that the greatest blow ever struck at liberty would be struck by America in the failure of her misston upon the earth.

This brings us to the other ground of his alarm—the matter of liberty of speech. Here also he was much more reasonable and philosophic than has commonly been realised. The truth is that the lurid individualism of

Carlyle has, with its violent colours, "killed" the tones of most criticism of his time; and just as we can often see a scheme of decoration better if we cover some flaming picture, so you can judge nineteenth-century England much better if you leave Carlyle out. He is important to moderns because he led that return to Toryism which has been the chief feature of modernity, but his judgments were often not only spiritually false, but really quite superficial. Dickens understood the change of democracy far better than Carlyle; just as he understood the merits of democracy far better than Carlyle. And of this fact we can produce one plain evidence in the matter of which we speak. Carlyle, in his general dislike of the revolutionary movement, lumped liberty and democracy together and said that the chief objection to democracy was that it involved the excess and misuse of liberty; he called democracy "anarchy or no-rule." Dickens, with far more philosophical insight and spiritual delicacy, saw that the real danger of democracy is that it tends to the very opposite of anarchy; even to the very opposite of liberty. He lamented in America the freedom of manners. But he lamented even more the absence of freedom of opinion. "I believe there is no country on the face of the earth," he says, "where there is less freedom of opinion on any subject in reference to which there is a broad difference of opinion than in this. There! I write the words with reluctance, disappointment, and sorrow; but I believe it from the bottom of my soul. The notion that I, a man alone by myself in America, should venture to suggest to the Americans that there was one point on which they were neither just to their own countrymen nor to us, actually struck the boldest dumb Washington Irving, Prescott, Hoffman, Bryant, Halleck, Dana, "Washington Allston—every man who writes in this country is devoted to the question, and not one of them dares to raise his voice and complain of the atrocious state of the law. The wonder is that a breathing man can be found with temerity enough to suggest to the Americans the possibility of their having done wrong. I wish you could have seen the faces that I saw down both sides of the table at Hartford when I began to talk about Scott. I wish you could have heard how I gave it out. My blood so boiled when I thought of the monstrous injustice that I felt as if I were twelve feet high when I thrust it down their throats." Dickens knew no history, but he had all history behind him in feeling that a pure democracy does tend, when it goes wrong, to be too traditional and absolute. The truth is indeed a singular example of the unfair attack upon democracy in our own time. Everybody can repeat the platitude that the mob can be the greatest of all tyrants. But few realise or remember the corresponding truth which goes along with it—that the mob is the only permanent and unassailable high priest. Democracy drives its traditions too hard; but democracy is the only thing that keeps any traditions. An aristocracy must always be going after some new thing. The severity of democracy is far more of a virtue than its liberty. The decorum of a democracy is far more of a danger than its lawlessness. Dickens discovered this in his great quarrels about the copyright, when a whole nation acted on a small point of opinion as if it were going to lynch him. But, fortunately for the purpose of this argument, there is no need to go back to the forties for such a case. Another great literary man has of late visited America; and it is possible that Maxim Gorky may be in a position to state how far democracy is likely to err on the side of mere liberty and laxity. He may have found, like Dickens, some freedom of manners he did not find much freedom of morals.

Some of his minor comments are of slight but material interest—notably his very characteristic summary of the question of the Red Indian. It marks the combination between the mental narrowness and the moral justice of the old Liberal. Dickens can see nothing in the Red Indian except that he is barbaric, retrograde, bellicose, uncleanly, and superstitious-in short, that he is not a member of the special civilisation of Birmingham or Brighton. It is curious to note the contrast between the cheery, nay Cockney, contempt with which Dickens speaks of the American-Indian with that chivalrous and pathetic essay in which Washington Irving celebrates the virtues of the vanishing race. Between Washington Irving and his friend Charles Dickens there was always indeed this ironical comedy of inversion. It is amusing that the Englishman should have been the pushing and even pert modernist, and the American the stately antiquarian and lover of lost causes. But while a man of more mellow sympathies may well dislike Dickens's dislike of savages, and even disdain his disdain, he ought to sharply remind himself of the admirable ethical fairness and equity which meet with that restricted outlook. In the very act of describing Red Indians as devils who, like so much dirt, it would pay us to sweep away, he pauses to deny emphatically that we have any right to sweep them away. We have no right to wrong the man, he means to say, even if he himself be a kind of wrong. Here we strike the ringing iron of the old conscience and sense of honour which marked the best men of his party and of his epoch. This rigid, and even reluctant justice towers, at any rate, far above modern views of savages above the sentimentalism of the mere humanitarian and the far weaker sentimentalism that pleads for brutality and a race war. Dickens was at least more of a man than the brutalitarian who claims to wrong people because they are nasty, or the humanitarian who cannot be just to them without pretending that they are nice.

New York, 1920. Exchange Court Building

Brook in the Black Mountains, Breconshire

What is America?

G. K. Chesterton

The following essay by Chesterton was published in chapter I in The Collected Works of G. K. Chesterton, *Vol. XXI, (Ignatius Press: San Francisco, 1990).*

I have never managed to lose my old conviction that travel narrows the mind. At least a man must make a double effort of moral humility and imaginative energy to prevent it from narrowing his mind. Indeed there is something touching and even tragic about the thought of the thoughtless tourist, who might have stayed at home loving Laplanders, embracing Chinamen, and clasping Patagonians to his heart in Hampstead or Surbiton, but for his blind and suicidal impulse to go and see what they looked like. This is not meant for nonsense; still less is it meant for the silliest sort of nonsense, which is cynicism. The human bond that he feels at home is not an illusion. On the contrary, it is rather an inner reality. Man is inside all men. In a real sense any man may be inside any men. But to travel is to leave the inside and draw dangerously near the outside. So long as he thought of men in the abstract, like naked toiling figures in some classic frieze, merely as those who labour and love their children and die, he was thinking the fundamental truth about them. By going to look at their unfamiliar manners and customs he is inviting them to disguise themselves in fantastic masks and costumes. Many modern internationalists talk as if men of different nationalities had only to meet and mix and understand each other. In reality that is the moment of supreme danger—the moment when they meet. We might shiver, as at the old euphemism by which a meeting meant a duel.

Travel ought to combine amusement with instruction; but most travellers are so much amused that they refuse to be instructed. I do not

Looking due north down Hirnant Valley

blame them for being amused; it is perfectly natural to be amused at a Dutchman for being Dutch or a Chinaman for being Chinese. Where they are wrong is that they take their own amusement seriously. They base on it their serious ideas of international instruction. It was said that the Englishman takes his pleasures sadly; and the pleasure of despising foreigners is one which he takes most sadly of all. He comes to scoff and does not remain to pray, but rather to excommunicate. Hence in international relations there is far too little laughing, and far too much sneering. But I believe that there is a better way which largely consists of laughter; a form of friendship between nations which is actually founded on differences. To hint at some such better way is the only excuse of this book.

Let me begin my American impressions with two impressions I had before I went to America. One was an incident and the other an idea; and when taken together they illustrate the attitude I mean. The first principle is that nobody should be ashamed of thinking a thing funny because it is foreign; the second is that he should be ashamed of thinking it wrong because it is funny. The reaction of his senses and superficial habits of mind against something new, and to him abnormal, is a perfectly healthy reaction. But the mind which imagines that mere unfamiliarity can possibly prove anything about inferiority is a very inadequate mind. It is inadequate even in criticising things that may really be inferior to the things involved here. It is far better to laugh at a negro for having a black face than to sneer at him for having a sloping skull. It is proportionally even more preferable to laugh rather than judge in dealing with highly civilised peoples. Therefore I put at the beginning two working examples of what I felt about America before I saw it; the sort of thing that a man has a right to enjoy as a joke, and the sort of thing he has a duty to understand and respect, because it is the explanation of the joke.

When I went to the American consulate to regularise my passports, I was capable of expecting the American consulate to be American. Embassies and consulates are by tradition like islands of the soil for which they stand; and I have often found the tradition corresponding to a truth. I have seen the unmistakable French official living on omelettes and a little wine and serving his sacred abstractions under the last palm-trees fringing a desert. In the heat and noise of quarrelling

Turks and Egyptians, I have come suddenly, as with the cool shock of his own shower-bath, on the listless amiability of the English gentleman. The officials I interviewed were very American, especially in being very polite; for whatever may have been the mood or meaning of Martin Chuzzlewit, I have always found Americans by far the politest people in the world. They put in my hands a form to be filled up, to all appearances like other forms I had filled up in other passport offices. But in reality it was very different from any form I had ever filled up in my life. At least it was a little like a freer form of the game called "Confessions" which my friends and I invented in our youth; an examination paper containing questions like, "If you saw a rhinoceros in the front garden, what would you do?" One of my friends, I remember, wrote, "Take the pledge." But that is another story, and might bring Mr. Pussyfoot Johnson on the scene before his time.

One of the questions on the paper was, "Are you an anarchist?" to which a detached philosopher would naturally feel inclined to answer, "What the devil has that to do with you? Are you an atheist?" along with some playful efforts to cross-examine the official about what constitutes an ἀρχή. Then there was the question, "Are you in favour of subverting the government of the United States by force?" Against this I should write, "I prefer to answer that question at the end of my tour and not the beginning." The inquisitor, in his more than morbid curiosity, had then written down, "Are you a polygamist?" The answer to this is, "No such luck" or "Not such a fool" according to our experience of the other sex. But perhaps a better answer would be that given to W. T. Stead when he circulated the rhetorical question, "Shall I slay my brother Boer?"—the answer that ran, "Never interfere in family matters" But among many things that amused me almost to the point of treating the form thus disrespectfully, the most amusing was the thought of the ruthless outlaw who should feel compelled to treat it respectfully. I like to think of the foreign desperado, seeking to slip into America with official papers under official protection, and sitting down to write with a beautiful gravity, "I am an anarchist. I hate you all and wish to destroy you." Or, "I intend to subvert by force the government of the United States as soon as possible, sticking the long sheath-knife in my left trouser-pocket into Mr. Harding at the earliest opportunity," Or again, "Yes, I am a polygamist all right, and my forty-seven wives are accompanying me on the voyage disguised as secretaries." There seems to be a certain simplicity of mind about these answers; and it is reassuring to know that anarchists and polygamists are so pure and good that the police have only to ask them questions and they are certain to tell no lies.

Now that is the model of the sort of foreign practice, founded on foreign problems, at which a man's first impulse is naturally to laugh. Nor have I any intention of apologising for my laughter. A man is perfectly entitled to laugh at a thing because he happens to find it incomprehensible. What he has no right to do is to laugh at it as incomprehensible, and then criticise it as if he comprehended it. The very fact of its unfamiliarity and mystery ought to set him thinking about the deeper causes that make people so different from himself, and that without merely assuming that they must be inferior to himself.

Superficially this is rather a queer business. It would be easy enough to suggest that in this America has introduced a quite abnormal spirit of inquisition; an interference with liberty unknown among all the ancient despotisms and aristocracies. About that there will be something to be said later; but superficially it is true that this degree of officialism is comparatively unique. In a journey which I took only the year before I had occasion to have my papers passed by governments which many worthy people in the West would vaguely identify with corsairs and assassins; I have stood on the other side of Jordan, in the land ruled by a rude Arab chief, where the police looked so like brigands that one wondered what the brigands looked like. But they did not ask me whether I had come to subvert the power of the Shereef; and they did not exhibit the faintest curiosity about my personal views on the ethical basis of civil authority. These ministers of ancient Moslem despotism did not care about whether I was an anarchist; and naturally would not have minded if I had been a polygamist. The Arab chief was probably a polygamist himself. These slaves of Asiatic autocracy were content, in the old liberal fashion, to judge me by my actions; they did not inquire into my thoughts. They held their power as limited to the limitation of practice; they did not forbid me to hold a theory. It would be easy to argue here that Western democracy persecutes where even Eastern despotism tolerates or emancipates. It would be easy to develop the fancy that, as compared with the sultans of Turkey or Egypt, the American Constitution is a thing like the Spanish Inquisition.

Only the traveller who stops at that point is totally wrong; and the traveller only too often does stop at that point. He has found something to make him laugh, and he will not suffer it to make him think. And the remedy is not to unsay what he has said, not even, so to speak, to un-laugh what he has laughed, not to deny that there is something unique and curious about this American inquisition into our abstract opinions, but rather to continue the train of thought, and follow the admirable advice of Mr. H. G. Wells, who said, "It is not much good thinking of a thing unless you think it out." It is not to deny that American official-ism is rather peculiar on this point, but to inquire what it really is which makes America peculiar, or which is peculiar to America. In short, it is to get some ultimate idea of what America *is;* and the answer to that question will reveal something much deeper and grander and more wor-thy of our intelligent interest.

It may have seemed something less than a compliment to com-pare the American Constitution to the Spanish Inquisition. But oddly enough, it does involve a truth, and still more oddly perhaps, it does involve a compliment. The American Constitution does resemble the Spanish Inquisition in this: that it is founded on a creed. America is the only nation in the world that is founded on a creed. That creed is set forth with dogmatic and even theological lucidity in the Declaration of Independence; perhaps the only piece of practical politics that is also theoretical politics and also great literature. It enunciates that all men are equal in their claim to justice, that governments exist to give them that justice, and that their authority is for that reason just. It certainly does condemn anarchism, and it does also by inference condemn athe-ism, since it clearly names the Creator as the ultimate authority from whom these equal rights are derived. Nobody expects a modern politi-cal system to proceed logically in the application of such dogmas, and in the matter of God and government it is naturally God whose claim is taken more lightly. The point is that there is a creed, if not about divine, at least about human things.

Now a creed is at once the broadest and the narrowest thing in the world. In its nature it is as broad as its scheme for a brotherhood of all men. In its nature it is limited by its definition of the nature of all men. This was true of the Christian Church, which was truly said to exclude neither Jew nor Greek, but which did definitely substitute something else for Jewish religion or Greek philosophy. It was truly said to be a net drawing in of all kinds; but a net of a certain pattern, the pattern of Peter the Fisherman. And this is true even of the most disastrous distortions or degradations of that creed; and true among others of the Spanish Inquisition. It may have been narrow about theology, it could not confess to being narrow about nationality or ethnology. The Spanish Inquisition might be admittedly Inquisitorial; but the Spanish Inquisition could not be merely Spanish. Such a Spaniard, even when he was narrower than his own creed, had to be broader than his own empire. He might burn a philosopher because he was heterodox; but he must accept a barbarian because he was orthodox. And we see, even in modern times, that the same Church which is blamed for making sages heretics is also blamed for making savages priests. Now in a much vaguer and more evolutionary fashion, there is something of the same idea at the back of the great American experiment; the experiment of a democracy of diverse races which has been compared to a melting-pot. But even that metaphor implies that the pot itself is of a certain shape and a certain substance; a pretty solid substance. The melting-pot must not melt. The original shape was traced on the lines of Jeffersonian democracy; and it will remain in that shape until it becomes shapeless. America invites all men to become citizens; but it implies the dogma that there is such a thing as citizenship. Only, so far as its primary ideal is concerned, its exclusiveness is religious because it is not racial. The missionary can condemn a cannibal, precisely because he cannot condemn a Sandwich Islander. And in something of the same spirit the American may exclude a polygamist, precisely because he cannot exclude a Turk.

Now for America this is no idle theory. It may have been theoretical, though it was thoroughly sincere, when that great Virginian gentleman declared it in surroundings that still had something of the character of an English countryside. It is not merely theoretical now. There is nothing to prevent America being literally invaded by Turks, as she is invaded by Jews or Bulgars. In the most exquisitely inconsequent of the *Bab Ballads*, we are told concerning Pasha Bailey Ben:—

> One morning knocked at half-past eight
> A tall Red Indian at his gate.
> In Turkey, as you'r' p'raps aware.
> Red Indians are extremely rare.

But the converse need by no means be true. There is nothing in the nature of things to prevent an emigration of Turks increasing and multiplying on the plains where the Red Indians wandered; there is nothing to necessitate the Turks being extremely rare. The Red Indians, alas, are likely to be rarer. And as I much prefer Red Indians to Turks, not to mention Jews, I speak without prejudice; but the point here is that America, partly by original theory and partly by historical accident, does lie open to racial admixtures which most countries would think incongruous or comic. That is why it is only fair to read any American definitions or rules in a certain light, and relatively to a rather unique position. It is not fair to compare the position of those who may meet Turks in the back street with that of those who have never met Turks except in the *Bab Ballads.* It is not fair simply to compare America with England in its regulations about the Turk. In short, it is not fair to do what almost every Englishman probably does; to look at the American international examination paper, and laugh and be satisfied with saying, "We don't have any of that nonsense in England."

We do not have any of that nonsense in England because we have never attempted to have any of that philosophy in England. And, above all, because we have the enormous advantage of feeling it natural to be national, because there is nothing else to be. England in these days is not well governed; England is not well educated; England suffers from wealth and poverty that are not well distributed. But England is English; *esto perpetua.* England is English as France is French or Ireland is Irish; the great mass of men taking certain national traditions for granted. Now this gives us a totally different and very much easier task. We have not got an inquisition, because we have not got a creed; but it is arguable that we do not need a creed, because we have got a character. In any of the old nations the national unity is preserved by the national type. Because we have a type we do not need to have a test.

Take that innocent question, "Are you an anarchist?" which is intrinsically quite as impudent as "Are you an optimist?" or "Are you a philanthropist?" I am not discussing here whether these things are right, but whether most of us are in a position to know them rightly. Now it is quite true that most Englishmen do not find it necessary to go about all day asking each other whether they are anarchists. It is quite true that the phrase occurs on no British forms that I have seen. But this is not only because most of the Englishmen are not anarchists. It is even more because even the anarchists are Englishmen. For instance, it would be easy to make fun of the American formula by noting that the cap would fit all sorts of bald academic heads. It might well be maintained that Herbert Spencer was an anarchist. It is practically certain that Auberon Herbert[1] was an anarchist. But Herbert Spencer was an extraordinary typical Englishman of the Nonconformist middle class. And Auberon Herbert was an extraordinarily typical English aristocrat of the old and genuine aristocracy. Everyone knew in his head that the squire would not throw a bomb at the Queen, and the Nonconformist would not throw a bomb at anybody. Everyone knows that there was something subconscious in a man like Auberon Herbert, which would have come out only in throwing bombs at the enemies of England; as it did come out in his son and namesake, the generous and unforgotten, who fell flinging bombs from the sky far beyond the German line. Everyone knows that normally, in the last resort, the English gentleman is patriotic. Everyone knows that the English Nonconformist is national even when he denies that he is patriotic. Nothing is more notable indeed than the fact that nobody is more stamped with the mark of his own nation than the man who says that there ought to be no nations. Somebody called Cobden[2] the International Man; but no man could be more English than Cobden. Everybody recognises Tolstoy as the iconoclast of all patriotism; but nobody could be more Russian than Tolstoy. In the old countries where there are these national types, the types may be allowed to hold any theories. Even if they hold certain theories they are unlikely to do certain things. So the conscientious objector, in the English sense, may be and is one of the peculiar by-products of England. But the conscientious objector will probably have a conscientious objection to throwing bombs.

Now I am very far from intending to imply that these American tests are good tests or that there is no danger of tyranny becoming the temptation of America. I shall have something to say later on about that temptation or tendency. Nor do I say that they apply consistently this conception of a nation with the soul of a church, protected by religious and not racial selection. If they did apply that principle consistently, they would have to exclude pessimists and rich cynics who deny the democratic ideal; an excellent thing but a rather improbable one. What I say is that when we realise that this principle exists at all, we see the whole position in a totally different perspective. We say that the Americans are doing something heroic or doing something insane, or doing it in an unworkable or unworthy fashion, instead of simply wondering what the devil they are doing.

When we realise the democratic design of such a cosmopolitan commonwealth, and compare it with our insular reliance or instincts, we see at once why such a thing has to be not only democratic but dogmatic. We see why in some points it tends to be inquisitive or intolerant. Anyone can see the practical point by merely transferring into private life a problem like that of the two academic anarchists, who might by a coincidence be called the two Herberts. Suppose a man said, "Buffle, my old Oxford tutor, wants to meet you; I wish you'd ask him down for a day or two. He has the oddest opinions, but he's very stimulating." It would not occur to us that the oddity of the Oxford don's opinions would lead him to blow up the house; because the Oxford don is an English type. Suppose somebody said, "Do let me bring old Colonel Robinson down for the week-end; he's a bit of a crank but quite interesting." We should not anticipate the colonel running amuck with a carving-knife and offering up human sacrifice in the garden; for these are not among the daily habits of an old English colonel; and because we know his habits, we do not care about his opinions. But suppose somebody offered to bring a person from the interior of Kamskatka to stay with us for a week or two, and added that his religion was a very extraordinary religion, we should feel a little more inquisitive about what kind of religion it was. If somebody wished to add a Hairy Ainu to the family party at Christmas, explaining that his point of view was so individual and interesting, we should want to know a little more about it and him. We should be tempted to draw up as fantastic an examination paper as that presented to the emigrant going to America. We should ask what a Hairy Ainu was, and how hairy he was, and above all what sort of Ainu he was. Would etiquette require us to ask him to bring his wife? And if we did ask him to bring his wife, how many wives would he bring? In short, as in the American formula, is he a polygamist? Merely as a point of housekeeping and accommodation the question is not irrelevant. Is the Hairy Ainu content with hair, or does he wear any clothes? If the police insist on his wearing clothes, will he recognise the authority of the police? In short, as in the American formula, is he an anarchist?

Of course this generalisation about America, like other historical things, is subject to all sorts of cross divisions and exceptions, to be considered in their place. The negroes are a special problem, because of what white men in the past did to them. The Japanese are a special problem, because of what men fear that they in the future may do to white men. The Jews are a special problem, because of what they and the Gentiles, in the past, present and future, seem to have the habit of doing to each other. But the point is not that nothing exists in America except this idea; it is that nothing like this idea exists anywhere except in America. This idea is not internationalism; on the contrary it is decidedly nationalism. The Americans are very patriotic, and wish to make their new citizens patriotic Americans. But it is the idea of making a new nation literally out of any old nation that comes along. In a word, what is unique is not America but what is called Americanisation. We understand nothing till we understand the amasing ambition to Americanise the Kamskatkan and the Hairy Ainu. We are not trying to Anglicise thousands of French cooks or Italian organ grinders. France is not trying to Gallicise thousands of English trippers or German prisoners of war. America is the one place in the world where this process, healthy or unhealthy, possible or impossible, is going on. And the process, as I have pointed out, is *not* internationalisation. It would be truer to say it is the nationalisation of the internationalised. It is making a home out of vagabonds and a nation out of exiles. This is what at once illuminates and softens the moral regulations which we may really think faddist or fanatical. They are abnormal; but in one sense this experiment of a home for the homeless is abnormal. In short, it has long been recognised that America was an asylum. It is only since Prohibition that it has looked a little like a lunatic asylum.

It was before sailing for America, as I have said, that I stood with the official paper in my hand and these thoughts in my head. It was while I stood on English soil that I passed through the two stages of smiling and then sympathising; of realising that my momentary amusement, at being asked if I were not an Anarchist, was partly due to the fact that I was not an American. And in truth I think there are some things a man ought to know about America before he sees it. What we know of a country beforehand may not affect what we see that it is; but it will vitally affect what we appreciate it for being, because it will vitally affect what we expected it to be. I can honestly say that I had never expected America to be what nine-tenths of the newspaper critics invariably assume it to be. I never thought it was a sort of Anglo-Saxon colony, knowing that it was more and more thronged with crowds of very different colonists. During the war I felt that the very worst propaganda for the Allies was the propaganda for the Anglo-Saxons. I tried to point out that in one way America is nearer to Europe than England is. If she is not nearer to Bohemia, she is nearer to Bohemians. In my New York hotel the head waiter in the dining-room was a Bohemian; the head waiter in the grillroom was a Bulgar. Americans have nationalities at the end of the street which for us are at the ends of the earth. I did my best to persuade my countrymen not to appeal to the American as if he were a rather dowdy Englishman, who had been rusticating in the provinces and had not heard the latest news about the town. I shall record later some of those arresting realities which the traveller does not expect; and which, in some cases I fear, he actually does not see because he does not expect. I shall try to do justice to the psychology of what Mr. Belloc has called "Eye-Openers in Travel." But there are some things about America that a man ought to see even with his eyes shut. One is that a state that came into existence solely through its repudiation and abhorrence of the British Crown is not likely to be a respectful copy of the British constitution. Another is that the chief mark of the Declaration of Independence is something that is not only absent from the British Constitution, but something which all our constitutionalists have invariably thanked God, with the jolliest boasting and bragging, that they had kept out of the British Constitution. It is the thing called abstraction or academic logic. It is the thing which such jolly people call theory; and which those who can practice it call thought. And the theory or thought is the very last to which English people are accustomed, either by their social structure or their traditional teaching. It is the theory of equality. It is the pure classic conception that no man must aspire to be anything more than a citizen, and that no man should endure to be anything less. It is by no means especially intelligible to an Englishman, who tends at his best to the virtues of the gentleman and at his worst to the vices of the snob. The idealism of England, or if you will the romance of England, has not been primarily the romance of the citizen. But the idealism of America, we may safely say, still revolves entirely round the citizen and his romance. The realities are quite another matter, and we shall consider in its place the question of whether the ideal will be able to shape the realities or will merely be beaten shapeless by them. The ideal is besieged by inequalities of the most tow-ering and insane description in the industrial and economic field. It may be devoured by modern capitalism, perhaps the worst inequality that ever existed among men. Of all that we shall speak later. But citizenship is still the American ideal; there is an army of actualities opposed to that ideal; but there is no ideal opposed to that ideal. American plutoc-racy has never got itself respected like English aristocracy. Citizenship is the American ideal; and it has never been the English ideal. But it is surely an ideal that may stir some imaginative generosity and respect in an Englishman, if he will condescend to be also a man. In this vision of moulding many peoples into the visible image of the citizen, he may see a spiritual adventure which he can admire from the outside at least as much as he admires the valour of the Moslems and much more than he admires the virtue of the Middle Ages. He need not set himself to develop equality, but he need not set himself to misunderstand it. He may at least understand what Jefferson and Lincoln meant, and he may possibly find some assistance in this task by reading what they said. He may realise that equality is not some crude fairy tale about all men being equally tall or equally tricky; which we not only cannot believe but can-not believe in anybody believing. It is an absolute of morals by which all men have a value invariable and indestructible and a dignity as intan-gible as death. He may at least be a philosopher and see that equality is an idea; and not merely one of these soft-headed sceptics who, having risen by low tricks to high places, drink bad champagne in tawdry hotel lounges, and tell each other twenty times over, with unwearied iteration, that equality is an illusion.

In truth it is inequality that is the illusion. The extreme dispro-portion between men, that we seem to see in life, is a thing of changing lights and lengthening shadows, a twilight full of fancies and distor-tions. We find a man famous and cannot live long enough to find him forgotten; we see a race dominant and cannot linger to see it decay. It is the experience of men that always returns to the equality of men; it is the average that ultimately justifies the average man. It is when men have seen and suffered much and come at the end of more elaborate experi-ments, that they see men under an equal light of death and daily laugh-ter; and none the less mysterious for being many. Nor is it in vain that these Western democrats have sought the blazonry of their flag in that great multitude of immortal lights that endure behind the fires we see, and gathered them into the corner of Old Glory whose ground is like the glittering night. For veritably, in the spirit as well as in the symbol, suns and moons and meteors pass and fill our skies with a fleeting and almost theatrical conflagration; and wherever the old shadow stoops upon the earth, the stars return.

[1] Auberon Edward William Molyneux Herbert (1838-1906) was an English radical and politician, political philosopher and author, an avowed republican and an enemy of all repressive legislation. He published *A Politician in Trouble about his Soul* (1884) and *The Voluntaryst Creed* (1908) and issued a monthly *Organ of Voluntary Taxation* (1890-1901).

[2] Richard Cobden (1804-1865) was en English politician and economist who studied economic and financial systems in the United States, Near East and Germany. He believed in free trade, the minimum of government at home and the minimum of intervention abroad. He published the pamphlet *England, Ireland and America*, opposing the defence of Turkey against Russia, and another pamphlet Russia, attacking the doctrine of the balance of power. He was a co-leader of the Anti-Corn-Law League.

New York, 1920

Return to the Vision

G. K. Chesterton

What follows is Chapter XIV of Chesterton's Book Sidelights on New London and Newer York and Other Essays *(Sheed & Ward: London,1932).*

The real case against Revolution is this; that there always seems to be so much more to be said against the old *régime* than in favour of the new *régime*. It is not so much that it is always a bad thing that things should burst; but that they so often burst in the wrong place. Thus the Bolshevist Revolution burst in the wrong place in the towns. These were so rare and unrelated to the rest of Russia, that it was almost as if a revolution in our big towns had begun in the lunatic asylums. The result was that there arose something so horribly inhuman and unnatural that it did really deserve to be called the Dictatorship of the Proletariat. In other words, it consisted of men who became tyrants while they were still slaves ... yes, ... even in the Socialist sense of wageslaves. The slavery peculiar to the town became the tyranny covering the countryside. And in the countryside, the men who had once been serfs and had become peasants, owning their own land, were forced to become slaves owning no land; because that is the law of the towns. All that would have been better, if the main explosion had come in the main bulk of the nation; if the Russian Revolution had been like the French Revolution. Much is said today against Rousseau and the romantic revolutionaries who idealised life on the land. But it is better to be romantic about a real thing like the land than to be realistic about an unreal thing like the Economic Theory of History. In an evil hour, Russia fell under the power, not of a French philosopher, but of a German Jewish economist. Karl Marx was the very opposite of a lover of the land. He was a typical townsman, as are most Jewish intellectuals of his type, and he could not understand

---

District of Santa Croce, Italy

peasants any more than the present Russian Government can. But the trouble burst in the wrong place; it burst in the town and permitted bookish people to enslave it by a book. Karl Marx became the Koran of all those half-Oriental tribes with something of the Moslem reverence for anything written on a piece of paper. For Marxians, like all material-ists, are of necessity mystics. For Matter is an unknown God; whereas Spirit was made flesh and dwelt among us.

That is only one example. A hundred others could be given of the way in which the cause of Revolution is so often right and the result of Revolution so often wrong. But the case can be put more favourably to the Revolutionary idea; and the point of the case is really this. There is a sense in which we may truly say that the fault of many revolutions was in not being revolutionary enough. I mean that the evil did not come through what they destroyed; but rather through what they retained. Certainly the combination of the two almost always left a false and un-fortunate heritage. An Englishman writing for an American paper may most naturally take the example of the American Revolution. I am far from certain how many Americans or Englishmen would agree with me. I sometimes have a dark suspicion that I should have to defend the American Revolution more often against Americans than against Eng-lishmen. But, in any case, my own personal view of it is this. I will not say that Americans were right to overthrow the power of King George; for in fact there was no power of King George to overthrow. England was not a monarchy. England was already an aristocracy. But Americans, in my judgment, were perfectly entitled to break away from that aristocracy. An aristocracy is a system which has its advantages and disadvantages; but for those who really wish to live the democratic life even the advantages were disadvantages. And, when all is discounted from the mere cant of emancipation, it is true that a poor man leaving the English countryside for the American coast did become a free man; even if he was starved or frozen in a blizzard or eaten by a grizzly bear. He had no longer a mas-ter or a lord. At home the advantage of aristocracy was having, a good squire; the disadvantage was having a bad squire. Some may even prefer a bad squire to a bear. But it is true, as far as it goes, that in breaking with aristocracy, the revolted colonies did open a democracy for those who care to be democrats. It was not the English things they ruined which ruined them. It was the English things they retained.

All the troubles of the Revolution came from being Conservatives. For instance, they were so persistently and pig-headedly Conservative that they preserved Puritanism. There was really no reason why that entirely local English or Scottish prejudice should have pursued them across the free Atlantic into the wide prairies of the land of promise. The Puritans who sailed in the *Mayflower* were altogether too respectful to the England of Elizabeth and Charles the First. They should have thrown their Plymouth religion into the sea somewhere; and started clean as Pagans, since it was impossible for them to start as Christians. The great Jefferson did indeed largely realise this; and made the philosophy of the Republic out of that normal and universal Deism which really is natural to most men, when they are neither Puritans, atheists nor Catholics. But I will firmly maintain, though I fear I shall not carry all my readers with me, that the Puritanism which was brought from Plymouth has produced, and is still producing, a crop of corruptions and difficulties which were really no part of the natural American situation at all. The destroyers of tea in Boston Harbour did not destroy sufficiently. The subscribers to the Declaration of Independence were not independent enough. Given the impossible position in England, between Puritans and aristocracy, it would have been better if they had drifted even further away. It would have been better if the New World had been something more like a New Creation.

I do not deal here directly with religion in the sense of religious proof, and its supreme claims; many are aware what particular creed would condition all my remarks on that side; as a Catholic I know well of what sacred thing the Puritans carried the fragments, and should always treat it and them with due regard. But, speaking of this single matter of simplifying American politics, and considering history apart from theology, so far as it can be considered, I repeat that it would be easier to reach a religious and political understanding today, if the Pilgrims had not been Puritans, and had not carried their sects and sectarian battles to the New World. Nay, in that sense it would be better if the natural religion of Americans had been like that of American Indians. They had better have lifted hands together to the Great Spirit walking above woods and clouds; a very natural religion; not unlike Jefferson's. For the Red God is at least a god of the beginnings; like the Red Clay of Adam; indeed we may say that, in the Bible, the First Man was a Red Man. Such a natural religion of origins might have eventually brought men nearer to ancient truths; even to the ancient truths of Christianity. And for my own faith (if it were here in question) Jesuits sometimes find it easier to convert Red Indians than Black Protestants.

It is true, of course, that at one time Puritanism was itself a Revolution. But it was a very remote Revolution; for all of us very remote in time and for Americans very remote in place. It was a curious crack in one corner of Europe, three hundred years ago, when all Europe was broken up by the upheaval of many other things, and many very contrary things, by the Paganism of the Renaissance, by the new pride of the Princes, by the greed and luxury of the New Rich. In any case, neither its virtues nor its vices are in the faintest degree sympathetic to the general spirit of the world today. It is a ruin, but a colossal ruin; and a ruin which is scattered over whole countries, and even whole continents, like the giant limbs of Ammon in the poem. And with that fact we come to another of the general considerations that must be taken into account in estimating the advantages and disadvantages of the revolutionary tradition. For everything is a tradition; even a Revolution.

It is a true point in the case against Revolution, that the world is so often cluttered up with the cold remains of old revolutions. What really stands in the way of the new novelty is the old novelty; which sometimes still considers itself new. For, after all, there are few institutions, however ancestral and antiquated, which do not work back to some sort of revolution. Not only American democracy, but also English aristocracy was created, in that sense, by revolution. What was called the Glorious Revolution of 1688 finally and firmly established that system of great squires from which the later emigrants escaped to find freedom in America. But I admit that it is a rather needless degradation of the word "Revolution" to apply it to the affair of 1688. The Glorious Revolution was not a revolution, even if it was a rebellion. As a matter of fact, it was a plot. It was the work of a few cold-blooded courtiers and conspiring nobles, betraying James the Second by a palace revolution in which the people had no part. The American Revolution was a real revolution, in whatever way the people were divided; in so far as its leaders appealed to a sort of abstract and primeval truth; like the makers of a new world. But even here, in the matter of the mere politicians of 1688, we may find the same point that I noted touching Puritanism. The American Republic really inherited rather too much than too little of the old party politics of England. We might say that the West has suffered only too much from the Westminster Election; just as it has suffered only too much from the Westminster Confession. The Party Man as well as the Puritan ought to have been drowned in crossing the Atlantic. Indeed I have more personal sympathy with those innocent and perhaps crazy enthusiasts who thought they were leaving all worldly pomps and fictions behind them when they set foot on the virgin land of the free. I sympathise more with the honest gentleman who threw his wig into the sea, before sailing into Boston Harbour. The act really amounted to a parable and even to a pun. He threw away the wig; it would have been better to have thrown away the Whig.

Nay, there is another injustice to America even in the common talk about Americanisation. In the mere worship of machinery, in the mere worship of money, in the headlong materialism that invents and exploits and sells with blind optimism, it is true that America on the whole advanced further; but it is not true that America advanced first. It seems to me only common fairness for an Englishman to admit that it was England that originally involved the world in this doubtful and dangerous departure from the traditions of Europe. To take the obvious example; the Steam Engine is as English as Shakespeare; though Puffing Billy has not remained such an inspiration as Poetic Will. I am not at all sure that, to a man of the time of Cobbett, for instance, England did not stand relatively for the town and America for the countryside. Much of the talk of emigrants, at that period, was rather of the sort that celebrates the West as what was afterwards called the Wild West. Heaven forbid that I should suggest that there is now anything resembling the Tame West; but in England there is less and less talk of anything beyond the West End. The urban limitation has closed upon us even more narrowly than upon the new cities, and what we call the West End has something of the character of the End of the World. Now the whole point of the old vision of America was that there was no End of the World. It was a reckless and romantic vision, of course, and many died of it in deserts and deep canyons; but that was the vision, and it is not always understood, especially since conditions have altered and limited even America liked a walled town. It is a real difficulty for historians that the strong motives of one generation are the stale jests of the next. A hundred American humorists, to say nothing of Mr. P. G. Wodehouse, have taught us to intone in a derisive chorus the famous phrase about "the great open spaces, where men are men." But there is something in it, for all that; if we only express it by saying that life in a modern town, whatever else it is, is not Normalcy. The Wild and Woolly aphorism is true; in the sense that if men are to be men, they will require rather more open spaces. Their real, original sociological object in going to America was to find those open spaces. It was *not* to find more engineers and electric batteries and mechanical gadgets in the home. These may have been the results of America; they were not the causes of America. So that here again, even in the case of the admittedly American energy in industrial machinery, I may be permitted the paradox of a doubt. I rather doubt whether America was founded to do these things. I rather incline to believe that America was founded to escape from these things. I darkly suspect that England was already beginning to be crushed between colliding cities, caught up in roaring and rending wheels, feeling the threat of the throttling industrialism that has since overpowered her, that men from England and Scotland and Ireland and Western Europe began to think of the unfathomable vistas of the new sunset lands. Therefore, while I should heartily support an English manresisting the Americanisation of England, I am not quite sure whether what he resists was not originally the Anglicising of America.

I write these words, therefore, in some sense to ease my national conscience. I am only too well accustomed to politicians and diplomatists, presuming to speak for England, who pay heavy and greasy compliments to the Fathers of the American Republic and the fighters in the American Revolution; who say exactly the right thing about George Washington, subject to a hazy idea that he was identical with Abraham Lincoln. It has always seemed to me that such men were only insulted by such praise. The men who made the Revolution in America are now mocked even in America, let alone England or Europe. But I for one feel it due to those great men to say that all subsequent trouble has not come from the things that they began, but from the things that they borrowed. It was not the conception of life outlined in the Declaration of Independence that was wrong; it was the thousand things that have come in since to perplex it; and many of them have come from England and from Europe. The great Revolution failed to attain those high levels of equality and luminous justice to which its first promise had pointed; not because Americans were wrong to resist a German called George the Third, but because they continued to revere a Frenchman called

Calvin, a Scotchman called Macaulay, an Englishman called Herbert Spencer, and all the rest of the dreary Whig and Puritan and industrial rationalism of what we call in England the Victorian Age. In this matter I am on the side of the old idealistic democrats. The vision was all right; it is the revision that is all wrong. America, instead of being the open agricultural commonwealth for which its founders hoped, has become the dumping-ground of all the most dismal ideas of decaying epochs in Europe, from Calvinism to Industrialism. Even the American features which most offend a European, the extravagant exaggeration of commercial competition, or mechanical invention, or journalistic violence, are not ideas of the Revolution. They are ideas that have immigrated into America after the Revolution. For my part, I wish that Jefferson's democracy had remained immune from them. I wish it had cared as little for George Stephenson as for George the Third. I wish it had been as remote from Lord Northcliffe as from Lord North.

New York, 1920

E.M. Card. D. Mercier

DON DE LA BELGIQUE 1926

The Nativity

G. K. Chesterton

The following Christmas poem by Chesterton was published in The Collected Poems of G. K. Chesterton *(Cecil Palmer: London, 1927)*

The thatch on the roof was as golden,
  Though dusty the straw was and old,
The wind had a peal as of trumpets,
  Though blowing and barren and cold,
The mother's hair was a glory
  Though loosened and torn,
For under the eaves in the gloaming
  A child was born.

Have a myriad children been quickened,
  Have a myriad children grown old,
Grown gross and unloved and embittered,
  Grown cunning and savage and cold?
God abides in a terrible patience,
  Unangered, unworn,
And again for the child that was squandered
  A child is born.

What know we of aeons behind us,
  Dim dynasties lost long ago,
Huge empires, like dreams unremembered,
  Huge cities for ages laid low?
This at least—that with blight and with blessing,
  With flower and with thorn,
Love was there, and his cry was among them,
  "A child is born."

Stained Glass Window, St. Catherine's Church, Bethlehem

Though the darkness be noisy with systems,
  Dark fancies that fret and disprove,
Still the plumes stir around us, above us
  The wings of the shadow of love:
Oh! princes and priests, have ye seen it
  Grow pale through your scorn;
Huge dawns sleep before us, deep changes,
  A child is born.

And the rafters of toil still are gilded
  With the dawn of the stars of the heart,
And the wise men draw near in the twilight,
  Who are weary of learning and art,
And the face of the tyrant is darkened,
  His spirit is torn,
For a new king is enthroned; yea, the sternest,
  A child is born.
And the mother still joys for the whispered
  First stir of unspeakable things,
Still feels that high moment unfurling
  Red glory of Gabriel's wings.
Still the babe of an hour is a master
  Whom angels adorn,
Emmanuel, prophet, anointed,
  A child is born.

And thou, that art still in thy cradle,
  The sun being crown for thy brow,
Make answer, our flesh, make an answer,
  Say, whence art thou come—who art thou?
Art thou come back on earth for our teaching
  To train or to warn—?
Hush—how may we know?—knowing only
  A child is born.

Bridge beside The Folly just north of Napton Lock

From the Mycenae Papers

Maurice Baring

The following piece is from Maurice Baring's book Dead Letters *(William Heinemann: London, 1925).*

Clytaemnestra to Aegisthus

MYCENAE

Honoured Sir,

I am sorry I was out when you came yesterday. I never thought that you seriously meant to come. I shall be very busy all next week, as Helen and Menelaus are arriving and I must get everything ready. Orestes was quite delighted with the cup and ball. You spoil him.

Yours sincerely,
CLYTAEMNESTRA

Clytaemnestra to Aegisthus

Most honoured Aegisthus,

One line to say that I have received your letter and *loved* it all except the last sentence. Please do not say that kind of thing again as it will quite ruin our friendship, which I thought was going to be so *real*.

Yours very sincerely,
CLYTAEMNESTRA

Fotheringhay, Northamptonshire

Clytaemnestra to Aegisthus

Most honoured Aegisthus,
   The flowers are beautiful, and it was kind of you to remember my birthday. But your letter is really too naughty. ...
   (The rest of the letter is missing)

Clyaemnestra to Aegisthus

MYCENAE

Most honoured Sir,
   This is to say that since you persist in misunderstanding me and refuse to listen to what I say, our correspondence must end. It is extraordinary to me that you should wish to debase what might have been so great and so wonderful.
                    Yours truly,
                    CLYTAEMNESTRA

Clytaemnestra to Aegisthus

MYCENAE

Most hounoured Aegisthus,
   I was much touched by your letter and I will give you the more trial you ask for so humbly and so touchingly.

   Paris has arrived. I don't know if you know him. He is the second son of the King of Troy. He made an unfortunate marriage with a girl called Œnone, the daughter of a rather disreputable river-person. They were *miserable* about it. He is very good-looking—if one admires those kind of looks, which I don't. He dresses in an absurd way and he looks theatrical. Besides, I hate men with curly hair. He has a few accomplishments. He shoots well and plays on the double flute quite well for a man who is not a professional; but he is totally uninteresting, and, what is more, impossible. But Helen likes him. Isn't it extraordinary that she always has liked impossible men? They sit for hours together sating to sating nothing at all. I don't in the least mind his paying no attention to me—in fact, I am too thankful not to have to talk to him; but I do think it's bad manners, as I am his hostess.

Helen is certainly looking better this year than she has ever looked; but she still dresses in that affectedly over-simple way, which is a pity. I don't know how long he is going to stay. I don't mind his being here, but Helen and he are really most inconsiderate. They use my sitting-room as though it were theirs, and they never seem to think that I may have things to do of my own, and they expect me to go out with them, which ends in their walking on ahead and my being left with Menelaus, whom I am very fond of indeed, but who bores me. He talks of nothing but horses and quoits. It is a great lesson to Queen Hecuba for having brought up her son so badly. Paris was educated entirely by a shepherd, you know, on Mount Ida. The result is his manners are shocking. Helen doesn't see it. Isn't it odd? I must say he's nice with children, and Orestes likes him.

I am your sincere friend,
CLYTAEMNESTRA.

Clytaemnestra to Aegisthus

MYCENAE

Most honoured Aegisthus,
We are in great trouble. I told you Helen was attracted by Paris. We of course thought nothing of it, because Helen always has flirted with rather vulgar men, and her flirtations were, we thought, the harmless distractions of a woman who has remained, and always will remain, a sentimental girl.

Imagine our surprise and dismay! Paris and Helen have run away together, and they have gone to Troy! Helen left a note behind for Menelaus saying she realised that she had made a mistake, that she hated hypocrisy, and thought it more honest to leave him. She said she would always think of him with affection. Poor Menelaus is distracted, but he is behaving beautifully.

Agamemnon is furious. He is overcome by the disgrace to his family, and he is so cross. We are all *very* miserable. Agamemnon says that the family honour must be redeemed at all costs, and that they will have to make an expedition against Troy to fetch Helen back. I think this is quite ridiculous. No amount of expeditions and wars can undo what has been done. I am sure you will sympathise with us in our trouble. I shouldn't have minded so much if Iphigenia wasn't grown up.

Electra has got whooping-cough, but she is going on as well as can be expected. I have no patience with Helen. She always was utterly thoughtless!

Your sincere friend,
CLYTAEMNESTRA.

Clytaemnestra to Aegisthus

MYCENAE

Most honoured Aegisthus,
There is no end of worry and fuss going on. Odysseus, the King of Ithaca, has arrived here with his wife, Penelope. They discuss the prospects of the expedition from morning till night, and I am left alone with Penelope. She has borrowed my only embroidery frame, and is working some slippers for her husband. They are at least two sizes too small. She talks of nothing but her boy, her dog, her dairy, and her garden, and I can't tell you how weary I am of it. She made me very angry yesterday by saying that I spoilt Orestes, and that I should be sorry for it some day. She is always casting her boy Telemachus in my teeth. Whenever Helen is mentioned she puts on a face as much as to say: "Do not defile me."

Your sincere friend,
CLYTAEMNESTRA.

From the Mycenae Papers

Clytaemnestra to Aegisthus

Most honoured Aegisthus,

My worst fears have been realised. They are going to make an expedition against Troy on a large scale. Odysseus is at the bottom of it. I cannot say how much I dislike it. All the Kings have volunteered to go, but the Fleet will not be ready for two years, so I am in hopes that something may happen in the meantime to prevent it.

Iphigenia is learning to make bandages, and says she will go to the front to look after the wounded. I am, of course, against this, and think it's absurd, but unfortunately she can make her father do what she likes. My only consolation is that the war cannot possibly last more than a week. The Trojans have no regular army. They are a handful of untrained farmers, and the town cannot stand a siege. It is all too silly. It is too bad of Helen to have caused all this fuss.

Your sincere friend,
CLYTAEMNESTRA.

P.S—No, of course I haven't written to Helen. She is as good as dead to me.

Clytaemnestra to Aegisthus
(Two years later)

My dear Aegisthus,

We have at last got some news. The Fleet has arrived at Aulis, and they are waiting for a favourable wind to be able to go on. At present they are becalmed. They are all well. Iphigenia writes that she is enjoying herself immensely. She has the decency to add that she misses me! I have not had a good night's rest since they have started.

Your most sincere friend,
CLYTAEMNESTRA.

Clytaemnestra to Aegisthus

My dear friend,

Please come here at once. I am in dreadful trouble. From the last letter I received from Agamemnon I understood there was something wrong and that he was hiding something. To-day I got a letter from Calchas, breaking to me in the most brutal manner an appalling tragedy and a savage, horrible, and impious crime! They have sacrificed my darling Iphigenia—to Artemis, of all goddesses! to get a propitious wind for their horrible Fleet! I am heartbroken. I cannot write another word. Please come directly.

Your friend,
CLYTAEMNESTRA.

Clytaemnestra to Aegisthus
(Two months later)

I see no reason why you should not come back; I have a right to ask whom I like to stay here. Do come as soon as possible; I am very lonely without you. Now that I no longer communicate with Agamemnon, in order to get news, I have written to Helen, and sent the letter by a very clever silk merchant, who is certain to be able to worm his way into Troy. Come as soon as you get this.

C.

P.S.—Agamemnon still writes, but I do not take the slightest notice of his letters. I trust the Trojans will be victorious. They have at any rate determined to make a fight for it. Our generals are certain to quarrel, Achilles and Agamemnon never get on well. And Achilles' temper is dreadful.

Clytaemnestra to Aegisthus
(Three months later)

I can no longer bear these short visits and these long absences. I have arranged for you to stay here permanently.

I wrote to Agamemnon last month a cold and dignified *business* letter, in which I pointed out that unless some man came here to look after things, everything would go to pieces. I suggested you. I have now got his answer. He agrees, and thinks it an excellent plan.

Odysseus wrote me, I must say, a most amusing letter. He says everything is at sixes and sevens, and that Priam's eldest son is far the most capable soldier on either side. He expects to win, but says it will be a far longer business than they thought it would be at first. Come as quickly as you can. Best and most beloved.

Your C.

Helen to Clytaemnestra
(Ten years later)

TROY

Dearest Clytaemnestra,

Your letters are a great comfort to me when I get them, which is very seldom. Everything is going on just the same. It is now the tenth year of the siege, and I see no reason why it should ever end. I am dreadfully afraid the Greeks will never take Troy.

I can give you no idea of how dull everything is here. We do the same thing and see the same people every day. We know exactly what is going on in the Greek camp, and most of the time is spent is discussing the gossip, which bores me to death. You are quite right in what you say about Paris. I made a fatal mistake. It is all Aphrodite's fault. He has become too dreadful now. He is still very good-looking, but even compared with Menelaus he is pitiable in every way and every bit as cross. Hector is very nice, but painfully dull. The King and the Queen are both very kind, but as for Cassandra, she is intolerable. She is always prophesying dreadful calamities which never come off. She said, for instance, that I would lose my looks and make a long journey in Egypt. As if I would go to Egypt from here! As to my looks, you know, darling, I never was vain, was I? But I can honestly tell you that, if anything, I have rather *improved* than otherwise, and among the Trojan women, who are absolute frights and have no more idea of dressing than sheep, I look magnificent. Andromache has got quite a nice face, and I really like her; but you should see her figure—it's like an elephant's, and her feet are enormous, and her hands red and sore from needlework. She won't even use a thimble! Cassandra always dresses in deep mourning. Why, we cannot conceive, because none of her relatives have been killed.

There is really only one person in the palace I can talk to-and that is Aeneas, who is one of the commanders. He is quite nice. What I specially like about him is the nice way in which he talks about his parents.

The Greeks are quarrelling more than ever. Achilles won't fight at all because Agamemnon insisted on taking away Briseis (who is lovely) from him. Wasn't that exactly like Agamemnon? I hope this won't make you jealous, darling, but I don't expect it will, because you have never forgiven Agamemnon, have you?

Everybody tries to be kind to me, and I have nothing to complain of. They all mean well, and in a way this makes it worse. For instance, every morning, when we meet for the midday meal, Priam comes into the room saying to me: "Well, how's the little runaway to-day?" He has made this joke every day for the last ten years. And then they always talk about the cowardice and incompetence of the Greeks, taking for granted that as I have married into a Trojan family I must have become a Trojan myself. It is most tactless of them not to understand what I must be feeling.

I suppose I am inconsistent, but the pro-Greek party irritate me still more. They are headed by Pandarus, and are simply longing for their own side to be beaten, because they say that I ought to have been given up directly, and that the war was brought about entirely owing to Priam having got into the hands of the Egyptian merchants.

I manage to get some Greek stuffs smuggled into the town, and the merchants tell me vaguely what people are wearing at Mycenae; but one can't get anything properly made here. Andromache has all her clothes made at home by her women—to save expense. She says that in times of war one ought to sacrifice oneself. Of course, I can't do this, however much I should like to, as the Trojans expect me to look nice, and would be very angry if I wasn't properly dressed.

I feel if I could only meet Odysseus we might arrange some plan for getting the Greeks into the town.

How is everything going on at home? There is a very strict censorship about letters, and we are all supposed to show our letters to Antenor before they go. I don't, of course. I daresay, however, many of your letters have been intercepted, because I have only heard from you five times since the siege began, and not once this year. Kiss the dear children from me.

Shall I ever see you again? I shall try my best to come home.
Your loving sister,
HELEN.

Clytaemnestra to Helen

MYCENAE

Dearest Helen,

Your last letter has reached me. I must implore you to be very careful about what you do. I hope with all my heart that the siege will be over soon; but if it is I don't think it would be quite wise for you to come back directly. You see everybody here is extremely unreasonable. Instead of understanding that Agamemnon and Odysseus were entirely responsible for this absurd war, Agamemnon has got his friends to put the blame entirely on you, and they have excited the people against you. It's so like a man, that, isn't it? I have been very lonely, because all our friends are away. Aegisthus is staying here just to look after the household and the affairs of the city. But he hardly counts, and he is so busy that I hardly ever see him now. There is a strong proTrojan party here, too. They say we had absolutely no right to go to war, and that it was simply an expedition of pirates and freebooters, and I must say it

53

is very difficult to disprove it. If there is any talk of the siege ending, please let me know *at once*. Electra has grown into a fine girl; but she is not as lovely as poor darling Iphigenia.

Your loving sister,
CLYTAEMNESTRA

Penelope to Odysseus

ITHACA

My darling Husband,

I wish you would write a little more distinctly; we have the greatest difficulty in reading your letters.

When will this horrid siege be over? I think it is disgraceful of you all to be so long about it. To think that when you started you said that it would only last a month! Mind you come back the moment it is over, and come back *straight,* by Aulis.

The country is looking lovely. I have built a new house for the swineherd, as he complained about the roof letting the rain in. Next year, we must really have a new paling round the garden, as the children get in and steal the apples. We can't afford it *this* year. The people have no sense of honesty; they steal everything. Telemachus is very well. He can read and write nicely, but is most backward about his sums. He takes a great interest in the war, and has made up a map on which he marks the position of the troops with little flags.

I am surprised to hear of Achilles' *disgraceful* conduct. If I were there I would give him a piece of my mind. I hope Ajax has not had any more of his attacks. Has he tried cinnamon with fomented myrtle leaves? It ought to be taken three times a day *after* meals. The news from Mycenae is deplorable. Clytaemnestra appears to be quite shameless and callous. Aegisthus is now openly living in the house. All decent people have ceased to go near them. I have had a few visitors, but nobody of any importance.

I am working you a piece of tapestry for your bedroom. I hope to get it finished by the time you come back. I hope that when the city is taken Helen will be *severely* punished.

We have taught Argus to growl whenever Hector is mentioned. I don't, of course, allow anyone to mention Helen in this house. Telemachus sends you his loving duty. He is writing to you himself, but the letter isn't finished.

Your devoted wife
PENELOPE.

Helen to Clytaemnestra

SUNIUM

Dearest Clytaemnestra,

Since I last wrote to you several important things have happened. Hector was killed yesterday by Achilles. I am, of course, very sorry for them all. All Cassandra said was, "I told you so!" She is so heartless. I have at last managed to communicate with Odysseus; we have thought of a very good plan for letting the Greeks into the city. Please do not repeat this. I shall come home at once with Menelaus. He is my husband, after all. I shall come straight to Mycenae. I doubt if I shall have time to write again. I am sending this through Aenida, who is most useful in getting letters brought and sent.

Please have some patterns for me to choose from. I hope to be back in a month.

Your loving sister,
HELEN.

Agamemnon to Clytaemnestra

SUNIUM

Dear Clytaemnestra,

We have had a very good journey, and I shall reach Mycenae the day after to-morrow in the morning. Please have a hot bath ready for me. I am bringing Cassandra with me. She had better have the room looking north, as she hates the sun. She is very nervous and upset, and you must be kind to her.

Your loving husband,
AGAMEMNON.

Odysseus to Penelope

THE ISLAND OF OGYGIA

Dearest Penelope,

We arrived here after a very tiresome voyage. I will not tire you with the details, which are numerous and technical. The net result is that the local physician says I cannot proceed with my journey until I am thoroughly rested. This spot is pleasant, but the only society I have is that of poor dear Calypso. She means well and is most hospitable, but you can imagine how vexed I am by this delay and the intolerable tedium of this enforced repose. Kiss Telemachus from me.

Your loving husband,
ODYSSEUS.

Clytaemnestra to Aegisthus

I am sending this by runner. Come back directly. I expect Agamemnon any moment. The bonfires are already visible. Please bring a good strong net and a sharp axe with you. I will explain when you arrive. I have quite decided that half measures are out of the question.

C.

Cooling Castle

L'Inquietude Juive

Charles Péguy

This Péguy essay is taken from Charles Péguy: Basic Verities, Prose and Poetry *(Pantheon Books: New York, 1948), translated into English by Anne and Julian Green.*

Etre ailleurs, le grand vice de cette race, la grande vertu secrète; la grande vocation de ce peuple. Une remontée de cinquante siècles ne le mettait point en chemin de fer que ce ne fût quelque caravane de cinquante siècles. Toute traversée pour eux est la traversée du désert. Les maisons les plus confortables, les mieux assises, avec des pierres de taille grosses comme les colonnes du temple, les maisons les plus immobilières, les plus immeubles, les immeubles les plus écrasants ne sont jamais pour eux que la tente dans le désert. Le granit remplaça la tente aux murs de toile. Qu'importe ces pierres de taille plus grosses que les colonnes du temple. Ils sont toujours sur le dos des chameaux. Peuple singulier. Combien de fois n'y ai-je point pensé. Pour qui les plus immobilières maisons ne seront jamais que des tentes.—Peuple pour qui la pierre des maisons sera toujours la toile des tentes. Et pour nous au contraire c'est la toile des tentes qui était déjà, qui sera toujours la pierre de nos maisons.—

C'est faire beaucoup d'honneur au monde moderne.—c'est en méconnaître le virus que de dire: Le monde moderne est une invention, une forgerie, une fabrication, le monde moderne est inventé, a été inventé, monté, de toutes pièces, par les Juifs sur nous et contre nous. C'est un régime qu'ils ont fait de leurs mains, qu'ils nous imposent, où ils nous dominent, où ils nous gouvernent, où ils nous tyrannisent; où ils sont parfaitement heureux, où nous sommes, où ils nous rendent parfaitement malheureux.

Jewish Unrest

Charles Péguy

To be elsewhere—the great vice of this race, its great and secret virtue, the great vocation of this people. A train journey for this people with fifty centuries of caravans in its memory, means a caravan journey. Any crossing for them means the crossing of the desert. The most comfortable houses, the best built from stones as big as the temple pillars, the most real of real estate, the most overwhelming of apartment houses will never mean any more to them than a tent in the desert. Granite replaced the tent with walls of canvas. These stones, bigger than the temple pillars, don't matter. This people is always on camel back. How many times have I not thought about this singular people for whom the solidest of houses will never be more than tents.—A people for whom the stones of houses will always be the canvas of tents. And for us, on the contrary, the canvas of tents was already, will always be the stone of our houses.—

It is doing the modern world far too much honour,—we disregard its venom by saying: The modern world is an invention, a forgery, a fabrication; the modern world is invented, has been invented, entirely fabricated by the Jews over and against us. That this is a regime made by their hands, imposed upon us, a regime which they have imposed on us, where they dominate us, govern us and tyrannise over us, where they are perfectly happy and where we are, where they make us perfectly unhappy.

C'est bien mal connaître le monde moderne, que de parler ainsi. C'est lui faire beaucoup d'honneur. C'est le connaître, c'est le voir bien superficiellement. C'est en méconnaître bien gravement, (bien légèrement), le virus, toute la nocivité. C'est bien en méconnaître toute la misère et la détresse. Premièrement le monde moderne est beaucoup moins monté. Il est beaucoup plus une maladie naturelle. Deuxièmement cette maladie naturelle est beaucoup plus grave, beaucoup plus profonde, beaucoup plus universelle.

Nul n'en profite et tout le monde en souffre. Tout le monde en est atteint. Les modernes mêmes en souffrent. Ceux qui s'en vantent, qui s'en glorifient, qui s'en réjouissent, en souffrent. Ceux qui l'aiment le mieux, aiment leur mal. Ceux mêmes que l'on croit qui n'en souffrent pas en souffrent. Ceux qui font les heureux sont aussi malheureux, plus malheureux que les autres, plus malheureux que nous. Dans le monde moderne, tout le monde souffre du mal moderne. Ceux qui font ceux que ça leur profite sont aussi malheureux, plus malheureux que nous. Tout le monde est malheureux dans le monde moderne.

Les Juifs sont plus malheureux que les autres. Loin que le monde moderne les favorise particulièrement, leur soit particulièrement avantageux, leur ait fait un siège de repos, une résidence de quiétude et de privilège, au contraire le monde moderne a ajouté sa dispersion propre moderne, sa dispersion intérieure, à leur dispersion séculaire, à leur dispersion ethnique, à leur antique dispersion. Le monde moderne a ajouté son trouble à leur trouble; dans le monde moderne ils cumulent; le monde moderne a ajouté sa misère à leur misère, sa détresse à leur antique détresse; il a ajouté sa mortelle inquiétude, son inquiétude incurable à la mortelle, à l'inquiétude incurable de la race, à l'inquiétude propre, à l'antique, à l'éternelle inquiétude.

Il a ajouté l'inquiétude universelle à l'inquiétude propre.—

To talk thus is to know the modern world very badly. It is to honour it far too much. It is to know and to see it very superficially. It is to very gravely (and very frivolously) disregard its venom and its noxiousness. It is to disregard all its destitution and distress. Firstly, the modern world is not properly designed. It is really more of a natural disease. Secondly, this natural disease is far graver, far deeper, far more universal.

No one profits by it and everyone suffers from it. Everyone is smitten by it. The moderns themselves suffer from it. Those who boast of it, who glory. in it, who rejoice in it, suffer from it. Those who love it best, love their disease. Those who pretend to be happy are as unhappy, are more unhappy than the others, more unhappy than we. In the modern world everyone suffers from the modern disease. Those who pretend to profit by it are as unhappy, more unhappy than we are. Everyone is unhappy in the modern world.

The Jews are more unhappy than the others. The modern world does not favour them particularly, does not benefit them particularly, has not given them a resting place, a residence of peace and quiet. Far from it. On the contrary, the modern world has added its own dispersion, its inner dispersion to their century-old dispersion, their ethnical dispersion, to their ancient dispersion. The modern world has added its unrest to their unrest. In the modern world they hold cumulative offices. The modern world has added its misery to their misery, its distress to their old distress. It has added its mortal unrest, its incurable unrest to the mortal, the incurable unrest of the Jewish race. To the unrest proper to the race, to its ancient, eternal unrest.

It has added universal unrest to unrest proper.—

Les antisémites ne connaissent point les Juifs. Ils en parlent, mais ils ne les connaissent point. Ils en souffrent, évidemment beaucoup, mais ils ne les connaissent point. Les antisémites riches connaissent peut-être les Juifs riches. Les antisémites capitalistes connaissent peut-être les Juifs capitalistes. Les antisémites d'affaires connaissent peut-être les Juifs d'affaires. Pour la même raison je ne connais guère que des Juifs pauvres et des Juifs misérables. Il y en a. Il y en a tant que l'on n'en sait pas le nombre. J'en vois partout.

Il ne sera pas dit qu'un chrétien n'aura pas porté témoignage pour eux.—Depuis vingt ans je les ai éprouvés, nous nous sommes éprouvés mutuellement. Je les ai trouvés toujours solides au poste, autant que personne, affectueux, solides, d'une tendresse propre, autant que personne, d'un attachement, d'un dévouement, d'une piété inébranlable, d'une fidélité, à toute épreuve, d'une amitié réellement mystique, d'un attachement, d'une fidélité inébranlable à la mystique de l'amitié.

L'argent est tout, domine tout dans le monde moderne à un tel point, si entièrement, si totalement que la séparation sociale horizontale des riches et des pauvres est devenue infiniment plus grave, plus coupante, plus absolue si je puis dire que la séparation verticale de race des juifs et des chrétiens. La dureté du monde moderne sur les pauvres, contre les pauvres, est devenue si totale, si effrayante, si impie ensemble sur les uns et sur les autres, contre les uns et contre les autres.

Dans le monde moderne les connaissances ne se font, ne se propagent que horizontalement, parmi les riches entre eux, ou parmi les pauvres entre eux—

The anti-Semites do not know the Jews. They talk about them but they do not know them. They suffer from them greatly of course, but they do not know them. Perhaps the rich anti-Semites know the rich Jews. Perhaps the capitalistic anti-Semites know the capitalistic Jews. Perhaps anti-Semitic business-men know Jewish business-men. For the same reason, I only know poor Jews and wretched Jews. There are some. There are so many that they cannot be counted. I see them everywhere.

It shall not be said that a Christian has not borne witness in their favour.—For twenty years I have tested them, we have mutually tested one another. I have always found them firm at their posts, as much as anyone could be, affectionate, firm, as purely tender as anyone could be, fond, devoted, of unshaken piety, firmly faithful, offering really mystical friendship, fond, unshakingly faithful to the mysticism of friendship.

Money is everything; it rules everything in the modern world so entirely and to such an extent that the social separation of the rich and the poor along horizontal lines has become infinitely graver, more cutting and more absolute, if I may say so, than the vertical separation between the Jewish race and the Christians. The hardness of the modern world towards the poor, against the poor, has become so entire, so terrifying and altogether so impious towards the ones and the others, against the ones and against the others.

In the modern world, acquaintances are made only, spread only, horizontally—the rich among themselves, the poor among themselves.—

Pauvre je porterai témoignage pour les Juifs pauvres.—Dans cette galère du monde moderne je les vois qui rament à leur banc, autant et plus que d'autres, autant et plus que nous. Autant et plus que nous subissant le sort commun. Dans cet enfer temporel du monde moderne je les vois comme nous, autant et plus que nous, trimant comme nous, éprouvés comme nous. Epuisés comme nous. Surmenés comme nous. Dans les maladies, dans les fatigues, dans la neurasthénie, dans tous les surmenages, dans cet enfer temporel j'en connais des centaines, j'en vois des milliers qui aussi difficilement, plus difficilement, plus misérablement que nous gagnent péniblement leur misérable vie.

Dans cet enfer commun.

Des riches il y aurait beaucoup à dire. Je les connais beaucoup moins. Ce que je puis dire, c'est que depuis vingt ans j'ai passé par beaucoup de mains. Le seul de mes créanciers qui se soit conduit avec moi non pas seulement comme un usurier, mais ce qui est un peu plus, comme un créancier, comme un usurier de Balzac, le seul de mes créanciers qui m'ait traité avec une dureté balzacienne, avec la dureté, la cruauté d'un usurier de Balzac n'était point un Juif. C'était un Français, j'ai honte à le dire, on a honte à le dire, c'êta a hélas un «chrétien», trente fois millionnaire. Que n'aurait-on pas dit s'il avait été Juif.

Poor myself, I will bear witness in favour of the poor Jews.—In this galley of a modern world I see them rowing at their bench, as hard and harder than the others, as hard and harder than we. They undergo the common lot as much and more than we. In this temporal hell of the modern world I see that they drudge and are tried like us and more than us. Worn out like us. Overworked like us. In these diseases, fatigues, neurasthenias, in all the overwork of this temporal hell, I know hundreds of them, I see thousands of them who painfully earn their wretched livings, as hard, harder, more miserably than we do.

In this common hell.

About the rich there would be much to say. I know far less about them. What I can say is that in twenty years I have gone through many hands. The single one of my creditors who behaved to me not only like a usurer, but what is saying rather more, like a creditor, like one of Balzac's usurers, the single one of my creditors who treated me with Balzacian harshness, with the harshness, the cruelty of one of Balzac's usurers, was not a Jew. He was a Frenchman, I am ashamed to say. One is ashamed to say that he was, alas, a Christian, a millionaire thirty times over. What wouldn't have been said, had he been a Jew?

Such Original Thought in
The Everlasting Man

James Morris

That the cave was a crèche!
Somewhere for the kids to play,
Pre-historic pre-school.

That Christ was born in a cave!
Beneath the earth,
An even more lowly birth.

That we learnt to write in Egypt,
Pictures becoming signs,
Semaphoring up the Nile.

That Babylon *was* pedantic,
A cold scientism,
Far from corybantic.

That 'the gods' behaved worse and worse,
The reverse of 'homely'
Virgil perceived.

That all primitive religions-
Had originally the One True God,
But forgot.

Looking east along the River Toscaig

That the rise of the Church,
Was always of itself, *sui generis,*
From the very first.

That 'The Dark Ages' was a period of Penance,
(Almost like a prison sentence)
For The Crucifixion.

View of Volcán Osorno from Frutillar, Chile

Looking south above the cliffs across the little bay of Norwich

The Pope in Britain, 2010: A Retrospect

Sheridan Gilley

SHERIDAN GILLEY *is Emeritus Reader in Theology in Durham University. He is a member of the Editorial Board of* The Chesterton Review *and of the Board of Trustees of the G. K. Chesterton Institute for Faith & Culture, UK. Dr. Gilley is the author of* Newman and His Age *(Darton, Longman & Todd: London, 2002).*

I dreaded the prospect of Pope Benedict's visit to Britain to beatify John Henry Cardinal Newman. The Roman Catholic Church had been experiencing nothing but bad publicity over its alleged attempts to shelter priestly paedophiles, and there was controversy over whether Newman was a homosexual, based in large part upon his wish to be buried in the same grave as his great friend and devoted assistant Fr. Ambrose St. John. Again, the more liberal English Bishops were rumoured to be opposed to the beatification, and my lack of confidence in the Catholic Bishops' Conference, formally in charge of the exercise, to organise the proverbial drinking session in a brewery was confirmed by the slowness of ticket sales for the various events, which provoked unfavourable comparisons with John-Paul II's wildly successful visit to Britain in 1982.

All this came on top of the highly theological character of Newman himself: he is not an obvious popular hero. His great achievements were intellectual and literary: a classic spiritual autobiography, the redefinition of the Anglican via media, the idea of the development of doctrine, the relationship of reason and the intellect to the spiritual life, and the role and limits of university education, and of conscience, the laity and papal authority. These are not directly practical matters, such as his rival Cardinal Manning's social crusades, which have a direct accessibility to the modern popular mind that does not like intellectuals anyway.

Monnow Bridge, Monmouth

71

There has, therefore, been an understandable hagiographic tendency to exaggerate Newman's good works among the poor. These existed, especially in his first years in Birmingham, in his humble mission in Alcester Street, ensconced in a former gin distillery, where the fledgling Oratory was overrun by a congregation of bug-ridden Irish immigrant paupers. Otherwise Newman's good works were largely at second hand, through his fellow Oratorians. Like many another flourishing Victorian church, the Oratory conducted poor schools, an orphanage and a chaplaincy to the workhouse. These, however, were not what Newman was essentially about. His best-known foundations were the Catholic University of Ireland and the Oratory public school, established in 1859 and still flourishing, originally for the sons of converts and of the old Catholic aristocracy and gentry. The Catholic University included the Dublin Catholic medical school, ultimately of great use to the poor, but both the University and the school were intended to educate elites, as was an Oxford Oratory, which Newman planned but which was embargoed in Rome, at the behest of his English Catholic critics.

The Pope, as another theologian and intellectual, has some of Newman's disadvantages. He also has the bad luck to be a German. He has generally been depicted as his predecessor's "Rottweiler" and Grand Inquisitor, a remote and unforgiving figure, with a Nazi past, though as an unwilling teenage conscript. He was thought most likely to denounce Britain for its sins. He has badly ruffled Anglican feathers by offering an "ordinariate" to preserve some Anglican traditions within Roman Catholicism for defecting Anglicans. Then, on the eve of his arrival, it was again derailed by another Belgian paedophile scandal, lovingly reported by the BBC, and by an unguarded statement from, of all people, the ecumenist Cardinal Walter Kasper, describing Britain as "a third world country." It seems that the Cardinal had meant to say that Britain is multicultural, with lots of immigrants, but he then diplomatically discovered that he was suffering from gout and remained behind in Rome.

More discouraging still was an aggressive secularist reaction to the prospective visit, characterised by the most astonishing abuse, as by the Oxford evolutionary scientist and professional atheist Richard Dawkins, author of *The God Delusion*, who described the Pope as "a leering old villain in a frock." Though floored by Eamon Duffy on Radio 4, the channel for middle-class Middle England, the Tudor historian David Starkey, the rudest man in Britain, was his usual offensive self. Duffy's parting shot was that even for non-Catholics, "the Pope is a good man in white defending virtue." The gay rights activist Peter Tatchell and some leading literary and scientific figures seemed determined to humiliate the Pope with public demonstrations of the new atheism. There was talk, stimulated by the jurist Geoffrey Robertson, who denied that the Vatican is a sovereign state, of arresting Benedict as a criminal for protecting paedophiles, and on the 15 September, the eve of the Pope's arrival, the left-wing liberal *Guardian* newspaper, the organ of the anti-papal movement, published a letter from fifty-five *bien pensants* opposing the visit, on various grounds, mainly of sexual ethics, to do with the Pope's opposition to abortion, condoms and homosexuality. Most if not all of the signatories, some of them distinguished, are members of the British Humanist Association.

There was also some opposition to the papal tour on the point of cost: as this was a state visit, from a head of state, the first such official visit to Britain by a Pope (John Paul's was purely pastoral), most of its expense (estimated at ten million pounds) will be borne by the hard—pressed taxpayer. But generally, the opposition was on dogmatically atheist or liberal grounds. The old Protestant nationalist No Popery was there, but in a minor key—Ian Paisley was at his post protesting in Edinburgh—but Holy Mother Church seems to have outlived that enemy only to find another. Anti-Catholicism is now liberal; as Philip Jenkins has described it, it is the anti-Semitism of the intellectuals.

Meanwhile chaos reigned, in the general uncertainty as to where the venues were to be.

The visit was saved, in part by the organisational ability of Chris Patten, Lord Patten, the last Governor of Hong Kong, who stopped the nonsense and sorted out the mess. Also notable were the heroic efforts of the Birmingham Oratory and the Birmingham archdiocese. Yet everything still seemed scuppered by the ferocious security arrangements, which severely discouraged attendance at the events, so that they were much smaller than John-Paul's. For the beatification ceremony in Cofton Park in Birmingham, I, as an "invited pilgrim," needed a prior invitation, then (by postal application, with a necessary reminder), a security pass, and also my passport, while the crowds of 60,000 were nearly all sponsored with security clearance through their parishes. I had to get up at 2 a.m. in a central Birmingham hotel for an expensive taxi drive at 4 a.m., which took half an hour, to a bus collection point, before the bus ride itself to a security check point as at Heathrow, including a bag search, and a long walk over slippery wet grass through the drizzle and darkness. There was no complaining, as it seemed that the Duke of Norfolk, the premier English Catholic layman as Earl Marshal of England, and the Anglican bishops, including the Bishop of Birmingham, had to do the same. I kept thinking of what daft things we Catholics do, and the odd sequence of events in my own life which had brought me here. The event was effectively closed to the unchurched poor, to anyone with no parochial connection or without a passport or a car, and there was no question of simply taking the nearest bus or train at the last minute and turning up in faith and hope, as for the last Pope's British rallies in 1982. I was lucky to meet two of my Durham Catholic professorial colleagues to drive me back to Birmingham at the end of the ceremony, or I would have been abandoned. Everything had to be pre-planned.

Yet there was an unexpected miracle at Cofton Park: the Pope appeared, the drizzle of the "sodden and unkind" Midlands all but ceased, and the sun came out: it was symbolic of the whole papal tour, which was a triumph. On its first day, September 16, a Thursday, Princes Street in Edinburgh became a grand avenue for the popemobile. The crowds, here as elsewhere, even in London, were untouched by the hostility of the metrosexual classes. The Pope was welcomed at the airport by the Duke of Edinburgh, and was received by the Queen in Holyrood Palace, and that meeting sealed the visit for many conservative Britons who think that she can do no wrong. As it was St. Ninian's Day, Benedict was preceded through Edinburgh by a parade of children from the schools dedicated to the saint, the proto-evangelist of Scotland. By beginning the visit in Scotland, which still has an old-fashioned Catholic population, of Irish and Highland origin, the Church appealed to a key flock of the faithful. The rally in Ballahouston Park in Glasgow was the lift off for large crowds, and the shy old pontiff showed an unexpected skill in kissing babies. He has a grace of gesture which seems to withhold something of himself. This is not John Paul II, but Benedict's blessing has its tenderness. That secured the enthusiasm of the tabloids, and the Pope's speech to the elite of the nation's politicians near a plaque commemorating St. Thomas More in Westminster Hall, on the dangers of secularism, interested the more thoughtful newspaper columnists.

Indeed, the sheer rudeness and shrillness of the secularist opposition provoked a response from even some of the humourists, an indelicate and wild and woolly bunch, like Hugo Rifkind, the son of a former Conservative Foreign Secretary and one of the immensely talented English elite of eastern European Jewish descent. Hugo suggested that humanists should be more humane. Peter Tatchell began to behave with dignity. There was to be no attempt at an arrest. By Saturday, September 18, on the eve of ceremony of beatification, *The Times*, which had been generally hostile to the visit, most notably in the grossly offensive cartoons by Peter Brookes, who had once depicted the Pope with a condom on his head, changed its tune altogether, and declared the event a success, while the evening prayer rally in Hyde Park dwarfed the counter humanist demonstration. Humanists nil, Pope 1.

The *Independent* newspaper on Saturday tried to persuade its readers through a dodgy poll that Catholics did not agree with the Pope about sex, but even the *Guardian* relented a little in the end, though still considering the whole shebang an anachronism. On the last day of the visit, the *Sunday Times* headline read "Rottweiler? No, he's a holy granddad." Of the "quality" newspapers, only the *Daily Telegraph,* known as The Torygraph, and its Sunday sister, were unstinting in their praise of the Pope and enthusiastic about his coming. At one time it might have been the heart of the opposition, but from a conservative Protestant point of view. The conservative *Spectator* was also enthusiastic, embodying the dark blue strand in the rainbow coalition of English Catholicism.

What really incensed the secularists about the papal rhetoric was the Pope's use of Nazi Germany as an example of an officially atheist state, drawing on his own personal experience and in the same breath, warmly thanking the British for their part in liberating Europe. This climaxed in Cofton Park in the Pope's opening reference to the day as Battle of Britain Sunday, marking its seventieth anniversary. Professor Anthony Grayling (once described to me by a BBC presenter as never allowing any good historic role to the Middle Ages) thought that he was being called a Nazi, but in the *Sunday Times*, Dominic Lawson, an atheist himself, though married to a Catholic, indicated the meaning of this point, quoting the great historian Michael Burleigh, who had also written in Benedict's defence: Hitler was an atheist, and his ultimate aim was the destruction of the Churches.

The media reportage richly illustrated the general attitude of the educated and media elites towards the Church, especially the BBC, which nonetheless proceeded to give superlative coverage to the Pope while he was here. Its main sin of omission was its failure to televise the his speech in Westminster Hall, but it came into its own in broadcasting the magnificent service of Evensong, with soaring trumpets and clouds of incense, in Westminster Abbey, the nation's pantheon. The two retired university professors of theology, the Pope and the Archbishop of Canterbury, seemed to enjoy each other's company, forgetting their differences in the pomp and circumstance of the occasion, as the splendour of Anglican ritual and music at their best lifted the visit to a higher plane. If only Catholics could worship so well.

The point of the Evensong, of course, was that the Church of England is a state church, with a recognised public role, in contradiction to the humanist wish to exclude Christianity from public life altogether. The Cofton Park ceremony was also extremely impressive: dozens of prelates and six hundred priests, and the fine setting of a kind of grassy bowl for the congregation, though with a rather naff central sanctuary, left over, it appeared by its style, from the 1970s. The sound system really worked. There was a good new setting of parts of the vernacular Mass by the distinguished Scottish composer, James MacMillan, who came on a bus like everyone else. But the occasion really came to life when the choir of two thousand thundered out the *Missa de Angelis* Nicene Creed in Latin, and some great Anglican hymns, concluding with "For All the Saints," as well as Newman's own hymns, "Lead, Kindly Light," "Firmly I Believe and Truly" and "Praise to the Holiest in the Height." A verse of the last was used as a tremendous acclamation for the beatification. It is not every saint who writes his own musical script.

I found myself in the second row of chairs on the grass, wedged around by the Knights of Malta in front and the Knights and Dames of the Holy Sepulchre behind me, the Knights in white crusader cloaks with red crosses, the Dames with black lace mantillas. Behind in green were the Knights of St. Gregory. How Chesterton would have loved this, as a Knight of the Holy Ghost. I had a pang of nostalgia for the old parochial confraternities with which any Catholic parish could put on just such a display. There was a gentle murmur of approval among the people around me when a row of English Catholic bishops were evicted from the sanctuary to make way for the papal retinue. The bishops are neither particularly well-known nor popular, though their leadership, the Archbishops of Westminster, Birmingham and Liverpool, are men of conspicuous ability. The motley crowds in Cofton Park also illustrated the shot in the arm for Catholicism from Britain's more recent waves of immigrants: Poles, Philippinos, Vietnamese, Nigerians. Even the *Guardian* found their restraint and good behaviour "very English." When the words and music stopped, there was an extraordinary silence. The Church's real crisis lies in the lack of recruitment to the clergy, which will come in this generation.

My own minor place in all this illustrates the extent of the media coverage. I took part with John Cornwell, the liberal Catholic author of a recent controversial book, *Newman's Unquiet Grave*, and with the Anglican historian Frances Knight, in a BBC Radio 4 programme about Newman in the series "Beyond Belief." It was over-controlled by the presenter, but one could get out something of what one wanted to say. I had already provided interviews to an Italian newspaper, and in Newman's Oxford College of Oriel to an Austrian television company. Then on the Monday before the Pope's arrival, I gave a lecture sponsored by the Birmingham Oratory, the Archdiocese of Birmingham and the University in a hall accommodating above three hundred people, including the Archbishop and the Vice-Chancellor. Then there was an interview with Radio Midlands and an address to the Manchester Catholic clergy. On Thursday I had a piece on Anglican-Catholic relations over four centuries in *The Times*, and on Friday a review of Cornwell's book, *Newman's Unquiet Grave*, in the Anglican *Church Times*. On Saturday, I spoke at a Newman Day in the Birmingham International Conference Centre with Fr. Ian Ker, Newman's biographer, Fr. Michael Lang, the liturgist, from the London Oratory, and Fr. Keith Beaumont, a member of the French Oratory, who has written an admirable short book on Newman for the beatification.

The huge conference hall was given free of charge for the day by the Birmingham City Council, which also paid for a stunning performance of Elgar's setting of *The Dream of Gerontius* in the Town Hall, and for a great civic banquet in the splendour of the Victorian classical council chambers attended by Princess Michael of Kent and the Archduke of Austria. The Council also spent a small fortune on policing and traffic control for Cofton Park, officially costing £80,000: I suspect much more.

I was told that the Cardinal's robes, which were on display in the city art gallery with his mitre and crozier, had been repaired at the Council's expense. Its generosity was extraordinary, even if one detects a certain civic pride and satisfaction that Birmingham has a saint, and Manchester does not. This balanced the Pope's reference to the errant Council which a few years ago, wanted to replace Christmas with Winterval ("Pope's battle to save Christmas:" *Daily Mail*). The celebration recalls Newman's rebuke to Monsignor George Talbot, who offered him a better congregation of hearers in Rome, that "Birmingham people have souls." There was another odd reminder of an older England at Cofton Park, which is near the now abandoned Mordor of the Longbridge car works: the young Tolkien lived round the corner in leafy surroundings, and re-created them as The Shire. Tolkien was the ward of one of the Fathers of the Birmingham Oratory, and it was Tolkien's great-grandson who designed the statue of Newman which now stands in the Park in his memory.

The concluding hours of the Pope's visit were spent at nearby Oscott College, where Newman was confirmed and received his minor orders from Bishop, later Cardinal, Wiseman, the first Archbishop of Westminster. Newman's Oratory was established first at Old Oscott, which he renamed Maryvale, now again a centre of theological learning. He was in many ways in Birmingham rather than of it, a city then with only a small population of mostly Irish Catholics, and with an Anglican Evangelical establishment and a civic elite dominated by Nonconformists, notably Unitarians and Quakers like the Chamberlains and the Cadburys. Newman's last public act was to persuade the Cadburys to assign a separate prayer room to their Catholic employees. Birmingham, like the Cadburys, sensed his greatness, and the vast crowd at his funeral was its homage. He is a saint for the world, not just for his city by adoption, but it has done him proud.

And so, now, has his native land.

Piazza del Duomo with the baptistry of San Giovanni, cathedral of Santa Maria de Fiore

Chesterton in America

Ian Boyd

IAN BOYD, *is the President of the G. K. Chesterton Institute for Faith & Culture, and Editor of* The Chesterton Review. *The following article was delivered at the Gerety Lecture at Seton Hall University on December 2, 2009. Fr. Boyd lectured on the same theme at the College of the Holy Cross in Worcester, MA, on March 25, 2010, and at the University of Notre Dame on October 4, 2010, on the occasion of the eightieth anniversary of Chesterton's visit to these universities.*

Chesterton's earliest writing about America is found in a fragment that he composed as a teenager. In it the central character

> . . . wished to discover America. His gay and thoughtless friends, who could not understand him, pointed out that America had already been discovered, I think they said by Christopher Columbus, some time ago, and that there were big cities of Anglo-Saxon people there already, New York and Boston, and so on. But the Admiral explained to them, kindly enough, that this had nothing to do with it. They might have discovered America, but he had not.

The passage is from a notebook that was published after his death by his biographer Maisie Ward entitled *The Coloured Lands*. Chesterton's actual discovery of America took place during two visits, the first of which was from early January until mid April of 1921 and the second, ten years later, a longer visit, from early October 1930 until late March 1931.

These visits to America came at a critical time in Chesterton's life. In 1921, though close to making his life-changing decision, he had not yet been received into the Catholic Church. When nine years later he visited

---

View of Boboli Gardens from Palazzo Pitti

America as a Catholic, he was welcomed with great enthusiasm at Notre Dame University, where he lectured for six weeks, and at Holy Cross College in Worcester, Massachusetts, where he received an honourary doctorate. His change in religion illuminates the difference in mood that marked his return visit to America. Although the lectures he gave on his second tour occurred in dozens of cities and were attended by audiences which were not predominantly Catholic, the atmosphere had changed: in 1921, his view of America had been somewhat pessimistic; in 1930 it was far more positive. In both instances, however, his reaction to America provides an excellent way of understanding Chesterton and the major themes of his social philosophy. They also throw light on what he learned from America.

In the course of his 1921 visit, Chesterton confirmed the public image that had gradually formed during the first two decades of his public life. He was proud to describe himself as a journalist, but he was a journalist of a most unusual kind. His meteoric rise to fame in the early years of the twentieth century had made him one of the best-known literary figures of the age. In addition to the hundreds of articles he wrote for newspapers and journals, he achieved fame by an inexhaustible flood of imaginative writing. During these years, he wrote biographies of Robert Browning, G. F. Watts, Charles Dickens and G. B. Shaw, as well as almost all of his highly regarded Dickens criticism. There were also a critical study of Victorian literature, a play, and a history of England. During these years he wrote the best of his verse, including his greatest poem, *The Ballad of the White Horse*. Incredibly he was also a novelist and a short-story writer, with nearly a dozen novels and what is his most famous fiction, the Father Brown stories.

He was recognised as an influential thinker. The ensemble of his writing represented a coherent philosophy of life so that, like a new Victorian sage, he had become the moral standard for a generation of readers in the English-speaking world and beyond. Not yet a Catholic, he nevertheless acted as a spokesman for Catholic beliefs. His account of how he came to Christianity was expressed in a religious and philosophical treatise—the famous *Orthodoxy*—which tells of his attempt to invent a new religion and of his subsequent discovery that, like America, it had been discovered long before and was called Christianity. "I did not make it," he writes, "God and humanity made it and it made me."

Though never disguising his Catholic sympathies, the creed he defended in this 1908 book was cheerfully ecumenical: "When the word 'orthodoxy' is used here," he explains, "it means the Apostles' Creed, as understood by everybody calling himself Christian until a very short while ago, and the general historical conduct of those who held such a creed."

Chesterton's fame before his first visit to America was based on his role as a moralist and as a defender of an endangered religious tradition. He admired of Samuel Johnson, appearing once in a pageant as that great English moralist whose thinking was very like his own. Fond as he may have been of debate, he understood that the malaise of the age would not be healed by mere argumentation. He (and the Anglo-Catholic group with which he worked) saw that it was pointless to address individuals without altering the moral atmosphere which was affecting people as decisively as the material world around them. Given that the collective mind he was attempting to influence was still in some sense Christian, his work was essentially that of catechesis rather than evangelisation.

Even his limitations were a help in performing this immense task. From the time of his marriage in 1901 to Frances Blogg, a devout Anglican, he had been in contact with a remarkable group of Anglo-Catholic theologians who were working out a strategy for the religious regeneration of England. He lectured for the Christian Social Union and wrote for their journal *Commonwealth*, as well as for less congenial journals, such as the *Church Socialist Quarterly*, *The Hibbert Journal* and A. R. Orage's *New Age*. He was a friend of Anglican social thinkers, including Henry Scott Holand, Bishop Charles Gore, Charles Masterman, and the radical Conrad Noel. Many of the ideas we identify as Chestertonian came from them. They were his teachers, but they also were influenced by him. Strangely, however, he was never an Anglican in the ordinary sense of the word. He seldom attended Anglican religious services, and he was never confirmed as an Anglican. In many ways, his religious position kept some of the vagueness of the Liberal Unitarian universalism that had characterised the religious atmosphere of his childhood.

But if these were limitations, they were limitations that made him a comfortable figure to his readers on both shores of the Atlantic. He was a sacramental Christian who could speak to evangelical Protestants and other such Christians unthreateningly, because he was not a Roman Catholic. His writings were all the more persuasive because he found room in them for anything good in contemporary society. He was thus able to maintain a genial friendliness with what seem to be irreconcilably hostile points of view. He was a Liberal in politics and a Catholic Christian in religion, even though the Liberal governments of his day were hostile to the Catholic ideas he championed. Typically, his novels seldom have a single hero or defend a single point of view. Like Adam Wayne and Auberon Quinn, the heroes of his first novel, *The Napoleon of Notting Hill* (1904), he is both an idealist and a critic of idealism. Like Evan MacIan and James Turnbull, the heroes of his most explicitly religious novel, *The Ball and the Cross* (1910), he is a spokesman for Catholicism and a critic of romantic Catholicism. He is like the Church he describes in *Orthodoxy*, welcoming a variety of apparently opposite points of view and keeping them intact in a complex balance.

It is important to remember that the Chesterton who arrived in New York at the beginning of 1921 was known to the American reading public. He himself had already noted that the English and Americans read each others' authors. Hawthorne and Mark Twain were as popular in Britain as they were in America, and Dickens and Thackeray were read by Americans even if they knew little about the backgrounds of these intensely English writers. So too with Chesterton. Most of his books readily found American publishers; and although their readers were unlikely to have fully understood the complex and idiosyncratic English background which provided the context for his writing, they had come to have an affection for an author whom they regarded as wise and humorous—an English Will Rogers, as it were.

To understand Chesterton's reaction to America in 1921, it is necessary to note another, submerged aspect of his complex personality. Much that seems surprising in Chesterton's philosophy of life can be accounted for by the distress he experienced in 1893-1894 when he was a student at London University's Slade School of Art. His mental and spiritual crisis of that time is known as solipsism. In chapter IV of the *Autobiography*, "How to be a Lunatic," Chesterton describes how this extreme form of idealism affected him:

At a very early age I had thought my way back to thought itself. It is a very dreadful thing to do; for it may lead to thinking that there was nothing but thought. At this time I did not very clearly distinguish between dreaming and waking; not only as a mood, but as a metaphysical doubt, I felt as if everything might be a dream. It was as if I had myself projected the universe from within, with all its trees and stars; and that is so near to the notion of being God that it is manifestly even nearer to going mad. I was not mad, in any medical or physical sense: I was simply carrying the skepticism of my time as far as it would go. And I soon found it would go a great deal further than most of the sceptics went. While dull atheists came and explained to me that there was nothing but matter, I listened with a sort of calm horror of detachment, suspecting that there was nothing but mind.

This mental crisis was also a moral crisis. Chesterton describes it "as a condition of moral anarchy within." He goes on to explain that the "the whole mood was overpowered and oppressed with a sort of congestion of imagination. As Bunyan, in his morbid period, described himself as prompted to utter blasphemies, I had an overpowering impulse to record or draw horrible ideas and images; plunging deeper and deeper as in a blind spiritual suicide." The entire experience is re-visited in *The Man Who Was Thursday* (1908) regarded as Chesterton's best novel. It is significantly sub-titled "A Nightmare."

Chesterton's reaction to the solipsistic nightmare from which he had quickly recovered, explains much about the world view which permeates all his writing. It might be said that he spent the rest of his life celebrating the discovery that he was not God. He insisted over and over again that basis of happiness was to be found in the gift of existence itself, a gift for which the only appropriate response was wonder and gratitude. One must learn, he said, to rejoice in those moments when one remembers that one is alive. Direct contact with simple material things had an immense importance for him. He disliked large-scale abstract ideologies such as socialism and monopoly capitalism, preferring small nations and small communities, such as the family and the village. While he hated British Imperialism he was intensely patriotic to England, and to his neighbourhood. After he had become a Christian, he found religious justification for this philosophy in the doctrine of the Incarnation. His favourite verse from the Creed was "*Et incarnatus est*" ("And the Word was made flesh and dwelt among us"), which is the distinguishing mark of Christianity. Like his beloved St. Francis, of whom he wrote a charming biography, he believed that the coming of Christ was itself an act of Redemption. Drawing upon this insight, he said, in a startling paradox, that the work of the devil is spiritual, whereas the work of God is material. As a sacramental Christian, he believed that the Christian community was itself the Sacrament of Christ because the sacraments were actions of Christ who had assigned to the Church his three-fold mission of healing, teaching and praying. Consequently, the life of every human being was a re-enactment of the Gospel story.

Such was the nature of the man who was welcomed to New York City on a chilly January day in 1921. Everything he then said about America and everything he then learned about America were related to the complex philosophy that it had taken him forty-seven years to develop. Even his witticisms expressed his Christianity. It is said that one of the questions an American reporter asked him even before the ship touched land—reporters, Chesterton pointed out, were like pirates who boarded the ship as soon as soon as it came into the harbour—was the age-old question about the book he would take with him to desert island: the Bible? Shakespeare? Dickens? There are different versions of Chesterton's reply, but in essence he said he would take a book entitled *A Hundred and One Ways to Make a Boat*. Here, in a single phrase, is an instance of Chesterton's ongoing concern with solipsism. The man on the desert island is a metaphor for the man trapped in his own mind, whose most pressing need is a boat that would take him back to his fellow human beings.

Chesterton in America discovered fresh confirmation of what he had come to believe. He tended to interpret events as symbols, and so he interpreted his American experience. While still on board, for example, he was thanked by an Irish-American reporter for all that he had done for Ireland. Chesterton indeed defended Ireland throughout his journalistic career, and in 1921 Ireland was a topic of special interest because of the war for independence. But Chesterton turned this small incident into a symbol about the meaning of America as a defender of the liberty, which was the central tenet of his own political philosophy. As the journalist was speaking Chesterton looking towards the Statue of Liberty, saw that the colossus was gleaming green in the morning light: "And then I suddenly remembered that this Liberty was still in some sense enlightening the world, or one part of the world. They had made it so much their home that the very colour of the country seemed to change with the infusion; as the bronze of the great statue took on a semblance of the wearing of the green."

In *What I Saw in America*, published the year after his return to England, Chesterton analysed what America represented. His vision is a combination of admiration and foreboding. He had visited many American cities: New York, Chicago, Philadelphia, Baltimore, Nashville, Oklahoma, Omaha and Albany. Everywhere he had received a hero's welcome, and slowly he formed his impressions into a single insight. There were, he said, two Americas. The first was located in cosmopolitan New York, which represented for him with everything he feared about modern commercialism. The second was the America of small towns and the countryside, and even of certain cities such as Boston, Baltimore and Washington, each of which exhibited an older civic tradition. While he liked Americans, he was uneasy about American life. Maisie Ward, explained his view with a question: "The whole question of America was: would the older, simpler, really great tradition win, or would it be defeated by the new and towering evil?"

All his comments on America were determined by this question. New York was to him a symbol of consumerist capitalism. Consider his comment about Broadway: "What a glorious garden of wonders this would be for anyone who was lucky enough to be unable to read." An illiterate farmer from Europe might imagine it to be a proclamation in letters of fire of some great national motto: "Liberty! Equality! Fraternity!" How disappointing to learn they were merely advertisements to make money. Of sky-scrapers, he admired the aesthetic appeal: "vertical lines that suggest a sort of rush upwards, as of great cataracts topsy turvy—the strong daylight finds everywhere the broken edges of things and the sort of hues we see in newly-turned earth or the white sections of trees." He found a true "imaginative pleasure" in what he called "those dizzy turrets and dancing fires." But his final judgment about them, like his comment about Broadway is dismissive: "If those nightmare building were really all built for nothing, how noble they would be."

On the great plains of the mid-West he found the America he admired. It was the society mocked by Sinclair Lewis in *Main Street*, but for Chesterton it represented the real strength of America. It appealed to him firstly because it was still—unlike England—agricultural. "We in England hear a great deal, we hear far too much, about the economic energy of industrial America, about the money of Mr. Morgan, or the machinery of Mr. Edison. We never realise that while we in England suffer from the same sort of successes in capitalism and clockwork, we have not got what the Americans have got; something at least to balance it in the way of a free agriculture, a vast field of free farms dotted with small freeholders."

Small-town America also appealed to him because it was a world of agricultural equality. He continues:

> And, even in places like that described as Main Street that comparative equality can immediately be felt. The men may be provincials, but they are certainly citizens; they consult on a common basis. And I repeat that in this, after all, they do achieve what many prophets and righteous men have died to achieve. This plain village, fairly prosperous, fairly equal, untaxed by tyrants and untroubled by wars, is after all the place which reformers have regarded as their aim. The march to Utopia, the march to the Earthly Paradise, the march to the New Jerusalem, has been very largely the march to Main Street.

The other aspect of the America Chesterton admired was represented by the older American cities. Boston and Philadelphia were for him locales of tradition and traditionalism. In Boston, Chesterton was received by the head of the Cabot family with what he describes as "kindness and hospitality." "Boston," he writes, "is very much a place of memories." Here he found things he loved which reminded him of England, and of things that had vanished from England: "There are old brown houses in the corner of squares and streets," he writes, "that are like glimpses of a man's forgotten childhood; and when I saw the log path with posts where the Autocrat may be supposed to have walked with the schoolmistress, I felt I had come to the land where old tales come true." In Philadelphia, he felt the presence of Penn and Franklin. Baltimore reminded him that the state of Maryland was "the first experiment in religious freedom in human history." He also visited Nashville and St. Louis where found the traditional American South. And in Washington, he found a city worthy of the great President after whom it had been named. It represented for him the ideal of George Washington: "the idea of the Republic that rises above modern money-making and endures." Chicago, he admits, is more than "the mere pork-packing yard that English tradition suggests," and he admires its setting on the shores of a great lake, but, as with many other cities, he found it "defiled and even diseased with industrialism."

Again and again he comes back to the theme of the two Americas. In a quiet hotel in Nashville, Tennessee, he found a faded picture on the wall: "And from the dark canvas looked forth the face of Andrew Jackson, watching like a white eagle." Jackson is another important symbol for Chesterton.

> I believe that there are even fewer among Englishmen than among Americans who realise that the energy of that great man was largely directed towards saving us from the chief evil which destroys the nations to-day. He sought to cut down, as with a sword of simplicity, the new and nameless enormity of finance; and he must have known, as by a lightning flash, that the people were behind him, because all the politicians were against him. The end of that struggle is not yet; but if the bank is stronger than the sword or the sceptre of popular sovereignty, the end will be the end of democracy.

In spite of his admiration for the people, especially in rural and small-town settings and in his respect for the tradition represented by Andrew Jackson—a tradition which he believed was embodied in the older cities—the view of America which he formed by the end of first visit was pessimistic. In the conflict between traditional America and the commercialism of New York, he saw that the latter was going to win. The city was invading the countryside and overwhelming it. The same was true of the traditional cities which incarnated the noble ideals of the eighteenth-century founding fathers. These cities were no match for the overwhelming power of commercial America; Jeffersonian democracy seemed dead.

There was moreover a religious difficulty. America was essentially a Protestant, and consequently a non-sacramental, nation. The dominant religious tradition was Puritan, especially in that rural America which had come closest to fulfilling Chesterton's vision of what a good society should be. One of the best-known sayings of Chesterton comes from *What I Saw in America,* his comment that America was a nation with the soul of a Church. President George W. Bush quoted these words a few years ago during a visit to Communist China. He took these words to mean that the Americans were essentially a religious people. And that indeed is part of what Chesterton meant. But Mr. Bush's interpretation is simplistic. It is true that ideals of the American Revolution seemed to Chesterton to be altogether large and admirable; unfortunately, by 1921, they had become ineffectual or even dead. But the religious ideals on which the nation had been built seemed to him small and life threatening, and these ideals he found to be much alive. Chesterton came to America during Prohibition, a social experiment that illustrated what he disliked about Puritanism, to which he preferred even Deism. On one occasion, he commented on the absence of a Thanksgiving Day in England. He suggested that the English should establish such a national holiday of their own on the same day as American Thanksgiving. There would, however, be one difference. The Americans would continue to celebrate the arrival of the Pilgrim Fathers; the English would celebrate their departure.

In the years that followed this first American visit Chesterton returned again and again to the triumph of Monopoly Capitalism. In 1927, he had been invited to give a talk at his *Alma Mater*, the University College in the University of London, an institution on the centenary of its founding. His topic: "Culture and the Coming Peril." After praising the great Liberal founders of the University, he went on to say that the greatest danger to the Christian culture of the West was not the Bolshevism of Soviet Russia but the globalised consumerist culture that was spreading from America to every part of the civilised world. He defined the coming peril in a curious phrase: "standardisation by a low standard." He claimed that the power of this consumerist culture to undermine traditional societies was greater than that of the totalitarian system of Communism. Given that men derive their behaviour from the surrounding culture, the new consumerism also represented a moral danger. He had explained what this danger was in an article he had written for *G. K.'s Weekly* on June 19, 1926. After insisting that the modern Catholic must defend morality against monopoly, he concludes:

For the next great heresy is going to be simply an attack on morality, and especially on sexual morality. And it is coming, not from a
few Socialists surviving in the Fabian Society, but from the living
exultant energy of the rich resolved to enjoy themselves at last with
neither Popery nor Puritanism nor Socialism to hold them back.
The thin theory of Collectivism never had any real roots in human
nature, but the roots of the next heresy, God knows, are as deep
as nature itself, whose flower is the lust of the flesh and the lust of
the eye and the pride of life. I say that the man who cannot see this
cannot see the signs of the times; cannot see even the sky-signs in
the street, that are the new sort of signs in heaven. The madness of
to-morrow is not in Moscow, but much more in Manhattan—but
most of what was in Broadway is already in Piccadilly.

Chesterton's second visit to America in the autumn of 1930 was as
cheerful as his first visit had been gloomy. Anyone who reads the American essays published in *Sidelights on New London and Newer York* (1932)
will notice a change in tone from *What I Saw in America*. This new
and more positive view of the country can be attributed to the Catholic
character of his second visit. He came to America as the guest of Notre
Dame University where he spent six weeks giving thirty-six lectures on
Victorian literature and Victorian history. His welcome at this Catholic
institution was enthusiastic. On the average five hundred students attended his lectures. There was another, perhaps more significant, reason
for Chesterton's pleasure in America. At Notre Dame he and Frances
lived, not in the splendour of what Chesterton had called the Babylo-
nian American hotel, but with an ordinary and normal American family. For the first time they experienced American hospitality in a domestic setting, and that setting was Catholic.

The importance of this Catholic ambience is difficult to exaggerate.
Chesterton had returned to England in the Spring of 1922; a year later
he had been received into full communion with the Catholic Church.
What this event meant to him was expressed in a poem he wrote on the
day of his reception, "The Convert." The poem concludes:

They rattle reason out through many a sieve
That stores the dust and lets the gold go free:
And all these things are less than dust to me
Because my name is Lazarus and I live.

Sacramental confession was in fact the beginning of a new life for Chesterton. Although evidently a very good man by any standard, he felt a deep need for the pardon that can be received only in the sacrament of Penance. When asked why he became a Roman Catholic, he replied that the short answer was that he wanted to be rid of his sins. The fact that he was returning to America as the guest of a Catholic institution was therefore the source of great satisfaction to him. Equally significant for him was the fact that the University he would be visiting was under the patronage of Mary the Mother of God, for Chesterton's devotion to Mary was central to his faith. In an essay published towards the end of his life in *The Well and the Shallows* (1935), he explains the role that Mary played in his conversion to Catholicism:

> I never doubted that the figure [of Mary] was the figure of the faith; that she embodied, as a complete human being still only human, all that this Thing had to say to humanity. The instant I remembered the Catholic Church, I remembered her; when I tried to forget the Catholic Church, I tried to forget her; when I finally saw what was nobler than my fate, the freest and the hardest of all my acts of freedom, it was in front of a gilded and very gaudy little image of her in the port of Brindisi, that I promised the thing that I would do, if I returned to my own land.

In receiving an honourary degree at Notre Dame, Chesterton commented on the difference between his first and second visit to America His new view of the country, he explained was closely connected to his discovery of Catholic presence and within that, of devotion to Mary, a distinguishing sign of Catholicism:

> I remember that, when I came to America before, about nine years ago, when I was not yet a Catholic, and when I had hardly realised that there were Catholics in America, my first sensation in this country was one of terror. I recall the first landing and that great hotel in New York, the Biltmore, the name of which held for me such terrifying possibilities. (Surely there would not be more of it!) It all seemed alien, although I quickly discovered what kind and generous people the Americans are. I did not feel at all like that when I came to America the second time. If you want to know why I felt different, the reason is in the name of your University. That name was quite sufficient as far as I was concerned. I would not have mattered if I had been in the mountains of the moon.

Wherever she has erected her pillars, all men are at home, and I
knew that I should not find strangers.

A further example of how Marian devotion affected his new view
of America is found in "The Arena," a poem he wrote about a football
game and dedicated to the University. In it he contrasts the arena of
Nero where the athletes saluted the emperor before going to a game
in which some would die, of them will do with Notre Dame's stadium
where young men invoke Mary as they engage in a bloodless sport: "We
about to live salute thee." The golden image on Nero's arena represents
for Chesterton everything that was wrong with the pagan world. The
statue of Our Lady on the golden dome of the university represents
everything Christianity had done to cleanse the world and restore innocence after the horrors of that cruel paganism:

> There uprose a golden giant
> On the gilded house of Nero
> Even his far-flung flaming shadow and his image swollen large
> Looking down on the dry whirlpool
> Of the round Arena Spinning
> As a chariot-wheel goes spinning; and the chariots at the charge.
>
> And the molten monstrous visage
> Saw the pageants, saw the torments,
> Down the golden dust undazzled saw the gladiators go,
> Heard the cry in the closed desert,
> *Te salutant morituri,*
> As the slaves of doom went stumbling, shuddering,
> To the shades below.
>
> Lord of Life, of lyres and laughter,
> Those about to die salute thee,
> At thy godlike fancy feeding men with bread and
> beast with men,
> But for us the Fates point deathward
> In a thousand thumbs thrust downward,
> And the Dog of Hell is roaring through
> The lions in their den.
>
> I have seen, where a strange country
> Opened its secret plains above me,

One great golden dome stands lonely with its golden image, one
Seen afar, in strange fulfilment,
 Through the sunlit Indian summer
 That Apocalyptic portent that has clothed her with the Sun.

She too looks on the Arena,
Sees the gladiators in grapple,
She whose names are Seven Sorrows and the Cause
of All Our Joy,
Sees the pit that stank with slaughter
Scoured to make the courts of morning
For the cheers of jesting kindred and the scampering
of a boy.

Chesterton then describes the game itself, between Notre Dame and Navy:

And I saw them shock the whirlwind
Of the world of dust and dazzle;
And thrice they stamped, a thunderclap;
and thrice the sand-wheel swirled:
And thrice they cried like thunder
On our Lady of the Victories,
The Mother of the Master of the Masters of the World.

The final stanza addresses Mary by the paradoxical titles of the Mother of Sorrows and the Cause of Our Joy:

Queen of Death and deadly weeping
Those about to live salute thee,
Youth untroubled; youth untortured; hateless war and harmless
mirth
And the New Lord's larger largesse
Holier bread and happier circus,
Since the Queen of Sevenfold Sorrow has brought joy upon the
earth.

The Catholic character of Chesterton's second tour of America was also underlined by his visit to Holy Cross College in Worcester, Massachusetts, where he received another honourary degree. The highlight of his visit to Holy Cross was the tribute he received from Paul Claudel, a world-renowned poet and dramatist, who was then the French

Ambassador to the United States. Claudel's words are a reminder of
what Chesterton meant, not only to American Catholics whom he was
meeting for the first time, but also for the entire Catholic world:

> I am delighted to bring my salutations to the great poet and the
> great Christian, G.K. Chesterton, during his tour of the United
> States. His books, for the past twenty years, have never failed to
> bring me joy and refreshment: and this feeling of regard is so ten-
> der and unusual that approbation is linked with admiration.
>
> During the past century, Catholicism almost everywhere has had
> to sustain attitude of defence: it preferred to take shelter in the
> past and in forms of refuge, or as one might say, in chapels se-
> verely cloistered and ornamented with rigid refinery. Chesterton
> thoroughly understood that in our religion Mystery is wed with
> Evidence, and our eternal responses with the most pressing and
> present exigencies. He is the man that threw the doors wide open
> and upon a world pallid and sick he sent floods of poetry, of
> joyousness, of noble sympathies, of radiant and thundering hu-
> mour,—all drawn from unfailing sources of orthodoxy. His on-
> ward march is the verification of that divine saying: "The Truth
> will make you free."
>
> If I were to state his essential quality, I would say that it is a sort
> of triumphant common sense—that *gaudium de veritate*, of which
> philosophers discourse;—a joyous acclaim towards the splendour
> and the powers of the soul, those faculties that were overbur-
> dened and numbed by a century of false science, of pedantic pes-
> simism, and of counterfeit and contra-fact. In the sparkling and
> irresistible dialectics of a great poet, he keeps always bringing us
> back to that infallible promise of Christ:—And I will refresh you:
> *Et Ego reficiam vos.*

Another feature of the visit to Holy Cross College also brought
home to Chesterton a reminder that the Catholic Church of which he
was now a member represented a larger and more varied world than the
one what he had previously known. The students at the College greeted
him in the languages of their immigrant forefathers, a revelation of the
ethnic richness of American Catholicism. Chesterton was greeted in Arabic, Armenian, Chinese, French, Gaelic, German, Greek, Hungarian,
Italian, Lithuanian, Polish, Portuguese, Spanish and Syriac.

The rest of Chesterton's second visit to America requires less comment. His original plan had been to return to England after his visits to Notre Dame and Holy Cross, but his agent persuaded him to extend his visit by embarking on a second tour of the country. Thus his 1930 visit continued until the Spring of 1931. In addition to lectures in the North-East and Mid-West, he travelled to the South and to California, as well as to British Columbia, his third visit to Canada. In 1921 he had come to Windsor, Ontario, from Detroit. In 1930 he had journeyed to the New World by way of the St. Lawrence River, disembarking at Quebec City, from where he had moved on to Montreal and Toronto, in each city addressing large and enthusiastic audiences.

The content of his talks throughout the second tour of America was similar to what he had said in his 1921 talks. Again he noted on the narrowness of the Puritan mind. "The essential of the Puritan mood," he said, "is the misdirection of moral anger." Puritanism he insisted, was a small spiritual idea in comparison with the large political vision of the founders of the American Republic. He even blamed the Puritans for what he regarded as the typically American worship of economic activity at the expense of contemplation. In Albany, he developped this theme:

> The people are too eager to build up: they spend their energy in building up something that will be taken down in few years. It has grown to be almost a religion with the people here.
>
> It is a very subtle thing. I don't know where it came from. It is the outgrowth of history, of the exhilarating climate and the pioneer spirit, I suppose. The Puritans came here full of ideals of religion as if a new light shone.
>
> That passionate energy for religion with which they came to this country passed away and the people have thrown their tremendous energy into business. It is the worship of activity for its own sake. They worship it without an objective. In England the rich classes that worship laziness are as bad. Neither is sound. It is a false religion.

In spite of such sombre comments, the tone of his second visit was overall remarkably cheerful. This change is all the more surprising when one recalls that America was then in the grip of the Great Depression. And yet Chesterton did not tell his audience that the economic disaster which the country was experiencing illustrated the truth of what he had predicted about the dangers of a financial system far removed from the realities of everyday life and of concrete realities. Chesterton did, however, remind his audiences that his criticism of American commercialism was in complete harmony with his criticisms of his own country. And if he praised a number of English things, such as "English inns, English roads, English jokes and jokers," he had, as he pointed out, always been a critic of British Imperialism:

> And when that perilous power and opportunity, which is given by wealth and worldly success, largely passed from the British Empire to the United States, I have applied exactly the same principle to the United States. I think that Imperialism is none the less Imperialism because it is spread by economic pressure or snobbish fashion rather than by conquest; indeed I have much more respect for the Empire that is spread by fighting than for the Empire that is spread by finance.

The serene cheer of his second visit is illustrated by the tone of the debates he took part in during his tour of the country. In New York he engaged in a genial debate with Clarence Darrow, a well-known lawyer and sceptic. The subject of the debate was the story of creation in the Book of Genesis. Reports make it clear that Darrow was no match for Chesterton. One observer wrote: "I have never heard Darrow alone, but taken relatively, when that relativity is to Chesterton, he appears positively muddle-headed. As Chesterton summed it up, he felt as if Darrow had been arguing all afternoon with his fundamentalist aunt, and simply kept sparring with a dummy of his own making. . . . Chesterton had the audience with him from the start, and when it was all over, everyone just sat there, not wishing to leave. They were loath to let the light die!"

It was also during this final tour of America that Chesterton invoked the memory of Abraham Lincoln in order to pronounce his admiration for the hidden America of small towns and humble people.

> Whilst I was in America, I often lingered in small towns and wayside places; and in a curious and almost creepy fashion the great presence of Abraham Lincoln continually grew upon me. I think it is necessary to linger a little in America, and especially in what many would call the most uninteresting or unpleasing parts

of America, before this strong sense of a strange kind of greatness can grow upon the soul. . . . It was out of this landscape that
the great President came, and one might almost trace a fanciful
shadow of his figure in the thin trees and the stiff wooden pillars. A man of any imagination might look down those strange
streets, with their frame-houses filled with the latest conveniences
and surrounded with the latest litter, till he could see approach-
ing down the long perspective that long ungainly figure, with the
preposterous stove-pipe hat and the rustic umbrella and deep melancholy eyes, the humour and the hard patience and the heart that
fed upon hope deferred.

On March 23, 1931, Chesterton and his wife left California. Arriving in New York on March 29, Chesterton gave a final series of lectures
and then returned to England and to his home in Beaconsfield where,
five years later, on June 14, 1936, at the age of sixty-two, he died.

It is almost ninety years since Chesterton made his first discovery
of America. What can one now say about his view of the country? In
many ways, the views he developped in America were prophetic, for the
globalised consumerist culture which he found in New York has had
the effects he predicted. Soviet Communism has collapsed, as he said
it would, but the Western world has also experienced the truth of what
Chesterton had to say about the more insidious danger represented by a
commercial culture which undermines traditional societies and coars-
ens moral life. I would go further and say that the current financial crisis
vindicates Chesterton's warning about the essential instability of our
modern form of Capitalism. A striking indication of the wisdom of
Chesterton's critique of Monopoly Capitalism can be found in Pope
Benedict's recent encyclical, *Caritas in Veritate*. At a recent Chesterton
Institute conference in Oxford, Philip Blond, an adviser for David Cameron, the British Prime Minister, described the encyclical as a Chesterton manifesto, with its praise for local initiatives and its insistence on
the need for de-centralisation and intermediate civic institutions. Pope
Benedict's recent initiative in inviting Anglicans into full communion
with the Church is another fulfilment of a Chestertonian prophecy. He
had once said that just as Protestants speak of certain figures from the
Middle Ages as "Morning Stars of the Reformation," he would prefer
to speak of "Morning Stars of the Reunion." Chesterton, himself is
surely such a one.

And yet there are things Chesterton wrote about America which have not stood the test of time. Whatever truth there is in his criticism of American Puritans should be balanced and corrected by what is now known about the virtues of American Evangelicals. They have turned out to be the best allies of American Catholics in the struggle to defend the right to life of unborn children. No group understands as well the truth of what Chesterton wrote about the new heresy, *viz.*, that it would be an attack on sexual morality. One may also regret that Chesterton failed to discover the hidden virtues of America's large cities. Had he spent more time in New York, he might have discovered that it was in fact a community of villages teeming with the life of the ordinary people whom he so much loved. Another failure in imagination concerns what Chesterton wrote about Jews. It is true that his writings on this subject have been badly misrepresented. His criticism was directed against a particular kind of Jewish secularism. In fact, at the beginning of his career, he had protested the persecution of Jews in Tsarist Russia, and at the end of his life he was among the first of English writers to denounce the Nazi persecution. How one wishes that he had had a chance to meet Rabbi Stephen Wise during his American travels. This leader of American Jewry defended Chesterton from the attacks of his American co-religionists. Shortly after Chesterton's death, he wrote:

> Indeed I was a warm admirer of Gilbert Chesterton. Apart from his delightful art and his genius in many directions, he was, as you know a great religionist. He as Catholic, I as Jew, could not have seen eye to eye with each other, and he might have added "particularly seeing that you are cross-eyed"; but I deeply respected him. When Hitlerism came, he was one of the first to speak out with all the directness and frankness of a great and unabashed spirit. Blessing to his memory!

The words of Rabbi Wise provide a good ending to a paper that has examined Chesterton's relations with America. The blessing of the Rabbi would be echoed by countless Americans who have found delight and wisdom in the writings of this great Englishman.

Chesterton at the College
of the Holy Cross

Dermot Quinn

DERMOT QUINN *is Professor of History at Seton Hall University. He serves on the American and UK Board of Directors of the Chesterton Institute for Faith & Culture, and is a member of the Editorial Board of* The Chesterton Review. *The following article was delivered at the conference "Chesterton in America and Holy Cross" on March 25, 2010 at the College of the Holy Cross.*

Fr. Boyd and I are delighted to be with you this evening to talk about Chesterton and America and Holy Cross. Each of those subjects, taken singly, is rather large. Taken together, they are entirely impossible. The blame lies with Monsignor Sullivan who believes (to adapt Chesterton) that if a thing is worth doing it is worth doing boldly— with high energy, efficiency, and enthusiasm. Coming into Worcester from the train you can see a sign that reads "Sullivan Tires." Well, not this Sullivan. He is the most indefatigable man I know and I thank him for inviting us tonight.

Tonight is devoted to a remarkable event in the history of Holy Cross and a notable moment in the Catholic history of America. Eighty years ago this year, G. K. Chesterton came to the United States for the second of two visits to a country he greatly admired and to which, over the years, he had devoted much thought. During that visit, for some memorable days in December 1930, he came here. Fr. Boyd will speak about Chesterton and America. Before that, let me, more briefly, say something about Chesterton and Holy Cross.

First, may I say that I have long admired Holy Cross at a distance but that now, seeing it face to face, I realise it is even better than I had

---

Petrohue, Chile

imagined. What I knew of it before, I knew from Father Anthony Kuzniewski's remarkable volume, *Thy Honored Name: A History of The College of Holy Cross, 1843-1994*, five hundred and fifteen pages long beginning with the sentence "this book is an abridgement of a longer manuscript... persons desiring a more detailed account of the college history should consult that source." In fact, persons desiring a more detailed account of the college history should probably consult a doctor, because it is hard to know what Father Kuzniewski left out, except the social security numbers of the current faculty. At any rate, he tells us that Holy Cross's foundation in 1843 was "an act of faith in God and in human potential." It is clear, one hundred and seventy years on, that that two-fold act of faith has been magnificently rewarded.

Of course there are little human details and oddities of personality that any official history, no matter how complete, must inevitably omit. I am thinking of legendary Holy Cross figures such as Father Joe LaBran who always exercised his ministry in a cowboy hat; of Father Francis J. Hart (known as "Mother" or "Ma") who was a great booster of athletics; of "Fuzzy" Foran who taught English; of J. Bryan Connors, famous for his grand manner, his cape, his flask and his glass—a Wheeler Hall Chesterton, you might say; of Father Charles Kimball (for whom Kimball Hall is named) who was nicknamed "the Roper" because he was always trying to rope young men into the priesthood.

These men would be called nonconformists if there were some kind of conformity against which their eccentricity could be measured. But Holy Cross, it turns out, is *full* of such people. The college has also had, in another sense, a distinguished history of dissent, a commitment to social justice that has expressed itself in striking and contrarian ways. I am thinking of Fr. Leonard Feeney who was ordered to teach English here when removed from the Harvard chaplaincy; of Philip Berrigan, who was briefly a student here before he went on the feature on the FBI's list of America's ten most wanted fugitives; of Michael Harrington, the socialist author of *The Other America*. I am thinking of student protesters in the early 1970s who occupied the radio station, among whom was Clarence Thomas. I am thinking of other Holy Cross graduates who went on to occupy other studios, including those of MSNBC, and actually broadcast from them. No one took much notice.

So, to know Holy Cross is to know the breadth and the depth of the Catholic world. It is a city on a hill, and to be associated with it is to be a citizen of no mean place. It is "a community," as Father John Brooks put it in 1983, "seriously committed to peace, to freedom, to equality, to social justice for all." So committed to peace, in fact, that the college's two newspapers are called *The Crusader* and, before that, *The Tomahawk*. I have often puzzled about that.

Part of your distinguished history is our subject tonight. To speak of Chesterton and Holy Cross is to speak, first of all, of Father Michael Earls, S.J., the man who brought him here. Father Earls is now a largely forgotten figure, but eighty years ago he represented a particular kind of American Catholic sensibility we would do well to rediscover, both for its own sake (as an expression of first generation ethnic patriotism) and for what it says to us about ways in which to be Catholic today in an age often inhospitable to a Catholic point of view. He was born in Southbridge, Massachusetts to Irish immigrant parents. He studied at Holy Cross, at Georgetown, in Montreal, and at the Jesuit novitiate in Maryland. He was ordained in 1912 and served as Professor of Rhetoric here from 1916 to 1926 and Professor of English from 1929 to 1931. His whole life was bound up with Holy Cross—a college he loved and which loved him in return. He is still here in spirit and, indeed, in stained glass —in the library. He has become, in death, the kind of icon that he was, in many ways, in life. He was the sort of person for whom Holy Cross was created in 1843; the sort of person, perhaps, for whom it still exists today.

What strikes me about Father Earls is that his life ran strikingly in tandem with Chesterton's. Chesterton was born in 1874 and died in 1936. Earls was born in 1873 and died in 1937. They were almost exact contemporaries. They also shared certain enthusiasms and certain antipathies. In no particular order, the enthusiasms were for Ireland, for light verse, for the singing of John McCormack, for convivial company. The greatest of their shared passions were, of course, for America and the Catholic Church. Their antipathies, again in no particular order, were towards nominalism in philosophy, decadence in art, indifference in religion, skepticism in belief. Chesterton regarded the 1890s as a decade of deep intellectual sickness, a time of what he called "moral anarchy," of "blind spiritual suicide." Father Earls did not go that far but he was still moved to condemn the "cheap flares and ironical criticism" of the

103

late Victorian period. The each represent, in other words, a conscious reaction against what John Coates has called the Edwardian cultural crisis—the collapse of the old certainties in religion, art and science, with nothing to put in their place.

Earls was no ordinary Jesuit—if there is, indeed, such a thing as an ordinary Jesuit. He was a poet, a playwright, a novelist, a short-story writer, a critic, a professor and, of course, a priest—the last of these the most important. Introducing himself to students, he called himself "a singular man with a plural name." He was certainly singular. In fact, he was Holy Cross's most notable literary figure of the early twentieth century, a kind of Massachusetts Robert Hugh Benson who could produce volume after volume of commercially attractive, devotionally powerful, occasionally sentimental, poetry and prose. His novels are *Wedding Bells of Glendalough* and *Marie of the House of D'Anters*. His books of poetry include *The Hosting of the King*, *The Road Beyond the Town*, *In the Abbey of the Woods*, and *Ballads of Peace in War*. He also wrote two collections of essays, *Under College Towers* and, in my view his best book, *Manuscripts and Memories*.

As a literary figure, Earls is a paradox. On the one hand, his poetry is extremely sentimental. If you have a taste for Houseman-esque evocations of Linden Lane, of Beaven Hall, of O'Kane's High Tower, he is your man. Reading Earls's verse is like eating dollop after dollop of double chocolate mousse. On the other hand, his prose is sharp and pungent, full of irritation at what he termed the "glib neologisms" and "ephemeral breathlessness" of contemporary literature. Modern poetry, he complained, was nothing but the "pitiable mouthings, the insistent ejaculations of inmates in an insane asylum." The Higher Critics were "miscreants of affected and stupid scholarship." And so on. He was belligerent and, at the same time, soft and syrupy, as if (to use a maritime metaphor) the USS Missouri also sailed under the flag of the Good Ship Lollipop.

This bombast suggests a man uncomfortable with the modern world but Earls was much closer to the contemporary literary scene than you might think. He maintained a wide correspondence with Louise Imogen Guiney, Joyce Kilmer, and, of course, Chesterton. Other correspondents included the California novelist Kathleen Norris (the best-paid female writer of her day) and lesser figures such as the Irish writer Peter Mc-

Brien, who lived in Derry (my own home town) and who died before reaching his full potential as a writer and critic. Earls liked McBrien but I confess I am in two minds about him. "We Catholics in Ireland," he wrote, "… lack artistic culture. In true religious culture we are the greatest little country in the world. Call into the cathedral here at 6 p.m. It is filled with business girls making the Stations of the Cross: true mystics. But, artistically, Derry, I'd say, would beat any city for complete lack of culture."

So, Earls was a contemporary figure but, somehow, not a modern one: and it is this tension, this ambivalence, that suggests his closest link with Chesterton—the Chesterton who said that we should be at once at home in the world and utterly astonished by it, the Chesterton who, as a Catholic, was thankful that he was not a child of his own time. Earls admired Chesterton, he said, because he championed "sane thoughts in literature, in philosophy, and history"—because he was "the apostle of common sense" when common sense (in art, in literature, in politics, in philosophy) was in decidedly short supply. Above all, Father Earls liked Chesterton's economic ideas, his "distributism," which advocated small proprietorships, family-owned businesses, regional co-operatives, the breakup of trusts and monopolies, a thousand little corner shops standing tall against big corporations and the servile state. Chesterton's book *The Outline of Sanity* (a sacred text of the distributist movement) was much admired by Father Earls, and you can see its influence in his own book *Manuscripts and Memories,* which complains of "the growing cloud-lands of capitalism and materialism" threatening the family, the neighbourhood, the community, and the Church. In Chesterton, he found a defender of those things that seemed so obvious they hardly needed defence at all.

That is why Earls invited him to Holy Cross in December 1930. It was Chesterton the Distributist he most wanted to promote, Chesterton the defender of the little man, Chesterton the scourge of modern economics. The brochure produced by Holy Cross to commemorate the visit, to which Father Earls contributed a preface, contains, among poems and other *Chestertoniana*, only one essay: *Some Heresies of Our Mass Production*. In it, Chesterton complained of the "demoniac logic" of modern industrialism. "As there is a machine for making the stick, there must also be a machine for making the machine. As the machine and the stick must be sold as often as possible, it must be broken as often as possible. … To this there is added salesmanship, which means inducing people to buy imperfect wheels as if they were perfect wheels; and mergers, ... and publicity. ..." Against mass production and mass consumption, against big banks and big business, against standardisation and low standards, he offered a return to the local, the simple, the down-to-earth. Eighty years on, and several global catastrophes later, I think he has a point.

Holy Cross, and Father Earls, showed Chesterton an America he had never seen before—an intensely ethnic, intensely Catholic, also an intensely anxious place. He encountered, more than on his 1920 visit, a *Catholic* America: an America of nuns and priests, of college football teams, of Irish names and Boston accents; an America that manifested, in its parishes and local attachments, the very communitarianism he had come to preach. It was even, in some ways, an America that was *too* American, too patriotic, too prone to think itself exceptional. (Earls himself spoke of America as "the goal of seeking centuries/since first from Aryan valleys went the train/of unrecorded men," the remark suggesting a Catholic version of the city-on-a-hill Puritanism with which he was surrounded in Yankee New England.

But there's no doubting the anxiety of 1930. "My first and second visits to America have some true significance," Chesterton wrote. "One began with the Boom and the other saw the start of the Slump." There had been "a profound revolution in the highly intelligent American people. Life-long Republicans were going to vote for Franklin Roosevelt. No one believed in Prohibition (least of all Chesterton). Wall Street had lost its allure. "Americans have seen more of plutocracy than anyone else," he wrote. "They may ... see through it sooner than anyone else." One industrialist told him that "the people must go back to the farm." Chesterton wondered why they had ever left it.

The visit was an enormous success. Chesterton planted an oak tree outside the library which still flourishes. He was greeted by students in Arabic, Armenian, Chinese, French, Irish, German, Greek, Hungarian, Italian, Lithuanian, Polish, Portuguese, Spanish, and Syriac. A pageant was organised in his honour, in which seven students formally welcomed him to the college dressed as Newman, Shakespeare, Cervantes, Chaucer, Dante, Virgil and Homer. He was also welcomed in words of unsurpassed eloquence by the French ambassador to Washington, Paul Claudel—words which Fr. Boyd will quote in a moment.

He was himself in sparkling conversational form. When those polyglot students commended him as a crusader for great causes, he replied that "I am not much of a crusader but all the world knows I am not a Mohammedan." When, sitting down to eat, someone used the term *hors d'oeuvre* he immediately translated it as "work horse." When he spoke of "Father Earls's terrifying hospitality," one knows instinctively what he means—full glasses and late nights and conversation about everything under the sun.

One cannot know those private conversations but one may speculate about them. Why did Earls love Holy Cross? Why did Chesterton wish to return? Earls loved it because it was local. He loved it because it was home. He loved it because it was everything he ever wanted in a place—it was American and Catholic and Irish and decent and true. And Chesterton wished to return because he surely recognised that there was some sort of Incarnational truth at work here. The God of Earth and Altar (to use the words of his wonderful hymn) chooses *this* earth, *this* altar, *this* time and place, to reveal to us the meaning of *all* time and of *every* place.

And Chesterton certainly loved the Incarnation—as, I suspect, all fat people do. There is a little story of his second visit to America—not from Holy Cross but from Notre Dame—that rather sums him up. During his time at South Bend, the man who got to know him best was his driver, Johnny Mangan.

"He came here to Notre Dame," Johnny wrote. "He was close to four hundred pounds, but he'd never give it away. He'd break an ordinary scale, I guess. I brought him out of the main building but he got stuck in the door of the car. Father O'Donnell tried to help. Mr. Chesterton said it reminded him of an old Irishwoman. "Why don't you get out sideways?" "I have no sideways.""

That was Chesterton—the man who had no sideways. The man who saw things as they were and told us face to face. The man who was, of all philosophers of the twentieth century, the one who could break any ordinary scale.

How blessed we are to remember him—and Father Earls—tonight.

Greetings from Fairyland: Chesterton, Science and the Natural World

Susie Byer

SUSIE BYERS *is Ph.D. candidate in the School of Humanities at the University of Western Australia in Perth, writing a thesis on the subject of G. K. Chesterton's attitude towards the natural world. She has previously worked as a tenants' advocate and social security advocate.*

Introduction

It may seem strange that a writer only tangentially concerned with the landscape-preservation issues of his day has, more than seventy years after his death, inspired a doctoral thesis on the possible application of his "philosophy of nature" to a new kind of ecology—and even stranger that he would be posthumously paired with Hannah Arendt in this project. And yet G. K. Chesterton's contribution to a potential "ecological populism" has led Richard Gill to write that

> [o]ut of the common ground between Arendt and Chesterton I believe we can begin to sketch an ecological politics which avoids the irrationalism and pantheism of the so-called "deep ecology" as well as the conformism of an "environmentalism" which would leave us both cut off from appreciating the objective value in nature as well as living a more humanly satisfying life.[1]

For Gill the potential for Chesterton's work to define a new kind of ecology lies in Chesterton's sense of "wonder" at the world, a trait which Gill believes Chesterton shared with Arendt. The value which, according to Gill, informs their work is a sense of gratitude at the very fact of being, the sheer luck of being born into a world populated by other

The Killhope water wheel

creatures. Gill has certainly identified an extremely important aspect of Chesterton's thought. Throughout his life, the values of gratitude and wonder remained essential to Chesterton's response to the world. They remained, however, part of a framework of theology, not ecology. Chesterton had a deeply religious attitude to the natural world that manifested itself in an anthropocentric approach to the relationship between nature and humans. This theological approach to nature led Chesterton to be suspicious of scientists' attempts to tear the secrets from God's creation. Despite professing respect for scientific endeavour, when it came to understanding nature, Chesterton preferred to be faithful to a notion of the world as "Fairyland," where no scientific laws could explain the miraculous and the magical.

Chesterton's religious persuasion did not impede his acceptance of certain scientific proposition. He accepted, for example, the plausibility of certain parts of evolutionary theory, provided that the soul was excluded altogether from evolution (this is discussed further below). Chesterton respected the natural world, then, as a creation of God, and since God had endowed man and no other creature with reason, a hierarchy existed between humanity and the rest of creation. Given the hierarchical nature of creation, Chesterton unsurprisingly refused to accept any theories (such as social Darwinism) that appeared to him to subordinate humanity's God-given intelligence and free will to the "laws" of the natural world. Chesterton's theological response to nature therefore directed his responses to scientific (and pseudo-scientific) theories of his time and conditioned his response to the modern world. As part of his critique of science, Chesterton also expressed doubt about the value of "progress" as both goal and assumption of his age, and he refused to accept the comfortable (in his view, lazy) belief that scientific and other advances were leading humankind towards a better future.

The Limitations of Science

Chesterton believed that science was limited in its explanatory power. Clearly, scientists had trouble with those phenomena that lay beyond the material world. In addition to this problem, however, Chesterton believed that it was possible for science (like any other ideology) to fall victim to passing fashions. He was concerned with scientific materialism, but also, in later decades, with the implications of the "new physics" which, he believed undermined the material reality which he believed necessary to balance the spiritual world. Chesterton was concerned to defend the existence of physical things just as he was concerned to defend the immaterial.

To deal first with materialism, Chesterton believed that this particular fashion was related to a kind of "scientific fatalism," which held that nature, once observed, would repeat itself indefinitely. He contrasted this approach with that of the "fairy tale philosopher," who is pleased when leaves are green because he knows that they could have been scarlet.[2] In Chesterton's mind, the fatalistic approach failed to attain its own standards of scientific proof: by adopting an attitude in which outcomes in the natural world are pre-determined, advocates of the scientific method did not meet the requirements for scientific rigour because they did not accept the limitations of their own knowledge. Chesterton believed that scientists were falling short of their self-professed standards by too credulously taking a pattern and turning it into a law. He was not alone in voicing these concerns: indeed, some of his criticism of the "infallibility" of science is reminiscent of epistemological critiques being advanced by contemporaneous philosophers such as Bertrand Russell (of at least some of whose work Chesterton was aware). Chesterton, for example, wrote that "All the terms used in the science books, 'law,' 'necessity,' 'order,' 'tendency,' and so on, are really unintellectual, because they assume an inner synthesis which we do not possess."[3] Bertrand Russell famously proposed in 1912 that

> The man who has fed the chicken every day throughout its life at last wrings its neck instead, showing that more refined views as to the uniformity of nature would have been useful to the chicken. [...] The mere fact that something has happened a certain number of times causes animals and men to expect that it will happen again. Thus our instincts certainly cause us to believe that the sun will rise to-morrow, but we may be in no better a position than the chicken which unexpectedly has its neck wrung.[4]

People, like Russell's chicken, are liable to fatal miscalculation if they attempt to predict everything that comes from nature on the basis that what has gone before will continue to be. Aside from being, in

111

Chesterton's eyes, scientifically indefensible, the endless repetition of natural phenomena was a stumbling-block to the possibility of miracles. Chesterton believed that to retain the possibility of the miraculous in nature was not bowing to dogma but was, on the contrary, retaining the capacity for free thought and liberty. He argued that "the assumption that there is something in the doubt of miracles akin to liberality or reform is literally the opposite of the truth," and that a man who cannot believe might be "honourable and logical" but is by no means liberal. On the other hand, a man who allows for the miraculous is a true freethinker because miracles mean "the freedom of the soul, and [...] its control over the tyranny of circumstance."[5]

Here, Chesterton is careful to defend the miraculous on the grounds of free thought. Indeed, one of Chesterton's great rhetorical strengths was the care he took to critique science according to its own terms, and not solely on the basis of received theological truth. For example, when criticising Darwinism, he (like many of Darwinism's opponents)[6] criticised the scientific evidence itself (and by the 1920s had concluded that Darwinism was on the way out).[7] The controversy that arose, partly in the pages of *G. K.'s Weekly*, between Hilaire Belloc and H.G. Wells, in which Belloc tried to demonstrate that the science in favour of Darwinism was flawed led Chesterton's paper to conclude that "Mr. Belloc has rammed his original proof up to the hilt, not only through a hole in the science of Mr. Wells, but [...] through an equally gaping hole in the science of Sir Arthur Keith."[8]

Eugenics

What was at issue for Chesterton in the rise of scientific materialism was the excision of the spiritual from contemplation of nature. He believed that "there is a mystical minimum in human history and experience, which is at once too obscure to be explained and too obvious to be explained away."[9] In a long passage in a book about the controversial "science" of eugenics, Chesterton outlined his concerns with the dominance of the scientific project in the early twentieth century, disputing claims that the established Church had too much power over the political process. He argued that rather than the Church, it was in fact Science (a word which Chesterton often capitalised) that was trying to "tyrannise through government." Science, that "great but disputed system of thought which began with Evolution and ended in Eugenics" was being forced on the population in schools and in statutes.[10] By the 1920s, however, Chesterton's feeling was that a backlash against science had started. After its invasion and domination of public discourse, the community had started to wonder whether the scientific paradigm was enough of a basis for a fulfilled life. Chesterton believed that it was becoming obvious to the population at large that scientific materialism had, over the course of its existence, "been used chiefly for the oppression of the people."[11]

One example of this oppression which particularly distressed Chesterton was eugenics, the "science" of selectively breeding humans to favour or diminish certain physical attributes. There were several reasons for Chesterton's disquiet about eugenics. Firstly, it was an artefact of the aforementioned materialism. In allowing for the possibility that not only physical characteristics but also behavioural traits could at least to an extent be controlled, eugenics eliminated both human (and supernatural) spirit and free will: something that Chesterton called a "humiliating heresy."[12] He did not accept that eugenics represented a triumph of the human will over biological circumstance, except to the extent that the will of the tyrannous minority was prevailing over the humble majority. Their individuality, which was Chesterton's concern, was to be crushed by the so-called "experts" who were to give themselves the power (belonging properly to God) to judge the worthiness of their fellows.

Chesterton was quick to point out the class implications of eugenics.[13] In his experience, scientific innovations were often applied selectively and oppressively, disproportionately affecting the poor (his newspaper *G. K.'s Weekly*, for example, waged a long campaign against the "feebleminded laws" which caused children of poor families to be removed into state care on flimsy evidence). Chesterton was firmly convinced that eugenics, and any attempt to impose the laws of the natural world onto people, were a plot against the working classes—a capitalist scheme to breed workers who were ever more efficient and more subservient. The story that Chesterton told was that capitalists, growing disappointed with the inefficiencies of a working class depressed and unhealthy as a result of industrial working conditions, had the choice of either improving their conditions (with the distasteful possibility that this might lead to more independence on the part of the workers) or changing the nature of the workers themselves. Eugenics was an expression of the latter path, a cheaper one than improving pay, working hours or status. The capitalist "could not alter or improve the tables or the chairs on the cheap. But there were two pieces of furniture (labelled respectively 'the husband' and 'the wife') whose relations were much cheaper." And, eventually, the capitalist could "divert the force of sex from producing vagabonds. And he could harness to his high engines unbought the red unbroken river of the blood of a man in his youth, as he has already harnessed to them all the wild waste rivers of the world."[14] Finally, eugenics represented a shocking supposition that humans could be bred like animals, which to Chesterton (for whom humans and animals were qualitatively and definitively different) signified a blasphemy of the highest order.

Chesterton was not the only Catholic to disparage eugenics[15]—the Catholic Church was important in its opposition, and in "holding out" against materialism more generally.[16] He was perhaps more unusual in the extent to which he identified eugenics as an imperative of capitalism. The impact of industrialisation on the poorer people, which caused some of his fellow citizens to give up entirely on the that social class, led Chesterton instead to give up on industrialisation. There is a sense in Chesterton's work that the correct order of things, in which people should look up towards God and look down towards the natural world, had been disrupted by modernity. Nature, interpreted through science, was coming to dominate people. Eugenics was just another example of the application of natural laws (mediated by science and the imperatives of capitalism and industrialisation) to humanity.

The New Physics

If Chesterton was disturbed by the base materialism of eugenics and other scientific "evils," one might expect him to be comforted by the dizzying implications of developments in physics in the twentieth century. The new physics, embodied in the popular consciousness by Albert Einstein, dissolved the floor from underneath previous materialist certainties about the world. Some religious thinkers welcomed the new physics as the "nemesis of materialism," but others were more cautious.[17] Chesterton, perhaps surprisingly, was one of those who was sceptical about some of the early twentieth-century advances in physics. It is not clear from his writing precisely how much he understood about discoveries in that area, but evidently he followed it enough to know that he did not like it:

> Science was supposed to bully us into being rationalists; but it is now supposed to be bullying us into being irrationalists. The science of Einstein might rather be called following our unreason as far as it will go, seeing whether the brain will crack under the conception that space is curved, or that parallel straight lines always meet.[18]

To Chesterton, the obsession with "facts" that characterised his youth had been replaced by extraordinary "fancies," and scientific propositions that seemed wildly improbable. In 1921, he discussed the "whole trend of natural philosophy in the last twenty or thirty years" which culminated in the bottom falling out of the cosmos. Although he did not comment on any specific cases where the new physics seemed incorrect (he probably, like other laypeople, had little chance of understanding them), but wrote of the "cumulative effect" of these discoveries, where "straight lines are curved," the "clock has altered" and the "very pattern of the world had changed." This new reality was a nightmare, in which "science is destroying what we thought we did know" to the point where "dancing to the tune of Professor Einstein, even the law of gravity is behaving with lamentable levity."[19]

The new physics, as historian of science Peter Bowler has pointed out, made it difficult for citizens of the twentieth century to hold to the view that everything was rigidly predictable."[20] Chesterton, despite his appetite for the surprising, did not rejoice at this development, having decided, at the same time as concluding that Darwinism was dying, that the new metaphysical imbalance was not so much in favour of materialism and rationalism as it was in irrationality and the dissolution of the "real." Chesterton had not intended, when he was railing against materialism, to dent faith in the importance of the natural (as opposed to supernatural) world, although his emphasis on "Fairyland" gives the impression that he had no faith at all in the probability of nature behaving as it should. The miracles in which Chesterton firmly believed were meant to be the exception, rather than the rule, and if the material and the supernatural became imbalanced then the result was either rigid rationalism or the vague solipsism with which Chesterton diagnosed many leading thinkers of the turn of the century. Chesterton connected atomic physics with the engulfing self-centredness of the "decadence" in which one could be sure of nothing but oneself (or perhaps not even that). His response to this problem was to energetically reaffirm the existence of the natural world.

Wonder at the World

Chesterton warned ceaselessly about the consequences of this decadence. He was constantly swinging his torchlight towards the externalities on display in wonderful, miraculous nature—illuminating the world for which he believed people should be grateful. This *idée fixe* eventually led him to the conviction that there existed a being outside of humanity—it seemed a logical requirement of the prominence of gratitude in his thought that there should be someone to whom one could express one's thanks. Chesterton did not explicate this chain of thought much further, but it seemed to him too unlikely that he could have received a world filled with such wonderful presents and there could be no one he could look to in thankfulness.[21] Thus, Chesterton progressed from the *existence* of the world to its *creation* by an external being.

"I had always vaguely felt facts to be miracles in the sense that they are wonderful," he wrote in *Orthodoxy*; "now I began to think them miracles in the stricter sense that they were *wilful*."[22] In Chesterton's view, the miracles of nature required a miracle-worker, the magic required a magician, and it was in his view unfathomable that the world could have come about without it having been willed to be so. In Fairyland, Chesterton chose to suspend some (although not all) natural laws, and replace what must be with what could be. In this way, divine involvement was necessitated in a way it was not if the natural world, following evolutionary laws, was capable of arranging its own affairs. If it was possible in Fairyland that a tree could grow tigers hanging on by the tail (as Chesterton argued it was), there must be one to whom the idea of tigers in trees was pleasing, and who had the capacity to bring it about: the Magician. In this sense, Chesterton's observations of nature led him directly towards a form of argument from first cause, which Chesterton dealt with in his biography of Thomas Aquinas. He argued that we do not need even St. Thomas, we do not need anything but our own common sense, to tell us that if there has been from the beginning anything that can possibly be called a Purpose, it must reside in something that has the essential elements of a Person.[23]

Chesterton's philosophy of science and the natural world, then, was premised on gratitude and wonder, and a certainty that things exist and that they matter, but that (indisputably in Chesterton's mind) what can be seen is not all that there is. The existence of miracles required that the laws of nature be mutable.

The Limitations of Chesterton's Science

Chesterton's scientific expeditions led Stanley Jaki, in *Chesterton, A Seer of Science*, to conclude that he should be ranked with Pierre Duhem (a French physicist and philosopher) and Émile Meyerson (a Polish epistemologist and philosopher) as an interpreter of science.[24] Jaki's conclusion probably exaggerates the sophistication of Chesterton's understanding of science. Jaki's work is extremely important for many reasons, however, not least in its intention to address the distinction that Chesterton made between science and "some scientifically illiterate moderns" caricature of it.[25] The trouble with Chesterton's conception of Elfland or Fairyland, however, is that it was not merely the frequency of green leaves that led scientists to unjustifiably assume that leaves would always be that colour—their conclusions were based on scientific research that was beyond Chesterton's expertise. Warnings about the dangers of using induction to make predictions were appropriated by Chesterton and rendered as an argument that there was nothing at all uniform or predictable about nature. In the end, William J. Scheick (who reviewed Jaki's book on Chesterton) was reasonable in his assessment that Chesterton's understanding of science was limited by the fact that he did not seem to read very much of it.[26] Limitations such as this that led a historian of twentieth-century science and religion to comment that Chesterton's essay "Science and Religion" (in which he posited that science was either infallible or false) "proposed a vision of science almost as simple-minded as [Hilaire] Belloc's."[27] This assessment, too, is an exaggeration. Chesterton's view of science was, of course, related to his theology. But his critiques of science were not "merely" romantic (as some have claimed) nor were they simply "anti-modern" (his complex relationship to modernity will be explored further below).

Chesterton's Vision of Science and Nature

Evolution is an illustrative case study for Chesterton's view of nature. It was a particularly troubling topic for Chesterton, because it spoke to his fundamental belief that humanity was separate from nature in a very basic way. In *The Everlasting Man*, he wrote that the "simple truth" was that man "does differ from the brutes in kind and not in degree."[28] Evolution threatened the assumption that humans were qualitatively different from beasts. Also, it was predicated on a notion of inevitability and the loss of a sense of individuality: a natural world populated by individual and purposeful creatures of God was replaced with something formless, indifferent and unavoidable. Discussing William Blake, Chesterton wrote that "Blake really insisted that man as the image of God had a right to impose form upon nature. He would have laughed to scorn the notion of the modern evolutionist—that Nature is to be permitted to impose formlessness upon man."[29] He felt that, with the loss of a creator and its replacement with an impersonal evolutionary force, nature was no longer a display of the will of God—it no longer meant anything, in fact. He was quick to point out the moral implications of this aspect of evolution, writing in 1908 that to respond to a "sweater" claiming that "sweating suits this stage of evolution," an eternal test, independent of an ever-evolving notion of "current morality," was necessary to prove that sweat-shop labour in any era was an unacceptable practice.

To Chesterton's mind, this formlessness involved the application to people of the laws of nature, and was imposed on humanity by scientists who ignored what, to Chesterton, seemed to be the obvious differences between people and animals. In *The Everlasting Man*, Chesterton describes some of the scientific conclusions drawn from fossil records, noting that even very early humans had the habit of drawing on walls, whereas animals have never acquired a taste even for bad art. "It is useless to begin by saying that everything was slow and a mere matter of development and degree," he wrote: "Monkeys did not begin pictures and men finish them [...] the wild horse was not an impressionist and the race-horse a Post-Impressionist." Art, in fact, "exists nowhere in nature except in man; and [...] we cannot even talk about it without treating man as something separate from nature."[30]

It was noted above that Chesterton believed humanity to be the only thing in the world endowed with reason. He believed also that people were the only creatures endowed with moral judgement. Nature for Chesterton was darkly inscrutable to the cogitations of the human mind, and so there was little point in looking to nature for guidance on moral questions. In his book on St. Francis of Assisi, Chesterton argued that Francis did not praise nature for its own sake. Nature was at all times treated as an important but subordinate part of God's creation. If the non-human realm is indeed one that is separate from but subordinate to humankind, it follows that it is dangerous to attempt to draw moral lessons from phenomena observed in nature. Chesterton in fact expressed disdain at the notion of "following nature" in any moral sense.

The idea of following nature or "returning to nature" was popular in some circles in Chesterton's time, and he was quick to stomp on it wherever he found it. In his book about Tolstoy, he wrote that the desire to return to nature is "in some respects rather like the heroic desire of a kitten to return to its own tail." Although a "simple and beautiful" object, one of the important qualities of a tail is that "it should hang behind."[31] Nature could be a source of much joy—it is evident from his writings that Chesterton found it so—but humanity must never be made obedient to it, for the simple reason that "the sense of the sacredness of every human being, the sense that he is different from nature, that he is above nature, is the whole essence and power and force of Christianity."[32] As such, there is no meaning in nature that we have not put there ourselves—"there is no principle in nature," Chesterton wrote. There is no equality, and neither is there inequality, and to read aristocracy into the anarchy of animals is just as sentimental as to read democracy into it. Both aristocracy and democracy are human ideals.[33] Often, too, nature-worship—most especially in the form of Social Darwinist "survival of the fittest" fantasies—has a habit of extracting mother nature's nastiest habits as models for human society:

> I sincerely maintain that Nature-worship is more morally danger-
> ous than the most vulgar man-worship of the cities; since it can
> easily be perverted into the worship of an impersonal mystery,
> carelessness, or cruelty. Thoreau would have been a jollier fellow
> if he had devoted himself to a green-grocer instead of to greens.[34]

In the austerity and vegetarianism of Chesterton's good friend George
Bernard Shaw he saw a trend toward people trying to adopt simpler lives
that were closer to "nature," and he was sceptical of both the motivation
and the outcomes of such trends. Chesterton was frustrated with what
he thought was a particularly artificial and unnatural simplicity—he believed that if one had to develop complicated theories to support one's
eating habits, then it was unlikely that one was acting "naturally" in any
meaningful sense. In 1905 he wrote that it did not matter if a man ate
a grilled or a plain tomato; it mattered if he ate "a plain tomato with a
grilled mind." The only kind of simplicity that Chesterton wanted to preserve was the "simplicity of the heart."[35] Chesterton's quest for "simplicity of the heart" led him away from following nature. He concluded that
scientific theories such as evolution as well as trends like vegetarianism
were in danger of reversing the man/ nature hierarchy that was so crucial
to his world view.

Stewardship

Chesterton's disinterest in scientific and moral approaches to nature
did not translate into a lack of care for it. He wanted to care for it, however, with a certain lightness: the common thread between "pantheism,
evolutionism, and modern cosmic religion" is that they all regard nature
as a mother, when the point of Christianity is that "Nature is our sister."
We should be:

> proud of her beauty, since we have the same father; but she has no
> authority over us; we have to admire, but not to imitate. This gives
> to the typically Christian pleasure in this earth a strange touch of
> lightness that is almost frivolity.

Chesterton's approach to nature bears the imprint of what is called
"stewardship," the notion that "man, sinful though he be, occupies a

position on earth comparable to that of God in the universe, as a personal possession, a realm of stewardship."[36] Environmental historian Clarence Glacken calls this idea "one of the key ideas in the religious and philosophical thought of Western civilisation regarding man's place in nature."[37] A crucial tenet of the stewardship tradition is that humans, who are responsible for nature, should never become so besotted with it that they subordinate themselves to it or forget that nature is just another creation of God, one which is not endowed with humanity's gifts of reason and self-reflection.[38] Stewardship, in short, is anthropocentric.[39]

Science and the Modern World

Did Chesterton's resistance to parts of the scientific project make him an "anti-modern" thinker? There is no doubt that he found aspects of the modern world to be deeply distasteful. He hated, for example, to see the English countryside torn up to make highways.[40] To him, this kind of practice represented an abdication of responsibility for the natural world (and in the context of the modern world an inevitable one) in which "man's" rightful control over nature was being wrested from him by the modern state.[41] It is not surprising then that Chesterton has often been dismissed as "anti-modern" or "romantic." Two years after Chesterton died, this view was already taking hold, with Raymond Las Vergnas describing him as being in a position where he had to reject science, and as being "spiritually hostile to the dry logic of abstract reasoning."[42] Later, Jay P. Corrin subtitled his book on Chesterton and Hilaire Belloc "the battle against modernity."[43]

On the other hand, some recent historians have started to approach Chesterton's relationship to the modern world in a different way. Anna Vaninskaya, for example, has pointed out that Chesterton was at home in the modern world of Fleet Street and the mass press, and that there was much in his work that distinctly fails to fall into the category of "anti-modern."[44] Chesterton's approach to science can in this respect be is enlightening, helping to expose Chesterton's relationship to the "modern." The evidence suggests that, rather than being utterly at odds with modernity, he was focussed on revolutionising the present, drawing inspiration from aspects of the past but not romanticising it in the manner of which he has often been accused. For example, his response to eugenics was to place it in a historical perspective incorporating the development of capitalism and the growing power of big business. His response to this question was not a "romantic" one but was actually quite hard-headed, and he was not merely "obstructionist" when it came to science (despite his hasty and sometimes unjustified rejection of some scientific theories). His theology itself, which was deeply bound up in his approach to science, was based on a more complex approach to the idea of "civilisation" than is often understood. He assumed, for example, that some manipulation of the natural world (whether in the name of science or of anything else) was in fact a *natural* thing and that, according to his principles of stewardship, humanity in fact had a duty to interfere with the forces of nature. Some mystery, however, needed to be left to nature for the sake of humility if nothing else, and to remind people that the unique position of the human race on earth did not grant them unlimited power or unlimited knowledge. Intriguingly, Chesterton conflated the forces of modernism (the advance of science and industrialisation) with those who resisted those forces in the name of nature and pronounced them both to be barbaric rather than civilised. His vision was based around a conception of what he believed was a healthy balance for the human soul, not around a notion of rejecting or embracing modernity.

Chesterton did not imagine himself to be operating within a paradigm of "pro" or "anti" modernity. He laughed at the use of the term "progress" as an end rather than a means, and believed that he had transcended debates about moving forwards or turning back the clock by providing a goal which appropriated what was useful from both the past and the present. In practice, however, he did have a generalised suspicion of many aspects of "modernity," such as increasing industrialisation, specialisation and mechanisation. It was his response to these questions though that simultaneously mark Chesterton out as more than a reactionary thinker and indicate the limitations inherent in an approach that assumes a polarised "pro" or "anti" response to modernity.

In an edited collection exploring the meanings of modernity in Britain from the late-Victorian era to the Second World War, Martin Daunton notes that British historiography has to date been marked by an acceptance of Martin Wiener's influential *English Culture and the Decline of the Industrial Spirit*, which narrated a history of economic decline caused by a wholesale rejection of modern values in favour of traditional and rural ones.[45] Later, Peter Mandler sought to challenge this orthodoxy, claiming instead that "before the first world war, English culture as a whole was aggressively urban and materialist, and the rural-nostalgic vision of 'Englishness' remained the province of impassioned and highly articulate but fairly marginal artistic groups."[46] In her social history of late Victorian and Edwardian Britain, José Harris remarked that "there were at all times many different perceptions of what constituted "the modern."[47]

What is of interest in Chesterton's approach to science is the way in which it illuminates some of this cacophony of responses to modernity. Neither "pro" nor "anti" science, Chesterton gleefully appropriates its own standards of evidence in order to criticise it. He provides an insightful critique of the consequences of the application of scientific ideologies to social questions, but does so in a way that is very much embedded in his very modern milieu: he revels in the innovations of modernity (such as the mass press and mass politics) which enable him to practise his distinctive style of popular journalism. Despite setting himself up as deliberately counter-cultural, Chesterton was deeply enough embedded in his own age that his rejection of the "modern" was incomplete. He wanted not to reject everything about the present day, but to challenge aspects of it on the basis of values that to him were timeless. His campaigns to that end were imperfect but sincere.

[1]   Richard James Gill, *The Wonder of the World: Hannah Arendt, G. K. Chesterton and Ecological Populism,* Ph.D. Thesis, University of Keele, 2001, accessed online at http://www.angelfire.com/folk/richardjgill/introduction.html on 30 April 2009. Gill, as he acknowledged in his thesis, was not the first to make a comparison between Arendt and Chesterton; see Margaret Canovan, "Chesterton and Hannah Arendt," *The Chesterton Review*, Vol. 7(2), 1981, pp. 139-53.

[2]   G. K. Chesterton, *Orthodoxy*, (The Bodley Head, London, 1957), first published 1908, p. 90.

[3]   Chesterton, *Orthodoxy*, p. 78.

[4]   B. Russell, *The Problems of Philosophy*, (Williams and Norgate, London, 1912), p. 98.

[5]   G. K. Chesterton, *Orthodoxy*, p. 218.

[6]   A. Ellegard, *Darwin and the General Reader: The Reception of Darwin's Theory of Evolution in the British Periodical Press, 1859-1872*, (University of Chicago Press: Chicago, 1990), pp. 333-4.

[7]   G. K. Chesterton, *Fancies versus Fads*, (Dodd, Mead and Company: New York, 1923), p. 214.

[8]   "And Tail: Science out-of-date," unsigned, *G. K.'s Weekly*, Vol. 5 (106), March 26, 1927, p. 307.

[9]   G. K. Chesterton, *The Uses of Diversity: A Book of Essays*, (Dodd, Mead and Company: New York, 1921), p. 18.

[10]   G. K. Chesterton, *Eugenics and other Evils*, (Ignatius Press: San Francisco, 1987), first published 1922, p. 345.

[11]   G. K. Chesterton, *Fancies versus Fads*, p. 215.

[12]   G. K. Chesterton, cited in D. Childs, *Modernism and Eugenics: Woolf, Eliot, Yeats and the Culture of Degeneration*, (Cambridge University Press: Cambridge, 2004), p. 11.

[13]   Chesterton placed a much greater emphasis on class than on race in his discussions of eugenics. When it came to race, he was, as Dan Stone noted tempted by the idea of "race-memory" or "racial instinct" (although he usually eschewed "scientific" race theories). See D. Stone, *Breeding Superman: Nietzsche, Race and Eugenics in Edwardian and Interwar Britain*, (Liverpool University Press: Liverpool, 2002), p. 116.

[14]   G. K. Chesterton, *Eugenics and Other Evils*, pp. 383-4.

[15]   Childs, *Modernism & Eugenics*, p. 4.

[16]   P. Bowler, *Reconciling Science and Religion: the Debate in Early-Twentieth-Century Britain*, (University of Chicago Press: Chicago, 1996), p. 22.

[17]   Bowler, *Reconciling Science and Religion*, p. 102.

[18]   G. K. Chesterton, *The New Jerusalem*, (George H. Doran: New York, 1921), p. 187.

[19]   G. K. Chesterton, *The New Jerusalem*, p. 168.

[20]   Bowler, *Reconciling Science and Religion*, p. 102.

[21]   Chesterton to my knowledge never engaged in a detailed way with the problem of evil, except to note the general fallenness of man and to emphasise the importance of free will.

[22]   G. K. Chesterton, *Orthodoxy*, p. 94.

[23]   G .K. Chesterton, *St. Thomas Aquinas*, (Ignatius Press: San Francisco, 1986), first published 1933, p. 536.

[24]   S. Jaki, *Chesterton, A Seer of Science*, (University of Illinois Press: Urbana, 1986), p. 26.

[25]   Jaki, *Chesterton, A Seer of Science*, p. 2.

[26]   W. J. Scheick, "Chesterton and Science," *English Literature in Transition, 1880-1920*, Vol. 30(3), 1987, pp. 366-8.

[27]   Bowler, *Reconciling Science and Religion*, p. 397.

[28]   G. K. Chesterton, *The Everlasting Man*, (Ignatius Press: San Francisco, 1986), first published 1925, p. 166.

[29]   G. K. Chesterton, *William Blake*, (Duckworth and Company: London, 1910), p. 162.

[30]   Chesterton, *The Everlasting Man*, pp. 166-7.

[31]   G. K. Chesterton, *Simplicity of Tolstoy*, (Arthur L. Humphreys: London, 1912), pp. 7-8.

[32]   "*Vox Populi, Vox Dei*," Lecure delivered at St. Paul's Church, Covent Garden, under the auspices of the London Branch of the Christian Social Union, March 16th, 1905. British Library Manuscript Add. 73286.

[33] G. K. Chesterton, *Orthodoxy*, pp. 171-2.

[34] G. K. Chesterton, *Alarms and Discursions*, (Dodd, Mead and Company: New York, 1911), p. 17.

[35] G. K. Chesterton, *Heretics*, (Garden City Publishing Company: New York, 1959), first published 1905, p. 136.

[36] C. Glacken, *Traces on the Rhodian Shore: Nature and Culture in Western Thought from Ancient Times to the End of the Eighteenth Century*, (University of California Press: Berkeley, 1967), p. 155.

[37] Glacken, *Traces on the Rhodian Shore*, p. 155.

[38] Glacken, *Traces on the Rhodian Shore*, p. 155.

[39] W. Jenkins, *Ecologies of Grace: Environmental Ethics and Christian Theology*, (Oxford University Press: Oxford, 2008), pp. 77-83.

[40] Letter from Chesterton to Mr. Langley Taylor of the Council for the Preservation of Rural England, 15th July, 1931, British Library Manuscript ADD 73240.

[41] Via, amongst other things, the Game Laws. Chesterton, *Eugenics and Other Evils*, p. 369.

[42] R. Las Vergnas, *Chesterton, Belloc, Baring*, (London, 1938), p. 8.

[43] J.P. Corrin, *G. K. Chesterton and Hilaire Belloc: The Battle Against Modernity*, (Ohio University. Press: Athens, 1981).

[44] A. Vaninskaya, "My Mother, Drunk or Sober: G. K. Chesterton and Patriotic Anti-Imperialism," *History of European Ideas*, Vol. 34, 2008, p. 546.

[45] M. Daunton and B. Rieger, "Introduction," in Daunton and Rieger (eds), *Meanings of Modernity: Britain from the Late-Victorian Era to World War II*, Berg, Oxford, 2001, pp. 1-2; M. Wiener, *English Culture and the Decline of the Industrial Spirit, 1850-1980*, (Cambridge University Press: Cambridge, 1981).

[46] P. Mandler, "Against 'Englishness': English Culture and the Limits to Rural Nostalgia, 1850-1940," *Transactions of the Royal Historical Society*, Sixth Series, Vol. 7 (1997), p. 170.

[47] J. Harris, *Private Lives, Public Spirit: Britain 1870-1914*, (Penguin Books: London, 1994), p. 35.

Chesterton and Belloc
Show the Way Forward!

Russell Sparkes

RUSSELL SPARKES *is Chief Investment Officer of the Central Finance Board of the Methodist Church in the UK. For six years he was Treasurer of the Linacre Centre, a Roman Catholic medical-ethics charity, and was also Chairman of the Chesterton Institute, a small charity promoting the thought of G. K. Chesterton, particularly its economic philosophy based upon Catholic social teaching. He is a member of the Keys, the Catholic Writers' Guild, and his books include:* G. K. Chesterton, Prophet of Orthodoxy *(Harper Collins,1996), an introduction to Chesterton's religious writings, and* Sound of Heaven—A Treasury of Catholic Verse *(St. Paul's, 2000). In 2008 he wrote,* Global Warming, Catholic Teaching on the Environment *for the Catholic Truth Society.*

Introduction

Distributism has been more or less completely forgotten in the mainstream media over the last seventy years. I have therefore been struck by two interesting new books that have appeared recently in the UK. While they originate from two very different viewpoints, each however shows a greater degree of sympathy with Distributist ideas than has been seen for many years.

The New Economics—a bigger picture is a review that is about to be published by *The Tablet* in London. It shows how people working on the radical fringes of economics have looked back to the Distributists for inspiration as a viable alternative to classical economics.

Petrohue Falls and view of Volcan Osorno, Chile

Red Tory—How Left and Right have broken Britain and how we can fix it was originally written as a review for *The Catholic Herald* in the UK. However, I have substantially revised and expanded for *The Chesterton Review*. Phillip Blond is a former lecturer in theology who shot to fame in the UK in 2009 with his public advocacy of social conservatism, or, in his phrase, "Red Tory." He has been described as the philosopher-king of the British Conservative party, and when he launched his own think tank, ResPublica, towards the end of 2009, the guest of honour was David Cameron, now British Prime Minister.

I thought that Blond's ideas therefore deserved a thorough description and analysis. It also seemed appropriate to show how they relate to some of the classic Distributist themes of the 1920s and 1930s, particularly as I am currently writing a book showing how Distributism emerged from a great and living tradition that included the guilds and William Cobbett, as well as land reform in Ireland. This is provisionally entitled, *When Globalisation Fails—the local alternative*.

The New Economics—a bigger picture
David Boyle and Andrew Simms (Earthscan, 2009).

While unemployment has not yet risen as much as feared previously, the credit crunch of 2008-2009 has led to the worst global economic slowdown since the 1930s. Fragile banking systems have appeared to come close to collapse, and the crisis has resulted in a surge in government borrowing leading to savage cutbacks in public spending.

Inquiries as to what has caused this slump will doubtless go on for many years, but the unquestioning application of "free-market economics" must take a large share of the blame. Indeed, even Alan Greenspan former head of the US central bank and high priest of unrestrained "market forces" now accepts that real-world economies do not operate as the textbooks say they do. The flaws of conventional economics are set out well in *The New Economics—a bigger picture*:

> Economics may have begun as a branch of moral philosophy, but it ignores the moral aspects of humanity, and other human aspects, as inconvenient for its theories. The result is a narrow eco-

nomic system, which fails to reflect the real world, and is hurtling towards human and environmental limits.

The book describes how standard economics is even coming under pressure from its own students for the increasing way it seems detached from the way real economies, and real people, actually work. It also criticises policymakers' unquestioning reliance upon these flawed models, and the way economic analysis has become the government's main analytical tool in areas like the Health Service where it was previously unknown. The authors should be praised for the clarity of their writing, and you certainly do not need fluency in higher mathematics to understand their book, unlike most economics texts. However the emphasis of *The New Economics* is not criticism of standard economic theory but rather to chronicle the rise of "new economics" over the least thirty years or so, which, rather like Adam Smith's pioneering studies of "political economy," seeks simply to understand what factors generate social wealth in its broadest sense.

What probably struck me most about this book is the way that its authors repeatedly talk about a "moral" or even a "spiritual" crisis. At first sight such talk of morality seems surprising; while it might be expected from conservative politicians, it should be noted that the new economics comes from a radical "leftwing" viewpoint where these terms are more rarely used. However, what is even more surprising, given this starting point, is the book's statement that the origins of the new economics derive from Catholic Social Teaching when publicised by Chesterton and Belloc as "Distributism."

> The one twentieth century movement that embedded elements of what is now the new economics was Distributism, inspired by Hilaire Belloc's 1912 book *The Servile State*, an influential diatribe against big business and Fabian collectivist policies. Distributism knitted together the old Catholic social doctrine of Pope Leo XIII that was so close to Belloc's heart, inspired originally by Ruskin via Cardinal Manning. ... At its heart was the redistribution of land and property so that everyone had some—on the grounds that small enterprises, smallholdings and small units were the only basis for dignity, independence and liberty.

Indeed, *The New Economics* shows how these ideas of Chesterton and Belloc are the roots and foundations of the new economics. The book's warnings about the negative impact of large supermarket chains would have delighted Chesterton, who repeatedly warned against big shops and "greedy grocers." Its policy recommendations of stringent anti-trust legislation to break up large corporations also come straight out of the Distributist campaign manual from the 1920s. *The New Economics* advocates breaking up the large banks whose speculations got us into this mess, ideas that are increasingly being taken up by regulators around the world.

If there is one writer whose ideas inspired the recent boom in new economics it was probably Fritz Schumacher and his famous 1973 book, *Small is Beautiful*. The authors note his preference for local based economics, just like the Distributists, and also where he got the idea from:

> An overarching principle for the movement of goods and services was described by Schumacher as "subsidiarity." It is an idea he took from Catholic Church that means things should be done at the lowest, or most local, practicable level with the aim of maximising social, economic, and environmental benefits.

It is probably fair to state that both the public and the authorities around the world are looking for new ideas on how the economy should be run following the evident failure of free-market economics in recent years. *The New Economics* certainly provides plenty to think about in this context.

Red Tory—How Left and Right have broken Britain and how we can fix it. Phillip Blond, (Faber & Faber, 2010)

Phillip Blond is a former lecturer in theology who shot to fame in the UK in 2009 with his public advocacy of social conservatism, or, to use his phrase, "Red Tory." (The phrase may be in use in Canada, but to the best of my knowledge it has never before been used in Britain.) His excellent new book, *Red Tory—How Left and Right have broken Britain and how we can fix it*, is primarily a detailed political and philosophical analysis of contemporary Britain. Blond has a good understanding of the evolution of leftish, thinking having grown up in an environment sympathetic to these views, while his philosophical skills enable him to point out their inherent contradictions with clarity and vigour:

> My leftish affiliation ended. Many of my left-wing friends suddenly seemed to me to be right-wing. ... Despite all their rhetoric, all they really believed in was unlimited choice and unrestricted personal freedom. They seemed in important ways to have been stripped of integral values and to have embraced a rootless cultural relativism. ... They seemed to delight in abortion, for example, and made it a fetish to choose, as if this were a real exercise of human freedom and unimpeded will, but they hated fox hunting because they thought it was cruel.

This philosophical analysis of the roots of modern left-wing politics is surely correct; it also clearly echoes what a certain Cardinal Ratzinger was saying over twenty years ago....Nevertheless, *Red Tory* illuminates the increasingly hostile relationship between New Labour and the churches, for all of Tony Blair's highly publicised religious beliefs. I am sure that many older Catholics like myself have felt puzzled by the overt hostility of the last Labour government to the Church. Think of the constant attacks on English Catholic schools in the name of "diversity," or the Government's obsessive fury about the gay-adoption row.

Go back thirty or forty years and there was a clear if informal alliance between the majority of Catholics and the Labour party. Indeed such a relationship was true in most Anglo-Saxon countries. A further question might be why the media normally presents the Church in a negative light; think of the way the Pope's Regensburg address was deliberately misinterpreted as "Islamophobic," often linked with innuendo about his boyhood conscription into the Hitler Youth.

In a sense *Red Tory* is a long essay, both philosophical and political, on what has gone so badly wrong over the last thirty years; in that respect it reminds me of Burke's *Reflections on the Revolution in France*, Chesterton's *What's Wrong with the World*, or perhaps even St. Augustine's *The City of God*, which reflected upon the moral chaos of the late Roman Empire shortly before its ultimate collapse. Indeed, there are definite echoes of the later in *Red Tory:*

They despised religion precisely because it put a limit on freedom by suggesting what they should choose. In fact they hated anything which limited whatever impulse they might have (Blond). 'They do not trouble about the moral degradation of the Empire; all that they ask is that it should be prosperous and secure. 'What concerns us', they say, 'is that everyone should be able to increase his wealth so that he can afford a lavish expenditure. ... Let the laws protect the rights of property and leave men's morals alone.' (Augustine).[1]

The book begins very strongly with an introduction almost incandescent with rage and sorrow at what has become of what was once universally acclaimed as one of the most civilised societies in the world. This is followed by a number of chapters with titles like "the errors of the left" and "the errors of the right," and "the illiberal Legacy of Liberalism" which examine the economic and social crisis of the last forty years. When I read these chapter titles it reminded me of Chesterton's works although there is no exact correspondence; perhaps *What's Wrong with the World Today*[2] should have been the book's subtitle.

The "illiberalism" chapter has a good demolition job on liberal guru Rawls. *Red Tory* makes the good point that his thesis that the state has to engineer equality of opportunity is as dogmatically materialist as any Marxist. These modern "neophiles" have no role for tradition, but worship at the altar of a "nihilistic liberalism that has over a long period of time almost completely eclipsed classical and Christian traditions of political life and argument." This is of course the opposite of the traditional virtue ethics that thinkers from Aristotle and Confucius onward have argued are essential for the flourishing of both individuals and societies, or in *Red Tory's* words:

> Liberalism has promoted a radical individualism which, in trashing the supposed despotism of custom and tradition concerning the nature of true human flourishing, has produced a vacated, empty self that believes in no common values or inherited creeds. But in creating this purely subjective being, liberalism has also created a new and wholly terrifying tyranny. For, in order to strip people of their cultural legacy and eliminate the idea that people should enjoy degrees of prestige according to their nature and capacity for virtue, and by making everyone instead the same sort of individual with basic physical needs and rights, an excess of centralised authority is required. ... In this way

the supremacy of the one lone, isolated individual quickly converts
into the supremacy of the one unquestionable state authority.

Blond does not overdo the nostalgia; his concern is the present, and
what might be done to improve it. However, when I think of the pride
that used to be taken in the British government's minimal interference
in ordinary people's lives; when I think of the way the courteous British
"Bobby" has been replaced by policemen who increasingly seem to kill
ordinary members of the public without any sanctions being taken (RIP
Ian Tomlinson and Charles de Menezes); when I think of the way that
Westminster used to be taken as a model as the mother of parliaments,
and now we have had a massive sleaze scandal involving false expenses
and a botched election where many people were not allowed to vote (Af-
rican observers, invited to observe this standard of excellence, openly
laughed); like the psalmist beside the waters of Babylon, I can only weep.

The book begins, just as Chesterton and Belloc did, by denouncing
what became known in 1931 as *The Whig Interpretation of History*[3], the
title of the historian Butterfield's supposedly revolutionary work. This
criticised the tendency, common in nineteenth century historical writing,
to see English history since the Reformation as a steady progress from
medieval savagery and superstition to the glorious Protestant triumph of
democracy. This thesis was however repeatedly attacked by Chesterton,
not least in his 1925 biography of *Cobbett*[4], which came out *six years*
before Butterfield's book was published. Here Chesterton noted how that
honest farmer William Cobbett had come to the conclusion, simply from
the evidence of his own eyes, that the landscape of southern England had
been much more intensively farmed in the past than in his day (1820s)[5]:

> Most of us know what was the accepted general version of history
> when we were at school. ... England had emerged out of a savage
> past to be the greatest empire in the world, with the best balanced
> constitution in the world, by a wise and well-timed progress or se-
> ries of reforms, that ever kept in mind the need of constitutional-
> ism and balance. ... Hence the country has been filled with a fresh
> and free population, made happy by humane and rational ideas,
> where once there only a few serfs stunted by the most baseless su-
> perstitions. ... but Cobbett began with the big fact that he could
> see with his own eyes, and with that he contrived, with tremendous
> reconstructive power, to turn all English history upside down.

Red Tory expresses a similar view, i.e., that the Middle Ages left us a relatively prosperous peasantry. (Blond does not mention works of economic historians, but there is widespread evidence that medieval contemporaries were often struck by how well-fed the English looked.) There was a strong system of local market economies with farmers exchanging their produce for locally manufactured goods in the market towns in the clear and transparent framework established by the guilds. These prosperous yeomen farmers did not disappear through some inevitable process, as historians influenced by either Whiggery or Marxist class analysis would suggest. In fact the reason for their decline was the way their common lands were taken away from them by enclosure in the Tudor period. I have always been struck by Chesterton's telling phrase on the economic consequences of the Reformation in the chapter entitled "The Rebellion of the Rich" in *A Short History of England.*[6] He bases it around the story of Thomas More:

> He (More) saw England passing from the medieval to the modern. Thus he looked forth, and saw many things and said many things; they were all worthy and all witty; but he noted one thing which as once a horrible fancy and a homely and practical fact. He looked over that landscape and said: 'Sheep are eating men.'

In other words common land that had once supported villages was now being turned into grazing land for the sheep of the rich. The first burst of enclosure under the Tudors was followed by its mass production in the eighteenth century as a Government dominated by rich landowners expropriated land on a massive scale using acts of Parliament. This incidentally created the starving poor who formed the desperate workforce which powered the Industrial Revolution. In *Red Tory's* words:

> Between 1750 and 1850 over 7.5 million access of open fields and common land were lost to private enclosure, licensed through Parliament. The agrarian peasant class who had previously farmed this land were driven from it into the large and expanding cities. ... there they formed the landless disposed mass that we now call the working class.

Blond's analysis is cogent and persuasive. He shows how from the 1960s the left abandoned its previously key concern for social justice in exchange for a cocktail of issues around identity politics, i.e., race, gender, and sexual identity, and the devastating impact this had on traditional working class morals and communities.

The new and toxic hedonism which arose in the 1960s destroyed the social bonds that had kept families together in the austerity of the 1930s. (*Red Tory* only briefly touches upon the way the women's movements may have empowered middle-class women, but by lowering male wages it ended up forcing working-class women out to work, to the detriment of family life. I would argue that immigration and technology also squeezed the middle and lower classes.)

Another negative factor was the way from the 1960s onwards the state began to destroy the extended family of the working class through demolition of slums, and forcibly relocated them to new tower blocks in housing estates a long way away. It is well known in policy circles that marriage socialises young men from poor backgrounds who turn from gangs to looking after their own family. But with marriage now an object of derision, is it surprising that poor estates are now terrorised by gangs just as births out of wedlock soar?

If you want to know the origins of the "sink estates" and "benefit culture" that disfigure so many of our cities, look no further than *Red Tory*. It argues that the new ideology of assertive hedonism had its most catastrophic impact on the working class, destroying the collective project of self-help that had helped the poor out of poverty from the Victorian period. At the same time, the Welfare State undermined the means by which they had done so via friendly societies, credit unions, and mechanics institutes. Like the Distributists, there is no doubting Blond's concern for the welfare of the poor yet, at the same time and like them, he argues that a universal system of welfare benefits has made self-reliance an obsolete virtue:

> Perhaps the chief reason the welfare state went astray is that the governing elite imposed a bureaucratic and centralised vision of the caring state upon a working class. ... Local requirements, organisation or practices were gradually ignored and rendered redundant. The welfare state, I believe, began the destruction of the independent life of the British working class.

The book also shows how the left's need to control, in the context of obvious social breakdown, has led to a surveillance state reminiscent of George Orwell's *1984*. It also explains clearly what has happened to recent British politics, not least why "New Labour" seemed so determined to follow in Mrs. Thatcher's footsteps.

> In truth, what New Labour offered was the worst of the left and the worst of the right. Concerning the left, statism of the most pernicious sort was imposed. Centralised standards were invented and imposed across a whole range of British public life. Sectors of the public realm largely untouched by Mrs. Thatcher were now forced into competition that empowered managers rather than consumers.

However, Blond is equally tough on the free-market ideology that Margaret Thatcher injected into the DNA of the Conservative Party. He argues that essentially this was based upon the same kind of obsessive individualism as the new left, with both left and right therefore worshipping the individualism of the market in a way that would have appalled an older generation of conservatives and socialists alike. *Red Tory* makes a number of good points about how both the new left and new right destroyed traditional social values. The book is highly critical about the surge in income inequality since the 1970s, warning that the lower paid risk becoming a new type of debt serfs.

> The lives of those at the bottom increasingly resemble those of a lower an abandoned caste. Indeed, what we have produced over the last thirty years is capitalism for the privileged few, and indebted servitude for the many. ... The last thirty years, under the aegis of both right and left, have introduced a new economic form via debt and low wages: serfdom. The radical politics of the future must address the needs of these new serfs.

Of course Belloc in particular repeatedly warned how the growth of slavery as a result of indebtedness had enfeebled the Roman Empire.[7] Indeed, although their names are only mentioned briefly in the book, the spirit of Chesterton and Belloc's "Distributist" warnings about economic and political power becoming concentrated in the hands of a small plutocracy resound throughout *Red Tory*. The book advocates a return to the "one nation" conservatism practised by Disraeli in the late nineteenth century, and also followed by Conservative governments in the 1950s. However, the inspiration for the book is not these Tory leaders but a Liberal member of Parliament from 1906-1910:

> Yet all intellectual efforts by Tories to construct a political economy for the poor pale beside Hilaire Belloc's 1912 tour de force, *The Servile State*. In these pages he denounces both capitalism and socialism—both, he argues, institute master-slave relations and both rely on dispossession. The capitalist monopolises land, ownership, and capital, thereby dispossessing the self-sufficient who are then forced to work for subsistence wages with no prospect of elevation. The socialist dispossesses the populace in the name of general ownership and a communal monopoly. From the perspective of the peasant or the worker both philosophies are exactly the same.

Red Tory ends with a section of practical recommendations with chapter titles like "the restoration of ethos" and "moralising the market." There is advocacy of "civil enterprises" based upon shared ethos rather than state imposition. The book believes that this ambition can be achieved through the formation of "free guilds" or voluntary professional associations, rather like a "fair-trade" brand.

Inevitably there are a few points that may be questioned. The book is very strong on politics and philosophy, less so in my opinion on economics. It is simply wrong for example to say that the medieval guilds encouraged monopoly, as one of their main objectives was to prevent it. In fact in their economic function the guilds were a key part of the medieval objective that commercial life should be an integrated expression of the Church's teaching. There was a code of mercantile ethics decreeing that craftsmen should make their goods honestly and well, that sellers should give good weight and be satisfied with reasonable profits. Chesterton got this, as so many things right, in his book *Chaucer.*[8] In it Chesterton examines two wealthy and respectable citizens making that famous pilgrimage towards Canterbury. They are a Doctor and a Dyer, the latter a master chemist and supplier of pigments. As Chesterton put it:

> The Doctor, in short, still exists as a roughly recognisable figure. The Dyer has totally disappeared....The reason why the Doctor is recognisable, and the Dyer is unrecognisable, is perfectly simple.

> It is that the Doctors not only were, but still are, organised on the *idea* of a Medieval Guild....The British Medical Council, which is the council of a Guild...does what a Guild was supposed to do. It keeps the doctors going; it keeps the doctors alive, and it does prevent one popular quack from eating all his brethren out of house and home. It sets limit to competition; it prevents monopoly.'

Still *Red Tory* has some good Distributist ideas. For example it advocates that the Post Office, which has branches in most towns and villages, should be used to revitalise local economies. (Of course, the recent New Labour government encouraged cost cutting and branch closures of the Post Office in order to polish it up for privatisation, which *Red Tory* opposes.) It suggests that the Post Office should be mutualised through the creation of community-owned enterprises, and should offer new services—petrol, food shops etc. This is surely right. In the UK in recent years there has been a wave of public house closures, but in a couple of villages the locals have bought their "local" as a co-operative, using it as a local shop and general resource. The ghost of Chesterton would surely be pleased. *Red Tory* also advocates better financial education and the provision of microfinance to help the poor. It ends with a call to arms, explaining why it believes only social conservatism can be a true way forward.

> We need a sustaining form of social conservatism, for only it can provide the bedrock upon which to stabilise the society it seeks to transform. It must avoid immersing the individual in a formless mass of relationships, whilst simultaneously recognising the claim of the common good over the free agency of the individual. ... At the same time, true conservatism needs to recognise crushing economic inequality and its harmful effects on precisely those institutions which conservatives instinctively cherish. This requires dedication to equity and fairness, to distributed wealth and asset ownership, as much as to inherited culture and ethical traditions.

Of course, Distributism in its time was also a philosophy. Chesterton and Belloc recoiled from the idea that the best humanity could achieve was a balance of grasping selfishness. In one of his editorials in *G. K.'s Weekly*[9] Chesterton wrote:

When I began it, I merely thought it reasonable that there should be one weekly paper to represent a reasonable alternative to conventional Socialism and academic Socialism. But I now realise... that we have taken on something much bigger than modern Capitalism or Communism combined. I realise that we are trying to fight the whole world; to turn the tide of the whole time we live in; to resist everything that seems irresistible. ... For the thing we oppose is something of which capitalism and collectivism are only economic by products. ... It is so vast and vague that its offensiveness is largely atmospheric; it is perhaps easier to defy than to define. But it might be approximately adumbrated thus; it is that spirit which refuses Recognition or Respect.

Like Chesterton, Philip Blond recognises that economic and social arrangements are at bottom moral ones. Adam Smith would have agreed. In turn these derive from philosophical and spiritual beliefs. On balance *Red Tory* does a good job of uncovering the twisted philosophical roots of modern politics.

[1]   St. Augustine, quoted in Christopher Dawson, *Enquiries into Religion and Culture*, (Sheed & Ward: London, 1933).

[2]   c.f. G. K. Chesterton, *What's Wrong With the World,* (Cassell: London, 1910).

[3]   Herbert Butterfield, *The Whig Interpretation of History*, (Bell: London 1931).

[4]   G. K. Chesterton, *William Cobbett*, (Hodder & Stoughton: London 1925).

[5]   William Cobbett, *The History of the Protestant Revolution In England and Ireland*, (originally published 1824), (TAN Books, 1988).

[6]   G. K. Chesterton, *A Short History of England*, (Chatto & Windus: London 1917).

[7]   c.f. H. Belloc, *Essay on the Restoration of Property*, 1928, revised 1936, London, The Distributist League, and also H. Belloc, *The Crisis of Civilisation*, (Fordham University Press: New York, 1937).

[8]   G. K. Chesterton, *Chaucer,* (Faber & Faber: London, 1932).

[9]   G. K. Chesterton, "Spiritual over Political," *G. K.'s Weekly*, 7 December 1929.

A New Europe—and a New UK?

Catherine Rachel John

CATHERINE RACHEL JOHN, *younger daughter of Donald Attwater, was born in 1926, and educated primarily at Abergavenny Girls High School and Cambridge University, where she read English and Early History of the British Isles. With long experience in writing for adults as a senior tutor for a correspondence college, she has also worked on topics of the liturgy and history of the Catholic Church. Out of this has come drama, including the scripts of* Becket and Seven Branches for Life *(music by Laurence Bevenot OSB) performed in Canterbury Cathedral in 1970 and 1975,* Keepers of the Light, *celebrations of the Celtic saints performed in 1975 and 1986, and* True Glory on Saint Cuthbert Mayne and his times. *Her prose works include A*dam Schall, A Jesuit at the Court of China *(1963) and* the Saints of Cornwall *(1981).*

Principles of Renewal

Distribution took its origin from Pope Leo XIII's celebrated encyclical *Rerum Novarum* (1891) as described in Allan Carson's interesting article "Third Ways"[1] (*The Chesterton Review*, Spring/Summer 2009). In the same issue Thomas Storck's review of *A Path of Our Own: An Andean Village and Tomorrow's Economy of Values* by Adam K. Webb refers to Pope Pius XI's *Quadragesimo Anno* (1931), and as its title indicates the two encyclicals are closely related, but the second one hardly seems to have entered into Distributist thought. This may have been partly influenced by Chesterton's death in 1936, but it has also been more generally neglected by English and American Catholics. Perhaps then I should not be surprised to read Mr. Storck's observations that Pope Pius XI's "project" was not generally received, let alone implemented.

Ponte Vecchio on the Arno

There seems to be no knowledge of the Christian Democrat movements in the countries of the European continent which were already playing a role in political and social life well before the outbreak of the Second World War. These were strongly but not solely Catholic-led, and by this time of writing are recognised major elements in all European countries except England and the rest of the UK.

They were fundamental to what has been called the resurrection of Europe after 1945. This meant almost the refounding of countries, and with the co-operation of the European Socialist parties, who were learning bitterly the perils of Communism and the necessity for democracy, they were creating the organisms we know as the European Union and, not least, the Council of Europe. These two formed the largest political parties in Europe, but not the only important ones, because the various systems also established for themselves in the individual countries as well as the general pattern made full room for the smaller groupings, not patronised as "minorities." Combined Christian Democrats now using the term European Peoples Party (EPP) form a civil political party which offers to the electorate aims, policies and methods like any other political party, with an emphasis on cohesion and clarity. Probably due to the necessity for vigorous Christian opposition to much in their community life there has been a tendency among American Catholics to sense a certain betrayal because the powerful EPP has not attempted to favour a theocracy, and they have misinterpreted inevitable papal critiques and warnings about right and wrong ways in Europe such as are to be found in relation to any country.

What could be named as the one most fundamental text in the new European process and which has come to be called, not very comfortably, the Principle of Subsidiarity, was drawn from Pope Pius XI's *Quadragesimo Anno*. The thought of course is not new: the expression has gone around the world:

> Just as it is wrong to withdraw from the individual and commit to the community at large what personal initiative and work can accomplish, so, too, it is an injustice, a grave evil, and a disturbance of right order for a larger and higher organisation to arrogate to itself functions which can be performed efficiently by smaller and lower bodies.

> This is a fundamental principle of social philosophy, unshaken
> and unchangeable, and it retains its full truth today. Of its very na-
> ture, the true aim of all social activity should be to help individual
> members of the social body, but never to destroy or absorb them.[2]

> Paragraph 79,
> The Encyclical Letter of Pope Pius XI,
> On Reconstructing the Social Order: 1931

I read it myself in an American publication called *The Social Justice
Review*, which was outlining a commentary of the nineteenth-century
Bishop of Mainz, William Emmanuel von Ketteler, on freedom, authority and the Church, with a special reference Liberalism. Much of this
latter will sound familiar to us, who have inherited practices without
necessarily associating them with a political ideology, e.g., emphasis on
free speech, universal suffrage, welfare, education, but all directed and
controlled by highly centralised government and its attendant powers
extended to the least details of our daily lives. In other words, a struc-
tural contradiction of the Principle of Subsidiarity. It may be noted that
Pope Benedict XVI in Part 2 of his first encyclical *Deus Caritas Est* refers specifically to Bishop Ketteler, *Rerum Novarum* and *Quadragesimo
Anno*, with the Principle.

A congress in 1999 of the European Peoples Party expressed its
"Respect for the Principle of Subsidiarity" in this way:

> Strict application and monitoring of the subsidiarity principle is
> both necessary and indispensable. We need a citizen-friendly Eu-
> rope which respects our regional, political and social differences,
> and which protects and promotes European regional identities,
> cultures and ways of life in all their diversity. The objective is a
> clear picture of how responsibilities are divided between Europe-
> an, national, regional and local levels.

While all these things were developing on the continent of Europe,
England in leadership of the rest of the United Kingdom continued to
follow its own way. Briefly it could be summed up by saying that the attempt was made to go on with national life and thought after the First
World War as if nothing: had happened. The long-term result of this
has been the confusion in which England finds itself today.

143

The Celts

It is essential for observers and sympathisers to distinguish between England and the countries and regions which for convenience sake we call Celtic: Scotland, Wales, Northern Ireland—even Cornwall. The terms Britain and British are complicated for historical reasons, but they are much misused, and we all need to be as precise as possible whom and what we are talking about. For instance, ecclesiastically and therefore culturally, the Church of England is what the name says, there is an entirely independent and very different Church of Scotland; Northern Ireland and Wales have no equivalents, only a variety of influential denominations, while Cornish Methodism is as important as Anglicanism. Politically, twentieth-century European experience has supported the "Celtic countries" in seeking modern public constitutional expression of their long, indeed ancient, national histories. At the present time the convolutions of political interests have enabled them to achieve varying levels of self-government, lately producing much that is valuable and significant, reflecting the activities of the many small countries of the European continent in re-establishing themselves after the Second World War.

This is one of the many elements in English people's uncertainty about who they are and so where they are going, or want to go. As always, this has long historical roots, with such significant dates as the Elizabethan Settlement (1559), the Revolution of 1688, the Parliamentary Reform of 1832, and the unfortunate fact in the twentieth-century that they came to identify themselves through over-simplification of gallant victory in two world wars, effectively ignoring the clash of ideas, beliefs and aspirations in the world all around them.

An underlying problem has been what was taught as English history, and very little teaching at all about the rest of the UK, let alone the countries of the European continent. Nobody expects a country, like smaller places and for that matter like smaller families, not to have a kind of mythology. But to a marked degree English mythology and history became intertwined so that the discovery in recent generations of many important serious inadequacies has contributed greatly to the uncertainties of the English about themselves, including their moral standing as a people inherent in their *amour propre*.

Ignorance

A major factor is the English ignorance of their political institutions. It may sound strange to many people of other countries that there is little if any formal instruction of youth, and was until recently little general adult interest, in such matters. It has been assumed that the English (and no doubt the British) are a naturally democratic, freedom-loving people, and that—it is not too much to say providentially, things will always work out well for them in the end. This makes it very difficult to enter on the reforms which recent events and experiences, political and financial, have made necessary. When challenged they are courageous, very intelligent, and highly inventive; they have been but are not now complacent, but they do not know where to start because they have not got the information. They would not now necessarily reject a plain statement or observation that the present parliamentary system is barely democratic, and that far from being the norm is largely out of step with those of the other developed democracies. But they cannot say except in the most obvious public instances and general personal experience where it goes wrong, let alone what sort of alternatives may exist.

The chapter on Elective Dictatorship in Lord Hailsham's book *The Dilemma of Democracy* (1978) contains a useful brief introduction to the British parliamentary system.

> The constitutional law of this island is based on the ancient prerogatives of the Crown, and the various Acts of Parliament by which these have been modified or extended. We [in England] have always possessed a strong central government, and when the powers of Crown and Parliament are united under a strong Administration, the legal powers of government are virtually unlimited. The limitations are moral and political, and are the result of conscious restraint or public opinion. They are not limitations imposed by law. In theory Parliament is supreme. There is nothing legally it cannot do, and practically nothing which, at one time or another, it has not done. It has prolonged its own life. It has taken away the lives or liberties of its fellow citizens without the semblance of a fair trial. It has confiscated property. It has ratified revolutions.

In this we are almost unique. The Congress of the United States, the French Assembly, the Bonn [now Berlin] Legislature, the Diet of Japan, the federal legislature of Switzerland, do not possess these powers or anything like them. Nor do the Parliaments of the various members of the Commonwealth to whom we have given independence. All possess powers limited by a constitution, which they have not the right to exceed. ... In our lifetime the use of [British governmental] powers has continuously increased, and the checks and balances have been rendered increasingly ineffective by the concentration of their effective operation more and more in the House of Commons, in the government side of the House of Commons, in the Cabinet within the government side, and ... in the Prime Minister within the Cabinet. The sovereignty of Parliament, absolute in theory, has become more and more the sovereignty of the House of Commons, and like all absolute rulers, the House of Commons, having more and more to do, and in consequence less and less time within which to do it, is becoming more and more the tool of its professional advisers, more and more intolerant of criticism, and less and less in control of the detail of what is done in its name.

Such considerations were wholly neglected by politicians and others of influence in public life, except a few objections on the grounds that what was elected could not by definition act despotically. Recently complaints have been made from fresh Members of Parliament that suggestions for change in certain things at Westminster were disapproved of on the grounds that they had long been there. At the same time the complete freedom of action described by Lord Hailsham has been exploited by the former Conservative government and spectacularly so by its successor, New Labour.

In the present confusion many very variegated patches are being proposed for the old garment, even some which might well tear it further and in any case are not coherent. It seems an extraordinary thing that—at the time of writing—no distinguished public voice has been heard making a preliminary proposal for a *genuinely independent* national convention—say, a Royal Commission—on the British Constitution.

Changes to the House of Lords (the idiosyncratic British Upper House) have already been made, but by New Labour in power. One of these affects the legal system, to which also other amendments have been brought in, equally without reference to the country as a whole. The judiciary and both lawyers in practice and students of law are striving to maintain actual principles. Many individuals and organisations now apply to the courts for redress in matters relating to governmental requirements and activities.

Full consideration would necessarily include the whole of United Kingdom. Complete independence for Scotland is already a matter for serious discussion; but in any case the country has already employed its new freedoms to reform the voting system for its own parliament, and instituting a practice of the various parties working together without losing their identities, very different from the Westminster constant and too often futile confrontation of the two or three large parties which has come to exasperate and even anger British citizens.

It is to be supposed that an independent Scotland would very early move to seek its own membership of the European Union. This, and the attitudes and practices among their fellow Celts, presents a striking contrast to the situation in England. It has to be remembered how much of what is called British or even English is London-led, where the approach to Europe has always been ambiguous.

The European Idea

The mistake made by parliamentary and other public leadership was to regard from the first what became the European Union as a revival of the old Europe of the past four hundred years and which finally came to its end in the Second World War. Realising that there was no longer a place for military intervention, England still regarded Europe as a place of commercial and financial rivalry. It has never accommodated itself wholly to what has been described as "co-operation is better than confrontation," and that therefore certain matters of Europe-wide legal and social organisation would have to be agreed. Used to the nineteenth-century policy of dealing with issues at home and abroad as they arise (and unwarned by its results for all concerned) the English have found very hard anything so far reaching in time, as well as space, as the European Idea.

In these notes I have been referring mainly to the European Union because it is the UK membership of this which engages the minds of so many public figures and the media, not least the BBC. It would be interesting to estimate what proportion of British, or at least English, people has even heard of the Council of Europe. This institution, which slightly pre-dates the beginnings of the European Union, is in its own way just as influential. There is no space here for an examination of it in detail, but a brief expression of its idea can be given. In the first place it is for all Europe, countries do not have to apply to join, and is thus very open to contributions from various interests.

Although in close contact with the EU, their buildings are adjoined in Strasbourg, the Council is not directly political. It concerns itself with the whole rich life of communities. For example:

> the European Convention of Human Rights, with its Law Court, the European Convention for the Protection of Minorities, including languages, and the revival in various ways of ancient Routes within and outside of Europe with their links between peoples, and their historic and cultural wealth, inspired by the Pilgrimage Routes to the ancient Spanish shrine of St. James of Compostela.

As will readily be seen, the Council of Europe was imbued from its inception with the Principle of Subsidiarity. In America and England natural human movements towards decentralisation are being called "localism" and in England also "bottom upwards." But the working of the clear ideas in the European continent has established the stability and fruitfulness not fully appreciated by the two generations born into England and USA since the end of the Second World War.

A group, Charter 88, has been exploring the English situation and in particular British constitutional problems. Its observation on the relationship between home and abroad goes to the heart of the matter:

> The national question is also a European question. Nowhere is the impact of Britain's failure to draw up a new constitution more disastrous than in its relations with the EU. Britain's position in Europe is bound to remain evasive and half-hearted until it has the self-respect that accompanies a modern, effective, democratic and secure constitution.

It is impossible to make forecasts: events and influences move so fast world-wide and, as we see in history, always to be allowed for is the unforeseen, not to say utterly undetected, in human beings and their affairs. I do not want to give the impression, even if such a judgment were admissible, that England is a land without hope. The country has a strong indigenous life, valuable organisations, large and small, and wise and constructive voices. The question is, how well and how soon these virtuous forces can make their way through a flood of confusion, often unintentionally but some of it intentionally destructive.

If there is no firm purpose of amendment the future would seem open to almost any calamity. Yet the very fact of such widespread disintegration opens opportunities for rebuilding the foundations of a new society and the gradual erection of its structures. This cannot be done with the unregulated haste which has caused so much damage in the impositions of recent governments; but it is a matter for urgency.

[1] *The Chesterton Review*, Vol. XXXV, Nos. 1& 2, Spring Summer 2009

[2] The Encyclical Letter of Pope Pius XI, On Reconstructing the Social Order, 1931. Paragraph 79.

Book Reviews

The Elusive Father Brown: The Life of Mgr. John O'Connor
Julia Smith
Gracewing: Leominster, UK, 2010
ISBN 978-0-85244-698-0

Father (later Monsignor) John O'Connor (1870-1952) was the priest after whom G. K. Chesterton created the character of Father Brown, the detective and hero of the numerous Father Brown mysteries. He was a friend of both Gilbert and Frances Chesterton, in fact the priest who received Chesterton into the Church, and well-connected to many others in the English Catholic intellectual community between the wars, including Eric Gill and David Jones. He was highly regarded by his friends, and Hilaire Belloc wrote that he "considered Father O'Connor to be one of the most intelligent men he had ever met." Although born in Ireland, Father O'Connor became a priest of the diocese of Leeds in the north of England and spent most of his priestly life as pastor of St. Cuthbert's parish in Bradford, Yorkshire. He was an avid collector of books and works of art, well-known in art circles, and was an important translator of the works of Paul Claudel into English.

Both as a friend of Chesterton's and in his own right Father O'Connor certainly deserves to be remembered. But there are two ways one can write the life of someone. If his life is outwardly sufficiently varied, then it is easy to know what to write about. On the other hand, if someone's external life has fewer compelling incidents, then a biographer should probably focus on his inner life, on the life of the mind, for example. And Father O'Connor presents enough material for this latter to be done. Appendix I of this work lists Father O'Connor's writings and translations, and while not

---

Looking down from the hill fort onto Abbotsbury

extensive, they would seem to offer sufficient matter for interesting analysis, especially on the two subjects which I will note below.

Unfortunately, however, Smith does not take this approach, and instead largely fills her book with accounts of meetings, dinners, entertainments, friends, friends of friends, and so on. We learn, for example, something about Father O'Connor's procuring of vestments, about the advice he gave on gardening, about which members of the Steinthal family played what roles in a birthday masque that Chesterton wrote, about the bacon and wine that he and Eric Gill dined on one fine March day, about the "sardines and beer or something tasty and Bohemian, perhaps meat pie with oysters in it with beer or stout to drink" which Father O'Connor suggested for a club dinner and about many other similar matters. Although the author touches on some of his possibly controversial writings, she does little more than touch on them and does not give the reader enough information to make a judgment of his own.

The two topics that Smith brings up that might have been treated more fully are Father O'Connor's ideas about liturgical reform and his relations with Eric Gill. Around 1928 Father O'Connor had written a booklet with the title, *Why Revive the Liturgy & How*. The author says it "was only circulated privately, probably because of the somewhat radical views expressed between its covers." Although Smith claims that Father O'Connor supported the idea of the priest facing *ad populum* during the liturgy and implies that he favoured celebrating Mass in the venacular, we do not get any detailed examination of Father O'Connor's booklet, which presumably might have given more of his ideas on the liturgy and his rationale for them. We get the statement that "his suggestions included many of the changes regarding vestments, language, the times and manner of communion, that would have to wait almost forty years to be implemented," but not enough to know exactly what he meant or wanted. When he built a new church in Bradford in 1934-35, it was a "round church," that is, with the altar in the center and pews around three or four sides. The photograph of the church's interior in the book shows it after it was remodeled in the 1960s, so it is not clear exactly what Father O'Connor's own arrangements were. But what is intriguing and worthy of discussion is to what extent Father O'Connor anticipated or would have favoured the changes in liturgical practice introduced after the Second Vatican Council. The liturgical movement of the first half of the twentieth century is currently a subject of study, and the extent to which its ideas did or did not lead to the reforms of the 1960s and 70s is a matter of research and debate. If Father O'Connor truly supported such things as the priest celebrating *versus populum* or the use of the vernacular, this would be valuable material for understanding the early liturgical movement, and it would be worth investigating as well how and where his views were formed, and to what extent they were shared by others within the English Catholic Church. But here we get only a small glimpse of what he thought and did, and even less on why.

The second matter Smith discusses more fully, but again without giving sufficient information as to what Father O'Connor really thought or said and why he did so. This matter is Eric Gill, his erotic art and in general his sexual life, including his behaviour toward his own daughters. Of course there is a fundamental difference in how we should evaluate Gill's erotic drawings and his sexual misdeeds. The first can be a matter for debate, the second hardly so. According to Smith, Father O'Connor figured in both matters.

Father O'Connor was apparently close friends of Gill and his family, the two frequently visiting each other, as well as Gill's favoured confessor, although it is not clear if he was his regular confessor. Gill carved several statues for St. Cuthbert's Church, including a set of stations of the cross. On his part, Father O'Connor supplied the text for the edition of the biblical Song of Songs that Gill illustrated (1925), and for the later (and less known) *The Song of the Soul* (1927), with text that he translated from St. John of the Cross. The first of these "caused something of an outcry in certain religious circles," Smith notes (108), because of "Eric Gill's somewhat explicit engravings of conjugal love between Christ and the female figure of his bride, representing his Church. ... " Someone of the stature of Father Bede Jarrett condemned it and "wished to have the book suppressed." Obviously the question of the portrayal of the nude and of sex in art is both complex and of perennial interest and importance, and one would like more discussion of Father O'Connor's thinking on the matter. Unfortunately Smith does not give us much of this, and says very little about the two of Father O'Connor's writings that might shed some light on his views, a 1930 article on Gill in

The Bookman and a 1943 review of his *Last Essays* in *Blackfriars.*

Smith does devote more space to Gill's sexual misbehaviour and Father O'Connor reactions. She herself seems intent on exculpating Gill, writing, for example of Gill's somewhat unusual attitude to sexual matters..., his incestuous relations with his sisters, his sexual experiments with his daughters, his naked cavorting with house guests. ... Gill is quite explicit in his *Diaries* about in what he and his daughters indulged, which was more in the nature of satisfying his curiosity rather than his passion," and "Gill's constant desire to know why something should be so was, according to his *Diaries*, often the reason for his visits to his daughters' bedrooms." One finds Gills's claim that he was motivated by "curiosity" or a "desire to know why something should be so" unconvincing. He already had more than ample knowledge of female sexuality, so we can hardly regard his attempt at self-vindication as anything more than white-washing. But, Smith assures us, "Father O'Connor was not only Gill's friend but a friend to all the family who would not have stood by and done nothing if any of them had shown signs of distress..." But can one really suppose that a Catholic priest at that time would have said or done nothing about incest, unless of course his knowledge had been obtained under the seal of confession?

Thus how much Father O'Connor really knew and what he might have learned only in confession is not clear. The author asserts that Father O'Connor was involved in Gill's decision to send his daughter, Elizabeth, to Switzerland for a time, Gill's main motivation being to "distract her from the attentions of [Hilary] Pepler's son. Gill disapproved of this on the grounds of their youth, but it also removed temptation from her father, as Father O'Connor no doubt pointed out." According to Smith, "Father O'Connor evolved his own apology for Gill's behavior and told both Gill himself and David Jones that those who led only a sheltered life were in no position to condemn the nude in art." This is a non sequitur, however, for the question of nudity in art is hardly the same as that of Gill's sexual wrongdoings, but Smith seems somehow to conflate the two. In any case, one would like to know more than Smith tells us of Father O'Connor's relations with and opinions both of Eric Gill's artistic project and of his personal behaviour.

Julia Smith has broken new ground by writing a biography of Father John O'Connor. It remains now for her or for others to probe some of the more interesting questions that will help illuminate his thought and at the same time shed further light on English Catholic life in the first half of the last century.

Thomas Storck
Westerville, Ohio

*   *   *

The Essential Belloc, a Prophet for Our Times.
Edited by C. John McCloskey,
Scott J. Bloch & Brian Robertson
Saint Benedict Press: LLC,
Charlotte, N.C., 2010:
ISBN 13: 978 1935 302 360

In the Introduction to, perhaps, his most contentious book, *Europe and the Faith*, Hilaire Belloc wrote:

> I say the Catholic "conscience of history—I say "conscience"—that is, as intimate knowledge through identity. ... For a man's way of perceiving himself (when he does so honestly and after

a cleansing examination of his mind) is in line with his creator's, and therefore with reality: he sees from within. Let me pursue this metaphor. Man has in him conscience, which is the voice of God. ... So it is with us who are of the Faith and the great story of Europe. A Catholic . . . understands (the story of Europe) from within. He cannot understand it altogether, because he is a finite being; but he is also that which has to understand. The Faith is Europe and Europe is the Faith.

In a letter to a friend, Hilaire Belloc confessed that he "was used to Insult, as I combine in one person three natures, all of them targets for insult in this country: a) Poverty, b) Papistry, c) Pugnacity." Probably those who insulted him did not much care about his poverty, and, when the thought seized him, he was quite capable of turning his pugnacity on his Papistry. "The Catholic Church," he remarked, "is an institution I am bound to hold divine, but for unbelievers, here is proof of its divinity, that no merely human institution run with such knavish imbecility would have lasted a fortnight." Clearly, Belloc thought that, as one critic put it, "far from denying the universality of the Roman Catholic Church, the author is rather showing that the Church was, by God's will and Providence, "incarnated" in and shaped by European civilisation, centered in Rome, and that *on its human side* the Catholic Church is Roman and European." These quotes reveal Belloc's personal conviction that integral to all culture is faith, and, therefore, "religion, not economics, is the heart of historical conflicts." In *The Essential Belloc, a Prophet for Our Times*, Editors C. John McCloskey, Scott J. Bloch, and Brian Robertson assert that Belloc was not nostalgic "for a Europe that once was." Rather, he was calling for the recapture of "the Incarnational aspect of history." Their book, a delightful compilation of mostly short extracts taken from sixty-two of the one hundred and fifty books listed in their bibliography, is a grand introduction to Belloc's personal commitment to that project.

Obviously a labour of love—the editors acknowledge help from friends, family members, the Hilaire Belloc Society—the extracts, though brief and even sometimes pithy, gather focus from the chapter headings under which they are grouped, and the short introductory notes that precede each of the ten sections. The temptation, of course, is to jump around from

Christendom in Crisis to *History and Historical Personages*, or sample *Friendship and the Inn* with *Songs and Verse*, especially if you have a extensive reading acquaintance with the Belloc cannon. I discovered that it does not really matter, because the effect of sequential reading or cherry-picking is almost exactly the same; that is, either way you come into contact with a compelling character made of a fascinating mixture of melancholy and ebullience, poetry and economic theory, pugnacity and humility, a restless pilgrim who saw in his "sacred Sussex . . . a reflection of Paradise." And you always recognise the voice, energetic, clear, uncluttered, dynamic, unselfconscious, prophetic, and constantly inclined toward breaking out into verse and song. "It is the best of all trades," he said, "to make songs, and the second best to sing them." And again, " let us love one another and laugh. ... Let us suffer absurdities, for that is only to suffer one another." Those who have read with delight *The Path To Rome* are aware that Belloc restlessly roamed European pilgrim routes, searching for the roots of his beliefs. But how many would recall the following meditation on his love for his native Sussex. "One's native place," he remarked, "is the shell of one's soul, and one's church is the kernel of that nut."

Similar compilations, for example, Heinz R. Kuehn's *The Essential Guardini*, feature much longer segments of their subject's books, while others, Ignatius Press' *The Quotable Chesterton*, warn the reader that these excerpts will be but short extracts from his extensive writings. Perhaps, given Belloc's vast corpus, it would be unfair to criticise the editors' selections. Still, there ought always to be room for the reader familiar with the person featured in the book to wish that his favourite passages had made the cut. In the poetry section, I looked to find the entire "Heroic Poem in Praise of Wine," but especially the final stanza. I know well the Nancy gate in the Lorraine town of Toul from which Belloc began his pilgrimage *Path to Rome*, having spent much of my military service in Toul. The descriptive passage included is excellent, but my first reading of Belloc's perilous, snowy mountain climb that nearly ended in disaster remains my most vivid memory of that long hike to the center of Christendom. And who that has experienced *The Cruise of the Nona* can forget the magical appearance from out of the Channel mists the British Fleet sailing across Sailor Belloc's bow toward its destiny in the battles of World War I.

On the other hand, the editors have managed to give us Belloc the Prophet in tersely stated thoughts such as: "That is the central social misfortune of our time. The small owner is on the way to ruin." Or on Islam, in "the major thing of all, Religion, we have fallen back and Islam has in the main preserved its soul. ... in the contrast between our religious chaos and the religious certitudes still strong throughout the Mohammedan world. ... lies our peril." In his editorial introduction, Scott J. Block, commenting on Belloc's *The Jews* written in 1922, remarks that Belloc "actually predicted the horror in the ghettos of Warsaw and the holocaust at the hands of the Third Reich."

Apropos the current controversy about Shakespeare as a recusant Catholic, Belloc remarked: "To a man acquainted with the Catholic Church and the society it produces, nothing is clearer than that the plays of Shakespeare were written by a man steeped in Catholic social tradition and for audiences in the same mood." Hear his meditation on the power of poetry. "How the mere choice and rhythm of words should produce so magical an effect no one has yet been about to comprehend, and least of all the poets themselves."

Perhaps the most revealing evaluation of his own disputatious character came in his essay *On the Place of Gilbert Chesterton in English Letters.* "All men one may say, or very nearly all men, have one leading moral defect. Few have one leading Christian virtue. That of Gilbert Chesterton was unmistakably the virtue of Christian charity: a virtue especially rare in writing men, and rarest of all in such of them as have a pursuing appetite for controversy—that is for bolting out the truth."

Finally, mention must be made of the volume's two introductory essays. Editor Scott J. Bloch, co-founder of the Hilaire Belloc society, in Kansas, and part of the founding of the International Hilaire Belloc Society in 1996, gives a graceful introduction to the accomplishments of his subject. I particularly appreciated his answer to the "canard of anti-Semitism," which he labels "the last desperate act of the politically correct mobs." In his preface, James V. Schall, S. J., has written his meditation on the book by asking us to consider "The Charm of Belloc." That word seems to me to suggest the desire to enchant, allure, or, most especially, to please, hardly the reputation of Belloc

the controversialist. In an essay "On Death," Belloc remembers an innkeeper who talked "to me over the table upon this business of Death, and as he talked he showed that desire to persuade which is in itself the strongest motive of interest in any human discourse." Persuasion is, it seems to me, at the heart of the Bellocian enterprise. But Schall has the last word. My Webster's defines the word, *Charm,* as "verse assumed to have magic power to help or hurt." Belloc's magic power is the poetic insight and direct force of his ideas. When coupled with an engaging and persuasive personality, and composed in a manner that reflects the transparent honesty of his Catholic conscience, his writing makes riveting reading. Whether it helps or hurts depends upon the disposition of the reading. But that Belloc's pen produced English prose and poetry of the first order, seems indisputable to me.

James P. McGlone
Department of Communications
Seton Hall University,
So. Orange, NJ

*   *   *

*The Social and Political
Thought of Benedict XVI*
Thomas R. Rourke
Lexington Books:
Lanham, MD, 2010
ISBN 978-0-7391-4280-6

Thomas Rourke, Professor of Politics at Clarion University in Pennsylvania, has written a comprehensive introduction to the theological-political thought of the man who now sits on the chair of St. Peter. But it is not, strictly speaking, the thought of Pope Benedict that we are dealing with here. For Rourke's book deals for the most part with the thought of Benedict *before* he became pope, that is, with the writings of Joseph Ratzinger as a private theologian, although he does include a summary of the encyclical *Caritas in Veritate*, and a short discussion of the two documents on liberation theology issued by the Congregation for the Doctrine of the Faith under Cardinal Ratzinger's aegis as prefect. Rourke, however, has chosen to refer, not just in his title but throughout the book to Benedict XVI "partly to avoid excessive and unnecessary formality and endless repetition of inelegant expressions such as 'then Cardinal Ratzinger' [and instead] opted for a simple and straightforward consistency" (8). This certainly makes sense, but

the usage does require the reader to keep in mind that we are dealing here, in large part, not with the magisterial teaching of a Roman Pontiff, but with the ideas and teaching of a private theologian, however eminent. Doubtless these ideas and insights have continued to influence Benedict since his elevation to the Papacy, but they still must be kept separate from the official teaching of the Church, even if they might often help us to understand the background to Benedict's actual papal statements.

In the Introduction, Rourke lays out the plan for his book and points out that any "attempt to categorise and organise [Benedict's] thought presents special problems, due to the comprehensiveness of his vision. Benedict does not treat theological and philosophical anthropology, faith and reason; the interactions among politics, reason, and faith; the consideration of freedom and conscience; threats to human life, and culture, as so many different, specialised topics. ... The reader will undoubtedly note a certain recurrence of major ideas" (5). This certainly is not a weakness in Ratzinger's thought, but a source of richness as he weaves recurrent themes together and shows the impact of ideas and principles on different areas of knowledge. In fact, Rourke says later of Benedict, "Harkening back to an earlier time wherein this sense of the whole was seen as desirable in intellectual life, Benedict's work crosses the typical academic borders. ... Whereas avoiding over-specialisation and compartmentalisation is a unique strength in Benedict, it does render it difficult to separate out the various fields Benedict addresses; nor is it possible to avoid overlap" (103).

Before discussing the more specifically socio-political aspects of his thought, Rourke, in chapter two, lays the groundwork for this by treating Cardinal Ratzinger's philosophical anthropology, that is, his understanding of the human person and of the anthropological foundations of the political community. Here we see a first instance of the fact that Joseph Ratzinger has often been presented as a caricature, and that not only by his foes but perhaps by his friends as well. Often in the secular or liberal Catholic media he has been presented as some kind of theological reactionary. Although any use of the term reactionary in theology is questionable, if it does apply to anyone, it certainly is not Joseph Ratzinger. We can see this, for example, in his ideas on the term

person in theology, in his attitude toward the Enlightenment and toward Church/state relations.

On the first point, Rourke brings out the perhaps unexpected fact that Ratzinger differs from St. Thomas on the implications of the theological concept of person. In contrast to Aquinas, who accepted Boethius's famous definition of person as an individual substance of a rational nature, Ratzinger sees person as purely relation. Rourke quotes from his 1990 essay, "Concerning the Notion of Person in Theology," that, "Relation, being related, is not something superadded to the person, but it *is* the person itself" (14). Now all theologians agree that when we speak of the Trinity, three persons obviously does not mean or imply three substances. But Ratzinger wishes to draw implications from this for other persons, including human persons. As he goes on to say in his essay, "This brings us to the second misunderstanding that has not allowed the effects of Christology to work themselves out fully [and sees] Christ as the simply unique ontological exception which must be treated as such." In other words, Ratzinger saw the usage of *person*, as applied in the doctrines of the Trinity and of the two natures in

Christ, as having implications for anthropology as well, something which Aquinas was unwilling to accept. But be that as it may, the discussion of Benedict's anthropological understanding of person highlights the fact that he often takes positions which might surprise those unacquainted with his writings and which perhaps reflect his background in the theological ferment that began in France and Germany in the 1940s and which has produced so many well-known theologians such as Henri de Lubac and Hans Urs von Balthasar.

In subsequent chapters dealing with revelation, reason and their relation to politics, with conscience and freedom, and with questions of culture and world religions, Rourke brings out Ratzinger's conditional acceptance of the Enlightenment of the eighteenth century, which he sums up in this way: "Benedict states at several points that he does not simply reject Enlightenment reason in politics. Rather, he asserts that its basic thrust of reasserting the role of reason in politics was justified" (125). For, "Benedict actually sees in the original ideal of the Enlightenment a kinship with the faith's absolute commitment to truth. Citing Horkheimer and Adorno, he contends that the Enlightenment is rooted in the conviction that the truth is absolute." Although his notion of enlightenment is not limited merely to the *Aufklärung* of the eighteenth century, neither does he entirely dismiss that epoch, and he "speaks approvingly of the modern Enlightenment in its intellectual roots" (36).

With regard to the relations between Church and state, Benedict argues in favour of a polity bound by the fundamental moral truths taught by the Church, but rejects the idea of a specifically Catholic political order. "Despite the fact that he rejects all of what many would see as historically more 'traditional' roles for the Church in a European context, Benedict continually finds that Christianity, not in any particular institutional form, but in its deepest nature as a faith, in fact has a great deal to offer politics, and its contribution is due almost entirely to the faith's understanding of reason as it relates to politics, religion, truth, and culture" (125). In fact one of the positive results that he believes came from the Enlightenment was its removal of politics from the auspices of the Church. "European Catholicism had its own equivalent of the state church system. In this sense. ... the Enlightenment was a powerful force for reinvigorating politics based on reason" (54).

Another point that Rourke brings up frequently, and that is one of the most fruitful aspects of Ratzinger's thought, is his emphasis on reason as a God-given and beneficial aspect of human life. Reason when properly employed, when linked to faith and not divorced from the first principles of the natural law, is vital to man's personal and social life. "In God there is a 'reason' behind the entire universe, and our own human reason is a reflection of that. This is what makes reason special, and gives it its exalted place in our pursuit of truth, of wisdom and understanding" (122). This, of course, was the burden of Pope Benedict's famous Regensburg address, where he contrasted the role of *Logos* in Christian thought with the largely arbitrary character of God as conceived in Islam.

Joseph Ratzinger's pre-papal writings on theology, philosophy, culture and related matters constitute a thought-provoking corpus which cannot fail to stimulate the thought of anyone who becomes acquainted with it. Thomas Rourke's work will have performed its chief task well if it leads the reader to investigate at first hand the complex, interesting and always fertile thought of a significant thinker of our time, a thinker whose subsequent career as Vicar of Jesus Christ guarantees him a permanent place in the history both of the Church and of European thought.

Thomas Storck
Westerville, Ohio

*   *   *

Hope in a Scattering Time: A Life of Christopher Lasch
Eric Miller
Wm B. Eedermans: Grand Rapids, MI, 2010
ISBN 13: 079 0802817693

When the *Culture of Narcissism* first appeared in 1979, author Christopher Lasch had long been a well-known public intellectual. Lasch had published the well-received *Haven in a Heartless World* the year before, and he had long been known as an astute critic on the left. But Narcissism was different. It was a bombshell, however, rocketing Lasch to the centre of the public conversation and even breaking into popular magazines such as *People*. The *Culture of Narcissism* directed its focus on the cultural dissolution of the preceding two decades.

Far from liberating, the "1960s" had unleashed pathologies that Lasch argued modern society had few means to combat. For Lasch, however, the book, though important, was only one stage in a journey that would take him from the progressivism of his Midwest upbringing through the various leftists ferments of the 1960s and 1970s, then in some ways back again. While not quite Chesterton in *Orthodoxy*, who set out in search of a truth that he found back at home, Lasch's intellectual and political journey lead him back again to his Midwestern American roots.

In this biography, Eric Miller analyses that journey and demonstrates why Lasch is worth reading now, even if some of his tools —such as his reliance on Freud —may be dated. Miller, an Associate Professor of History at Geneva College, places Lasch in the context of his time, and shows how he became increasingly separate from his secular, liberal allies toward something more like conservatism. *Hope* follows its subject in great detail, and Miller clearly has done thorough research in the correspondence and archives. Born in 1934, Lasch was raised in a secular Midwestern household infused with the progressive notions of the era. His father was a

newspaper editor who moved to Chicago in part because of the increased conservatism of the Omaha, Nebraska paper where he had previously worked. His mother, Zora, whom the elder Lasch met had the University of Nebraska, where he studied as an undergraduate before going up to Oxford as a Rhodes scholar. They are not, in other words, the typical picture one would have of the Midwest, but then that picture is often drawn by those who would dismiss the middle of the nation as provincial rubes. This background always remained important to Lasch, and may explain his desire to teach and live in smaller towns, most significantly in a small town outside the University of Rochester, where he spent a significant portion of his career. He felt some alienation from urban life even as a young graduate student in history at Columbia in the mid-1950s which he attended after Harvard University.

Even from his graduate school experience, Lasch struggled with the problem of liberalism and its many variants. He was from the outset a defender of liberalism, and remained so to some extent throughout his life. Yet it took him a lifetime to fully delineate and define what that liberalism was. In the 1940s and 1950s, Lasch was witnessing a transformation of liberalism, from a uniquely American blend of populism, localism, and mild progressivism at first, which then moved after the New Deal and the civil rights movement to a reliance on bigger centralised government. In the 1960s and 1970s liberalism became a "lifestyle," devoted to personal freedom and consumerism, and then finally changed into a politically correct ideology focused on abstract equality and gender politics toward the end of his life. Lasch's best books are a reflection of his struggle with liberalism as it entered its various phases. In the end, he found himself defending a liberalism not much different from what used to be called "the American way of life," based on community, family, and traditional mores, including respect for distinguished intellectual achievement. This put him at odds with his fellow liberals, for whom distinction could not be recognised in a worldview dominated by an oppressive sense of equality and who further could not defend what they considered a "premodern" worldview.

Haven, which was subtitled *The Family Besieged*, was a defence of the family, and grew in part out of a series of essays he had done for the *New York Re-*

view of Books in 1975. This enraged certain parts of the Left, for whom the family was either an oppressive patriarchal construct or a tool of industrial capitalism. Lasch, instead, saw it for what it was: a training ground for the virtues and as defense against a words to world that saw people as either objects of government manipulation or "consumers" of capitalist phantasms.Lasch, however, never became what in America would be considered a conservative, though the 1980s many conservatives were engaging with his ideas. He clearly had no connection with the neoconservatives. Their embrace of capitalism, Lasch thought, trumped any professed devotion to traditional values, and when the two conflicted, capitalism won out indeed, Lasch thought—perhaps not entirely fairly—that for many neoconservaives, traditional values were important only insofar as they could support a capitalist order of a certain sort. On the other hand, Lasch had little patience for the "traditionalist" conservatives as well. If the neoconservatives thought too much about capitalism, the traditionalists thought too little about it, preferring instead to develop the theories of a "managerial elite" that manipulates the country. Lasch's liberalism would not allow ho to him reject anti-capitalism as a foundation of his social crititique. In the end, however, he sounded very much like Russell Kirk, although Lasch was the more rigorous social scientist whereas Kirk emphasised creating a "counter-narrative" infused with the moral into that of modernity.

While Lasch became friendlier toward religion as he aged, and began to see in it a socially positive force, he never embraced a particular faith. His respect always had a distance to it, and he never fully embraced the argument that "religion" as a category did not really exist. Only particular faiths, with particular cultural expressions, can create and sustain culture, including the kind of liberal culture he wanted to preserve. *Hope in a Scattered Time* is a helpful reminder of the work of one of American's great intellectuals, and a reminder that the American tradition contains within it the resources for regeneration.

Gerald J. Russello
Fellow
G. K. Chesterton Institute for
Faith & Culture

*   *   *

Quest for Shakespeare: The Bard of Avon and the Church of Rome,
Joseph Pearce
Ignatius Press, 2008
ISBN: 978 1586172244

Even though Father Henry Sebastian Bowden, aided by the unparalleled scholarship of Richard Simpson, set forth a groundbreaking argument for Shakespeare's Catholicism over a century ago (*The Religion of Shakespeare*, 1899), interest in the Bard's faith waned in subsequent decades as academicians turned to allegedly more important matters such as his seeming psychosis, questionable sexual orientation, and, of course, whether he existed at all. Famished by such inane musings, loyal Shakespeareans were more than happy to feed on the plays and poems themselves, confident that they could be savoured for their sheer beauty regardless of the author's faith (or lack thereof). After all, years of meticulous research had led no less an expert than Peter Ackroyd to declare that Shakespeare was "a man without beliefs."

Joseph Pearce aims to expose the utter nonsense of Ackroyd's judgment. He takes great pains to prove "beyond all reasonable doubt" (24) that Shakespeare was raised a Catholic and remained a Catholic. Yet the author does more than simply rehash the abundant evidence for Shakespeare's Catholicism; he tries to persuade all who happen to care that it is crucial for us to know the faith of the man who penned these treasures if we wish to appreciation fully their timeless worth. "What if our understanding of Shakespeare is essential to our understanding of ourselves as reflected by Shakespeare?" (18). Shakespeare, Pearce suggests, not only holds a mirror to our humanity, he himself is that mirror.

Pearce's first order of business is to debunk the ongoing "anti-Stratfordian" myth that Shakespeare was anyone (the Earl of Oxford, Christopher Marlowe, Daniel Defoe, Anne Hathaway, or even Her Majesty the Queen) but the child born to John and Mary of Stratford, baptised at Holy Trinity Parish on the 26th of April, 1564, tutored by the Simon Hunt (who later became a Jesuit priest after studies in Rome), married to Anne Hathaway in November of 1582, and deceased on the Feast of Saint George in 1616, his fifty-second birthday.

Even those who concede Shakespeare's existence have serious doubts as to whether he

had attained the requisite level of education to write so deftly. In response, Pearce, noting that Elizabethan England was one of the most educated civilisations in history, lists several contemporaries of Shakespeare raised in even more meagre circumstances than the Bard: Christopher Marlowe's father was a shoemaker, Alexander Pope's a draper, and Ben Jonson's stepfather a bricklayer. Neither does the objection that Shakespeare was too young to compose such sublime verses hold much water: Christopher Marlowe was only twenty-three and Ben Jonson twenty-six when their first plays were successfully produced. Some scholars have even dared to discredit the authenticity of Shakespeare's work on the basis of his shaky signature (a sign of infirmity, they say), a hypothesis for which Pearce shows little patience.

These obstacles removed, Pearce reviews the copious evidence that William's parents, fellow villagers, and closest friends were all recusants. The fact that John Shakespeare bequeathed the family house to his son indicates that William himself persevered as a Catholic to the end despite the excruciating pressure to forsake the "old religion." Stratford it seems was a bastion for "Church papists," people who dutifully attended services at the local parish while practising Catholicism at home. That there was a communal dimension to this resistance is clear from the fact that the medieval paintings inside the town parish were whitewashed rather than defaced as a way for the Queen's subjects to comply in good conscience with the law she reinstated to "destroy all shines … pictures, paintings, etc."(33). Yet the most significant puzzle piece consists in the famous "will" found tucked away in the rafters of the family home in 1757. This document, written circa 1581, imitates the devotional formula composed by Saint Charles Borromeo to supply clandestine Catholics with a means to profess their desire to receive the "last sacraments" in the absence of a priest. Copies of this "Testament," which had been widely promoted by Jesuit Fathers Edmund Campion and Robert Persons, had also been disseminated in Warwickshire. As these ran short, the faithful, including John Shakespeare, were forced to handwrite their own copies based on the original Borromeo model.

Pearce also discusses the significance of "Domina Jane Shakspere," a likely relative of William and subprioress of the Wroxall

Priory in 1525, as well as Isabella Shakespeare, prioress in 1457 and likely the inspiration for the homonymous heroine of *Measure for Measure*. Other familial connections suggest that Shakespeare himself risked his good name and fortune for being Catholic. His mother sprang from well-to-do Arden stock and had close relatives implicated in the so-called "Somerville Plot." Her cousin Edward, for example, was hanged, disembowelled, beheaded, and quartered for his alleged involvement. Persecution against Catholics only worsened as the years passed, though the Shakespeares and other Stratfordians eventually developed ways to live respectably and peaceably without abandoning their beloved religion.

When it comes to the elusive "lost years" (1579-1592), Pearce treads cautiously but confidently, opining that Shakespeare did not study abroad but nonetheless accumulated a vast amount of learning. A portion of this period must have been spent in Lancashire where William maintained close family connections with like-minded recusants. It is less clear as to whether, pace Evelyn Waugh's captivating fantasy of William attending the Jesuit's Mass, Shakespeare had any personal acquaintance with

Father Campion. Pearce does, however, cite compelling evidence that Campion lodged in the Lancashire area several times, thus enhancing the possibility of a personal acquaintance with William.

In the end, Pearce asserts that the relationship with Campion may be a moot point. The facts concerning Shakespeare's immediate family are alone sufficient to make a clear case for his Catholicity, and that is the main purpose of this volume. In a sequel, Pearce plans to outline a critical method for reading the Bard's plays, sonnets, and poems "with fresh and unprejudiced eyes" (173). In two appendices to the present book, Pearce gives us a taste of what is to come. Yet I cannot help wondering if it might have been more effective to interweave the two tasks. If Shakespeare's work is the mirror Pearce claims it to be, then it would make sense to trace the contours of his life with the aid of the writings themselves, be they fictional or poetic. Pearce, however, errs toward dividing the process sharply into two distinct steps: first a proof of Shakespeare's Catholicism, then an explanation of how we are to read his works accordingly. Of course, there is nothing intrinsically wrong with such a method, provided it does not mis-

lead teachers of Shakespeare into thinking that students will understand Shakespeare only after having gained prior knowledge of his Catholic faith. However, part of the immense joy of experiencing Shakespeare for the first time is to discover that you can follow his plays without preliminaries. All you need is a working comprehension of English and a place to sit (or stand) in the theatre. Though it would be hard to disagree with Pearce that Shakespeare's drama "comes to life in the light of the Catholic life of the playwright" (173), it would be a shame to ignore the rapture that envelopes an audience who may not even know when or where Shakespeare lived, let alone what he believed.

Daniel B. Gallagher,
Pontifical Gregorian
University, Rome

*　　*　　*

The medieval towers of San Gimignano loom over the town of San Gimignano

Film Reviews

Doomed Bourgeois in Love: Essays on the Films of Whit Stillman,
Mark C. Henrie,
ed. Wilmington [DE]: ISI, 2002
ISBN 1-882926-70-6

The Last Days of Disco With Cocktails at Petrossian Afterwards.
Whit Stillman
New York: Farrar, Straus and Giroux, 2000
ISBN 0-374-18339-2

Barcelona & Metropolitan: Tales of Two Cities
London: Faber and Faber, 1994
ISBM 0-571-17365-9

Each of these books is, in one way or another, derived from Whit Stillman's films *Metropolitan* (1990), *Barcelona* (1994) and *The Last Days of Disco* (1998). My review will therefore be as much concerned with the films as with the books. I begin by noting that Stillman himself acted as scriptwriter as well as director, and that he was as obsessive in directing as he had been in writing; according to the actors, he choreographed every gesture, virtually every turn of the head and curl of the lip. He knew exactly what and whom he wanted to maximise the effect of these productions. It's as if the author in Chesterton's play *The Surprise* entered the action at the beginning of the first act instead of the second. Stillman's obsessive attention to minutiae encourages the (multiple) viewer—or student of the published scripts of *Metropolitan* and *Barcelona* (*Tales of Two Cities*) and of Stillman's novel based on *The Last Days of Disco*[1]—to a careful examination of the smallest detail, such as the acronym for Illinois High-Speed Motor Company, IHS Motors that features in *Barcelona* and recurs incidentally in *Last Days*. "IHS" is used in New Testament manuscripts as an abbreviation

---

The island of Isola Bella

for the name of "Jesus," in Greek, ΙΗΣ(ΟΥΣ). This firm, for which the "Bible-dancing goody-goody" Ted Boynton works, embodies the virtues of capitalism—"sales"— and as such is worthy of his dedication to its heroes: Franklin, Emerson, [Dale] Carnegie and Bettger. This unobtrusive hint points to the thesis of *Barcelona*: that American commercialism, despised in Europe, is a "culture" and "philosophy" in which "customers become friends"; in other words, it is a sort of distributist reworking of classic capitalism and, as such, authentically Christian. As the film closes, Ted and his cousin, Fred, have returned to the States to enjoy the American version of the sacred meal: barbequed hamburgers—the real thing, not the *ersatz* European version—which their Spanish brides have learned to respect and even to relish.[2] Similarly, light-hearted discourses on the merits of detached collars (*Metropolitan*), the right way of shaving (*Barcelona*), and Disney's *The Lady and the Tramp* (*Last Days*) are actually about tradition, parental responsibility, and marriage, which again are completely consonant with Stillman's Christian agenda. And the films certainly *are* talky, full of clever dialogue in a sort of cinematic version of the book-length debate between Turnbull the athe-

ist and MacIan the believer in *The Ball and the Cross*.

The conviction that these films merit such close scrutiny is born out by *Doomed Bourgeois in Love: The Films of Whit Stillman*. Of the nine essays in the book, six are devoted to the films—two apiece—and three to more general topics: comedy, irony and poetry. The book closes with three previously published reviews of the films and a discussion of the novelised form of *Last Days*. Their focus, generally, is on patriotism, virtue and tradition, the social concerns of the films that provide the framework for a strong religious theme generally more hinted at than stated, like the Bible—lying, significantly, under a copy of *The Economist*—which Ted Boynton reads as he gyrates around his apartment to the music of Glen Miller; Stillman, like Chesterton, prefers to keep his Christian commitment implicit. As a consequence, these essays, perceptive as they are, tend to downplay the deeply religious purposes of the films. Two essays, by Joseph Alulis[3] and R.V Young,[4] for example, are devoted to tracing parallels between Jane Austen and *Metropolitan*. Young views it as a contemporary retelling of *Mansfield Park*: the quiet heroine (Fanny Price/Audrey Rouget) eventually wins the affection of Tom Townsend away from her attractive but unworthy rival (Mary Crawford/Serena Slocum). Tom, however, is no Edmund Bertram. Initially, a cynical outsider to the privileged members of the U.H.B. (urban haute bourgeoisie), he describes the book as "notoriously bad." We later discover that he has not read it, preferring to go directly to secondary sources for his opinions. One of them is outrageous: "everything that Jane Austen wrote seems ridiculous from today's perspective." Audrey Rouget, who is, in another way on the fringe of the U.H.B., surely responds in Stillman's voice: "Has it ever occurred to you that today, looked at from Jane Austen's perspective, would look much worse than ridiculous?" Austen's *Persuasion*, in some ways similar in plot to *Mansfield Park*, provides another parallel to *Metropolitan* that Alulis explores: two outsiders ultimately come together, but "in a manner that conforms to the standards of her society."[5] Tom's conversion—not too strong a term—is signaled by his actually reading *Persuasion* and his coming to recognise that the conventional manners of the U.H.B. represent an admirable tradition of civility, whether or not it continues. A Chesterton parallel here would be Adam Wayne's defence of doomed district in *The Napoleon of Notting Hill*.

As in all comedy, there is an underlying note of sadness as we come to realise that the U.H.B., like the disco club of *Last Days*, is doomed: "a meteorite is headed straight for it."[6] Their disappearance as a class represents an impoverishment of society at large. Something good will have been lost. This sense of loss acts as a corrective to a discussion between Tom and his strongest critic, Charlie Black, about Fourierism, a utopian socialist movement of the nineteenth century reminiscent for Chestertonians of distributism. To Charlie's claim that the closing of Brook Farm, an American version of Fourierism, proves that it was a failure, Tom replies that the fact that each of us will die does not mean that he has been a failure. The point of the movie, that the U.H.B. is a noble social arrangement, stands even though by the end of the film it no longer exists as a recognisable group.[7] Every human society will end one day or another, but we are not thereby prevented from assessing it as a success or a failure. And its success is well described by Joseph Alulis's Austenesque summary of *Metro-*

politan, which is in fact applicable to all three films "The just regime is the one that awards prerogative only to a class composed of persons possessed of practical wisdom and only insofar as they possess it."[8] The whole of *Pride and Prejudice* could be read as a commentary on this statement, or *Persuasion*, towards the end of which the heroine, Anne Elliot, anticipates Stillman's scripts: "My idea of good company, Mr. Elliot, is the company of clever, well-informed people, who have a great deal of conversation; that is what I call good company."[9] But Stillman's original take on Austen is his claim that it is the American form of democratic aristocracy that makes this good company possible: "The bourgeois regime—our regime—encourages virtue."[10] In other words, as Mr. Elliot replies, "'You are mistaken,' said he gently, 'that is not good company; that is the best.'"[11] In *Barcelona* the same point is made: American innocents abroad—shades of Mark Twain—in their encounter with dissolute Europeans discover that honesty in business is not only good; it is the basis of virtuous living.

Much of the effectiveness of the films arises from the affection Stillman has for his characters; flawed as they may be, "we end up simply liking them,"[12] as we cannot help liking the eccentrics in *The Club of Queer Trades* or, especially, Innocent Smith (*Manalive*). That the best of Stillman's characters are religious directs attention to what I believe is his main purpose: to show that the U.H.B. in their various guises function as well as they do because they are Christians. Consider Audrey Roguet. Her sterling worth is implied by her attendance—with her mother, the only parent, incidentally, that appears in any of the films; the U.H.B. are otherwise on their own—at the splendid Christmas service in the Church of Saint John the Divine, while poor Tom is reduced to Jingle Bells on a tiny television set. To the thoughtful and articulate Charlie Black are allotted the opening words of *Metropolitan*. They constitute a sort of psychological proof for the existence of God, in that everyone senses that his interior monologue is in fact a dialogue that must therefore have an auditor, *et voilà*, God. More interesting, in a way, is the character Nick Smith played by Chris Eigerman, who appears in all three films in essentially the same role, that of the smart-alec truth-sayer.[13] He actually uses the word "sin" to describe his fornication, when the other characters are accusing him of hypocrisy for denouncing in others what he has been guilty of himself: "like many other great moralists and preachers, [he] had been eloquent on a point in which [his] own conduct would ill bear examination."[14] Driving the point home, *A Mighty Fortress is Our God*, the opening music of *Metropolitan*, recurs when Nick is off for a gruesome visit with his divorced father and his stepmother. In Luther's theology, for one to acknowledge his sinfulness is to assure his salvation.[15]

Secular critics have universally ignored the religious character of Stillman's work. And excellent as they generally are, the essays in *Doomed, Bourgeois, in Love* do not in my estimation give sufficient attention to the Christian underpinning of the films, although, of course, they can hardly ignore it: "Whit Stillman's films are ... Christian."[16] But I go further in saying that *The Last Days of Disco* is actually an allegory in the tradition of *The Pilgrim's Progress*, that ultimate statement of classical Calvinism. In interviews, Stillman has not called attention to his religious commitment, perhaps because he knows that the influence of the films would be much reduced if its Christian inspiration were emphasised. *The Spitfire Grill*, initially admired, was severely criticised once its religious backing was "unmasked." A warning bell may already be ringing the in the minds of my readers: the fact that no one, including Stillman, has described *Last Days* as an allegory is best accounted for on the supposition that it isn't one. Consider Peter Augustine Lawlor's "Nature, Grace and *The Last Days of Disco*." Despite the title, it discusses the film completely on the level of the story, especially with regard to the differences between men and women;[17] it is an essay full of insight. Furthermore, in an oft-quoted piece of dialogue from Barcelona, Stillman himself seems to rule out allegory or even much digging into symbolism:

> *Fred*: One thing that keeps cropping up is this about "subtext." Songs, novels, plays—they all have a subtext, which I take to mean a hidden message or import of some kind.
> Ted nods.
> *Fred*: So subtext we know. But what do you call the meaning or message that's right there on the surface, completely open and obvious? They never talk about that. What do you call what's *above* the subtext?
> *Ted*: The text.
> *Fred*: (*Pause*) Okay. That's right. ... But they never talk about that.

The meaning of *Barcelona is* "completely open and obvious." Fred, the naval officer, and Ted, the businessman, confront the naïve, comic, and ignorant anti-Americanism of the pseudo-sophisticated Europeans, and Ted, at least, does so as a Christian. *Last Days*, too, has overt religious content: "Grace, ultimately, is the subject of *Disco*."[18] I accept that observation but committed as I am to allegory—see, e.g., my earlier reviews of *Into the Wild* and *The Magician*—I find it too limited. Let me, therefore, present my argument and leave adjudication to others. I begin by noting that every successful allegory must also be simply a good yarn, as in, supremely *The Man Who was Thursday.* Mere symbolism is wearying; mere plot trivial. The success of art lies in a union of the two, which Stillman certainly achieves. And so I interpret *Last Days* as an allegory of the history of salvation as the old dispensation gives way to the new, a remote but effective parallel to the biblical use of story as a vehicle of revelation.

The very title—*The Last Days*—is loaded with Christian significance. It refers immediately to the second coming of Christ, at the end of time, but in the New Testament it is also connected with the destruction of the Jewish temple by the Romans in A.D. 70. I see the disco club in the film as representing the temple in Jerusalem under the old covenant. Many seek admission, but only a few, the "chosen people," are admitted; once inside they find a sort of ideal society superlative in what it offers in talk, dance, and friendship, as the revealed religion of Judaism was superior to the paganism of its neighbours. Details, again, are important. There's Dan, for instance, who as his name suggests is prophetic, in this case as a strong advocate for the cause of social justice. Similarly, the main female characters have old-fashioned names: Charlotte (who represents the gentiles) and Alice (who represents Israel). Like the Jews, Alice is busy producing a book: she and Charlotte work in publishing. Her success in this highly competitive field comes from her recommending a book by the brother of the Dali Lama on Tibetan monasticism that Charlotte had rejected. Later, when the author turns out to have been a fraud, Alice recoups simply by shifting it from non-fiction to self-actualisation. As the prophet Dan(iel) says, "mumbo-jumbo of all kinds has been highly commercial throughout the history of book publishing. The first printed book was the Bible." Charlotte, on the other hand, after losing her job, decides to go into television.

These admittedly arcane interpretations are supported by Charlotte's convincing Alice to compromise her principles in her relationship Tom, a lawyer specialising in ecological causes, which for many today is as close to religion as they come. The biblical parallel to this scientism would be the paganism of the nations surrounding ancient Israel. And, as it was with Israel, so with Alice: the encounter is disastrous. Later in the film, Holly (= holy) comforts Alice by telling her that it's altogether possible that she will meet someone who loves her so much that he will marry her anyway. Accepting Alice as symbolic of the chosen people, we now look for her true bridegroom. In the Old Testament it was the Lord God himself,[19] but in the New it is Jesus, and his bride is the new Israel, "the Israel of God."[20]

Enter a character named Jesus, here used in its Hebrew form, Josh(ua). Like Jesus, Josh attracts attention: "Until that night it never occurred to me how handsome Josh might be considered by women not to mention other men." In one scene people in the club stare in admiration as he passes: "Never was anything like this seen in Is-

rael."[21] The "emptying out" of the Incarnation, by which "the Father is greater than I"[22] is reflected in a charming scene between Josh and Alice. She notes that his clothes are slightly big. Josh answers, "I'm still waiting for my growth spurt. My father and my brother are both over six feet . . . Tall people tend to have great personalities— this kind compassionate comprehension of the rest of the world . . . My father and brother are that way." Even the literal Lawlor can say that "[Alice] sees something of God in Josh's singular devotion"[23] Josh appears when the film is well underway, like the long-desired of Israel. His identity is confirmed when he passes through a locked door—he kicks it open—to be greeted with "Christ! Are-you-out-of-your-mind?!" The speaker of these words, the venal Des (Eigerman) who works at the club, may be identified with the section of Judaism that refused to recognise Jesus (Josh) as the Messiah. Des continually contradicts him, calling attention to the fact that Josh had spent time in an insane asylum: "people were saying, 'He is beside himself.'"[24] Des's identifying of Josh as the Christ may be compared to Caiaphas's similar identification of the Messiah:[25] they were both right without knowing it. Furthermore, like Jesus, Josh drives the moneychangers out of

177

the temple, in this case as an assistant D.A. in charge of a raid on the club that resulted in the arrest of its directors for tax evasion.

Alice, under the influence of Charlotte's axiom that "opposites attract,"[26] accepts Des's attentions for a time but eventually realises that the faithful Josh is her true partner. In the novel, more is made of this switch. Alice has a favourite aunt, Janet, who had worked for Simon & Schuster back in the old days, when it was a good place to be. For Alice, Janet's marriage to Uncle Jack proved not only that opposites attract but also that they complement one another in what seemed to be an ideal marriage. The reality is that Janet has been devastated by discovering, out of the blue, that Jack is an adulterer. In the film Josh makes the same point in an exposition—a sort of sermon—of Aesop's fable of the tortoise and the hare. Humourously, Josh imagines a rematch: "That [first] race was almost certainly a fluke. Afterward, the tortoise is still a *tortoise* and the hare still . . . a *hare*." He makes the same point in his discussion of *The Lady and the Tramp* by defending the faithful Scottie who truly loves Lady, only to be supplanted by the dissolute tramp. The union, Josh says, is doomed, for people don't change: once a tramp, always a tramp. Des disagrees, claiming that the tramp's love for Lady has made him into a better person. The parallel with the Alice-Josh-Des relationship is obvious, and Des's continuing promiscuity indicates the Alice, in choosing Josh, is wiser than Aunt Janet had been. The third other quasi-sermon comes at the end of the film. As with the U.H.B., the disco goers no longer exist as an identifiable group: "Disco is dead!" But Josh prophetically proclaims that the good thing that disco represented can never disappear. It's too important, too elementally human, and as church bells ring in the background Josh expostulates with the remnant of the disco crowd:

> "Disco will . . . never be over, . . . Disco will always live in our minds and hearts. Something like this that was this big and important and this great, will never die. . . . Oh, for a few years, maybe for many years, it will be considered passé and ridiculous. It will be misrepresented and caricatured and sneered at—or, worse, completely ignored. . . . Disco was . . . *too great* and *too much fun* to be gone forever! It's got to come back someday."

At the end of the film, Alice joins Josh on a subway, and, with the disco hit *Love Train* on the soundtrack, they begin dancing, to be joined by the entire group of passengers in the car and then by the people on the platform. The temple is has been destroyed, but the Gospel message moves beyond the old dispensation into the world.

Back when I was still teaching, I sometimes used *Last Days* as an essay topic: "Granted that Josh represents Jesus, is he a Protestant or a Catholic Christ?" The answer is really quite obvious. To begin, there is a strong Protestant ethos in all three films. The U.H.B., for example, would certainly have included traditional New-England Protestantism as one of its characteristics. Hence Audrey and her mother worship in an Episcopal church. Similarly, Protestant hymns are prominent in the action. The use in *Metropolitan* of Luther's *A Mighty Fortress* has already been noted, and *Amazing Grace* and *Dear Lord and Father of Mankind* are important to the action of *Last Days*. That the former is sung by Charlotte indicates that conversion is possible even for a "wretch" like her. And the latter, which had functioned as a sort of mantra for Josh during his mental illness, is a

prayer for obedience to God's will: "Not as I will, but as thou willt."[27] Taylor Nichols, who played Charlie Black, the Christian apologist in *Metropolitan*, was then cast as the dancing Bible-reading goody-goody in *Barcelona*. When Fred breaks in on him and asks "What is this? . . . some strange Glenn Miller-based religious ceremony?" Ted answers, "No. Presbyterian." Later, Presbyterian Ted prays aloud at the bedside of a comatose Fred. Greta, his future wife, a Catholic, joins him, silently. Their prayers are heard.

Protestantism emphasises preaching and individual recourse to the Bible, while Catholicism is essentially a sacramental religion. It's a matter of proclamation versus rite. In classical Protestantism, the individual joins himself to Christ by an act of faith: "For God so loved the world that he gave his only Son, that whoever believes in him should not perish but have eternal life."[28] The Church then comes into existence as the union of all those who have already been saved. In Catholicism, on the other hand, the Church has always existed: "We shall belong to the first Church, the spiritual one which was created before the sun and moon."[29] It is thus the sacramental action of the Church that in the rite of baptism delivers the catechumen from sin and makes him a member of Christ's body: "Truly, truly, I say to you, unless a man is born of water and the Spirit, he cannot enter the kingdom of God."[30] The sheer talkiness of the films reveals a commitment to the power of the spoken word, leading, logically, to Josh's final discourse on the glories of disco. When the group separates after his speech, Josh is on his way to lunch with Alice, which in the allegory may be interpreted as a reference to the wedding feast of the Lamb, but it takes place off camera, i.e., in heaven. The real proclamation of the Gospel occurs on the subway train, as Josh and Alice dance contagiously to *Love Train*, and the message spreads, first of all to the other travellers in the car and then to the people on the platform, all of whom join in the dance.

Whit Stillman's films appeared at four-year intervals during the nineties, but it is now more than a decade since the release of *The Last Days of Disco*. I wonder if the turmoil in Anglicanism—which has attracted worldwide interest and whose parallels in other Protestant churches differ only by being less publicised—has not shaken his confidence in a tradition that is being abandoned by the Christian U.H.B., by Protes-

tant businessmen and soldiers, and by his "disco" devotees.[31] As Des, the truth-saying cynic of *Last Days*, says, "For a group to exist, I think someone has to be willing to admit they're part of it."[31]

Daniel Callam, C.S.B.
Holy Rosary Church
Toronto, ON

[1] Quotations have been taken from the printed sources, although they differ slightly from the actual films.
[2] Christian Kopff, "Europe and America in *Barcelona*," *Doomed*, p. 97, notes that a certain degree of misunderstanding continues even to the end in that Europe and America keep somewhat apart.
[3] Joseph Alulis, "In Defense of Virtue: Whit Stillman's *Metropolitan*," *Doomed*, pp. 63-83.
[4] R.V. Young, "From Mansfield to Manhattan: The Abandoned Generation of *Metropolitan*," *Doomed*, pp. 49-62.
[5] Alulis, p. 71.
[6] In the novelised form of the film there are additional scenes and sometimes the dialogue has been altered. The narrator is Jimmy Steinway who has a job in advertising.
[7] James Bowman, "Whit Stillman: Poet of the Broken Branches, *Doomed*, p. 39, notes: ". . . it is far from clear whether any such thing [as the U.H.B.] actually exists."
[8] Alulis, p. 65.
[9] Jane Austen, *Persuasion*, ch. 16.
[10] Alulis, p. 81.
[11] *Persuasion*, ch. 16.
[12] Mark C. Henrie, "At Whit's End," *Doomed*, p. xiii.
[13] Other characters appear and reappear in the films. Audrey Rouget,

glimpsed dancing at the disco, is as perceptive as ever. Charlotte describes being interviewed by her: "I didn't get the job." Similarly the villainous Rick Von Sloneker from *Metropolitan* reappears as the criminal owner of the disco and is still pompously ridiculous. For one thing, he hates advertising: no *kerygma* at his club.

[31] A premonition of what has actually come to pass in Protestantism may be found in Nick Smith's comment, "Our generation is probably the worst since . . . the Protestant Reformation. It's barbaric, but a barbarism even worse than the old-kind. Now barbarism is cloaked with all sorts of self-righteousness and moral superiority."

*　　*　　*

[14] *Persuasion*, ch. 11.

[15] Cf. *A Mighty Fortress is Our God*: "*Mit unsrer Macht ist nichts getan,/Wir sind gar bald verloren;/Es streit't für uns der rechte Mann. . . .*"

[16] Peter Augustine Lawlor, "Nature, Grace, and *The Last Days of Disco*," *Doomed*, p. 133.

[17] Lawler, p. 140. Cf. also Mary P. Nichols, "Whit Stillman's Comic Art," *Doomed*, p. 13: "Religion makes an appearance in *Last Days* in a more muted form than in *Barcelona*. . . . Nor does religion [there] receive the serious attention it does in *Metropoliltan*."

[18] David M. Whelan, "The Apotheosis of Disco," *Doomed*, p. 121.

[19] Is 62.5.

[20] Gal 6.16.

[21] Matt 9.33.

[22] Jn 14.28.

[23] Lawlor, p. 145.

[24] Mk 3.21.

[25] Jn 11.49.

[26] Cf. the opening paragraph of the novel, p. 5: "Opposites attract, unfortunately, and the cost in terms of subsequent despair, ruinous legal actions, divorce, fatherless—or motherless—families, cracks in the social welfare system and people falling through those cracks, even suicide and violence, is incalculably horrible."

[27] Matt 26.39.

[28] Jn 3.16.

[29] 2 Clement 14.1.

[30] Jn 3.5.

San Bento Monastery,
Rio de Janeiro, Brazil

News & Comments

Joseph Sobran: God's Satirical Soldier

— The following article by Jack Kenny was published in the American Public University *online edition on October 5, 2010.*

Like most conservatives, Joseph Sobran, enjoyed being a contrarian, flatly contradicting the conventional wisdom, which he liked to describe as "what everybody thinks everybody else thinks." Joe Sobran wasn't "everybody" and he was only too happy to challenge, in his own special way, many of the things that "everybody knows." Things like "You can't turn back the clock." "Who turned it ahead?" asked Sobran, who may have been the best since G. K. Chesterton at challenging the assumption that change is necessarily progress. *National Review*, his literary and ideological home for roughly two decades, had declared its mission in terms of high drama: "It stands athwart history yelling Stop...." Sobran simply quoted Hamlet: "The time is out of joint." It was typically Sobran. Even when he was passionately engaged, as he was on so many of the social and political issues of our time, he communicated a marvelous calm, analytical mien with words that so clearly and brilliantly punctured the myths, illusions and outright lies that permeate what has become an essentially pagan culture. He helped us appreciate the seriousness of contemporary threats to life, liberty and just plain decency in America, even as he made us laugh at the absurdity of them.

Sobran was flat out fun to read and he obviously found it fun to lampoon, for example, environmentalists hell-bent on protecting every species but the human. "Why is it always our planet Gore is trying to save?" he asked about the ecological crusades of the for-

---

The seaward side of Spurn Head

183

mer Vice President. "Why doesn't he stay home and take care of his own?" When Seymour Hersh published a book about the Kennedy presidency called *The Dark Side of Camelot*, Sobran confessed, "I didn't know there was a bright side." When the lurid stories of prisoner abuse at Abu Ghraib in Iraq made the news, Sobran put it in perspective: "There goes all the good will we built up through years of bombing Arab cities and starving Arab children." His passion and wit were wedded inseparably, most notably on the subject of legalised abortion. To my knowledge, no other widely circulated columnist took on what John Paul II labeled the "culture of death" as frequently and fervently as Sobran did. "Abortion," he wrote in his book, *Single Issues*, "violates every decent human instinct—so much so that its indecency must be clothed in euphemism." And Sobran ridiculed the euphemisms with a logic and wit George Orwell might have envied.

The deliberate, premeditated killing of an infant in the womb is, as "everyone knows," Sobran wrote, now only a matter of "terminating a pregnancy." Woman are no longer "with child," they are merely pregnant, "not 'with' anything particularly." Words like "killing" or "baby" are out, of course. "But it's still acceptable to say 'rape' and 'incest' rather than 'involuntary intercourse' and 'excessive family intimacy,'" Sobran observed. "True some women still say things like 'The baby [sic] is kicking,' but that merely shows that they are insufficiently open to new ideas. I even saw a book on the newsstand titled *Caring for Your Unborn Baby*, when the author obviously meant 'Caring for Your Fetal Matter.' But such gaffes are probably protected by the First Amendment."

By the end of his life he was calling himself a "reactionary utopian" and a "reluctant anarchist," but he was always much more a genuine conservative than many who wear that mantle, while giving limited lip service to conservative cultural values and devoting their full energies to the necessity of cutting marginal tax rates and rushing to war at the drop of a hat or the tilt of a turban. Strange, he noted, that the only people being accused of "single-issue politics" are those who have focused on the single issue that lies most directly at the heart of a decent society. "What," he asked, "could be more barbarous than the killing of an unborn child, by the choice of its mother, through the agency of a doctor and with the blessing of the state?"The issue being buried by a neglect that is anything but benign is as old as the Garden of Eden, where mortals dared to know good and evil apart from the will of the Creator. "Do we dare assume the role of the enemies of creation?" Sobran asked. With the legal sanction for the killing of an estimated 4,000 babies a day, it seems America has dared to assume precisely that role.

Nearly thirty-eight years after *Roe v. Wade*, even most pro-lifers may have a hard time fully appreciating just how radical is that decree from our judicial Caesars. Sobran, for all his wit and learning, was like the small boy in the Hans Christian Andersen story who saw right through the emperor's imaginary clothes. "Under its pretended neutrality," he wrote, "the Court has given a positive answer to the religious question: it has defined us, operationally, as an atheistic people, a people for whom no moral considerations may obstruct the claims of convenience and hedonism assisted by the advanced techniques of killing."

Sobran's death last week at age 64, from complications arising from diabetes, silenced in our time a voice and a pen employed relentlessly against America's covenant with death. He will be, God willing, one more soldier in the company of the saints in Heaven. We will do well to continue his battle on earth, recalling always the exhortation of Saint Paul:

"Let us not be weary in well doing; for in due season we shall reap if we faint not." (Galatians 6:9)

Joseph Sobran

Letter to Gilbert K. Chesterton

— The following letter was written by Pope John Paul I in the book *Il-lustrissimi: Letters From Pope John Paul I* (Little Brown & Company: Boston, 1978). Translated from the Italian by William Weaver.

In What Sort of World...

Dear Chesterton,

On Italian television, these past months, we have seen Father Brown, that unpredictable priest-detective, a typical creation of yours. Too bad Professor Lucifer and the monk Michael did not also appear. I would have been happy to see them, as you described them in *The Ball and the Cross*, traveling in an "airship," seated side by side, Lent next to Carnival.

When the Ship is over St. Paul's Cathedral in London, the professor hurls blasphemy at the Cross. And the monk says: "I once knew a man like you, Lucifer.... This man also took the view that the symbol of Christianity was a symbol of savagery and all unreason. His history was rather amusing. It is also a perfect allegory of what happens to rationalists like yourself. He said, as you say, that it was an arbitrary and fantastic shape, that it was a monstrosity, loved because it was paradoxical. Then he began to grow fiercer and more eccentric; he would batter the crosses by the roadside.... Finally in a height of frenzy he climbed the steeple of the Parish Church and tore down the cross, waving it in the air, and uttering wild soliloquies up there under the stars. Then one still summer evening as he was wending his way homewards, along a lane, the devil of his madness came upon him with a violence and transfiguration which changes the world. He was standing, smoking, for a moment, in the front of an interminable line of palings, when his eyes were opened. Not a light shifted, not a leaf stirred, but he saw as if by a sudden change in the eye-sight that this paling was an army of innumerable crosses linked together over hill and dale. And he whirled up his heavy stick and went at it as if at an army. Mile after mile along his homeward path he broke it down and tore it up. For he hated the cross and every paling is a wall of crosses. When he returned to his house he was a literal madman.... He broke his furniture because it was made of crosses. He burnt his house because it was made of crosses. He was found in the river."

Lucifer was looking at him with a bitten lip.

"Is that story really true?" he asked.

"Oh, no," said Michael, airily. "It is a parable. It is a parable of you and all rationalists. You begin by breaking up the Cross; but you end by breaking up the habitable world...."

The monk's conclusion, which is also your own, dear Chesterton, is correct. If you take away God, what remains, what does mankind become? In what sort of world are we reduced to living?

But, it is the world of progress, I hear some say, the world of well-being!

Yes, but this vaunted progress is not everything that was hoped: it also brings with it missiles, bacteriological and atomic weapons, the current process of pollution: things which—if provision is not made in time—threaten to bring catastrophe on the whole human race.

In other words, progress with human beings who love one another, considering themselves brothers, children of a single God the Father, can be something magnificent. Progress with human beings who do not recognise God as a universal Father becomes a constant danger.

Without a parallel moral process, interior and personal, that progress develops, in fact, the most savage dregs of mankind, making the human being a machine possessed by machines, a number manipulating numbers, "a raving barbarian," Papini would have said, "who instead of a club can wield the immense forces of nature and of mechanics to satisfy his predatory, destructive, orgiastic instincts."

I know: many people think the opposite of you and of me. They think that religion is a consolatory dream: it is supposed to have been invented by the oppressed, imagining a nonexistent world where they later will recover what is stolen from them today by their oppressors; it is supposed to have been organised, entirely for their own advantage, by these oppressors, to keep the oppressed under their heel, and to lull in them that instinct of class which, without religion, would impel them to struggle.

It is useless to point out that it was precisely the Christian religion that fostered the wakening of the proletarian consciousness, exalting the poor, announcing future justice.

Yes, they answer, Christianity awakens the consciousness of the poor, but it paralyses it, preaching patience and replacing the class struggle with faith in God and gradual reformation in society!

Many think also that God and religion, directing hopes and efforts towards a future, distant paradise, *alienate* man, prevent him from fighting for a more immediate paradise, to be achieved here on earth.

It is useless to point out to them that, according to recent Council, a Christian, precisely because he is a Christian, must feel more committed than ever to fostering progress, which is for the good of all, and to supporting social advancement, which is meant for everyone. The fact remains, they say, that you think of progress for a transitory world, while waiting for a definitive paradise, which will not come. We want paradise here, as the end of all struggles. We already glimpse its rise, while your God, by the theologians of *secularisation*, is called "dead." We agree with Heine, who wrote: "Do you hear the bell? On your knees! They are carrying the last sacraments to God, who is dying!"

My dear Chesterton, you and I do indeed fall on our knees, but before a God who is more alive than ever. He alone, in fact, can give a satisfying answer to these three problems, which are the most important for everyone: Who am I? Where do I come from? Where am I going?

As for the paradise to be enjoyed on earth, and only on earth, and in a near future, as conclusion to the famous "struggles,"

I would like people to listen to someone more gifted than I and—without denying your merits—also than you: Dostoevski.

You remember Dostoevski's Ivan Karamazov. He is an atheist, though a friend of the devil. Well, he protests, with all his atheist's vehemence, against a paradise achieved through the efforts, the toil, the sufferings, the torment of countless generations. Our posterity happy thanks to the unhappiness of their forebears! These forebears who "struggle" without receiving their share of joy, often without even the solace of glimpsing the Paradise emerging from the Inferno they are going through! Endless multitudes of the maimed, the sacrificed, who are merely the humus that serves to make the future trees of life grow! Impossible! Ivan says, it would be a pitiless and monstrous injustice.

And he is right.

The sense of justice that is in every man, of whatever faith, demands that the good done, the evil suffered, be rewarded, that the hunger for life innate in all be satisfied. Where and how, if not in another life? And from whom if not from God? And from what God, if not from the one of whom Francis de Sales wrote: "Do not fear God in the least, for He does not want to do you harm; but love Him greatly, because He wants to do you great good"?

The one that many are fighting is not the true God, but the false idea of God that they have formed: a God who protects the rich, who only asks and demands, who is envious of our progress in well-being, who constantly observes our sins from above to enjoy the pleasure of punishing them!

My dear Chesterton, you know as well as I, God is not like that, but is at once good and just; father also to prodigal sons; not wanting us poor and wretched, but great, free, creators of our own destiny. Our God is far from being man's rival that He wanted man as a friend, calling him to share in His own divine nature and in His own eternal happiness. And it is not true that He makes excessive demands of us; on the contrary, He is satisfied with little, because He knows very well that we do not have much.

189

Dear Chesterton, I am convinced, as you are: this God will become more and more known and loved, by everyone, including those who reject Him today, not because they are wicked (they may be better than either of us), but because they look at Him from a mistaken point of view! Do they continue not to believe in Him? Then He answers: I believe in you!

June 1971

Pope John Paul I

INTRODUCTION

P. D. James

— *The following introduction to* Father Brown The Essential Tales *(Modern Library Classics: New York, 2005) was written by P. D. James, bestselling author of celebrated literary mystery novels, many of them featuring her poet-detective, Commander Adam Dalgliesh of New Scotland Yard. Recent books include* A Certain Justice, Death in Holy Orders, *and* The Murder Room. *Previously she served in the police and criminal justice departments of Great Britain's Home Office. She has received honourary doctorates from seven universities and in 1991 was made a life peer as Baroness James of Holland Park. She lives in London and Oxford.*

Gilbert Keith Chesterton, who was born on Camden Hill in London in 1874 and died in 1936, can be described in terms which are hardly ever used of a writer today; he was a man of letters. All his life he earned his living by his pen and he was as versatile as he was prolific. After his education at the intellectually prestigious St. Paul's School, he went on to study at the Slade School of Art and was talented as an illustrator, particularly of the novels of his lifelong friend, Hilaire Belloc. Chesterton gained a reputation as a novelist, essayist, critic, journalist, and poet, and although much of this copious output, particularly on social, political, and religious subjects, has proved ephemeral, his book about Charles Dickens, published in 1906, remains an influential work, and a few of his poems, including "The Donkey," the vigorous narrative poem "Lepanto," and "The Rolling English Road," continue to appear in anthologies of popular verse.

But although much has been lost, what remain in the public imagination, and are still read with pleasure and admiration, are his detective short stories featuring a Roman Catholic priest, Father Brown. These first appeared in *The Innocence of Father Brown*, published in 1911, and were followed by four further volumes, *The Wisdom of Father Brown* (1914), *The Incredulity of Father Brown* (1926), *The Secret of Father Brown* (1927), and *The Scandal of Father Brown* (1935). The character is based on a friend of Chesterton's, Father John O'Connor of St. Cuthbert's Church in Bradford, to whom *The Secret of Father Brown* was dedicated.

All G. K. Chesterton's writings, including the Father Brown stories, show, however subtly, the influence of his religious faith (he was received into the Roman Catholic Church in 1922) and of his image of the world. He had a great romantic view of England, an almost medieval nostalgia for a simpler, rural and happy land, remote from technology, materialistic big business, and monolithic state power. It was a view that he shared with Hilaire Belloc, earning them from George Bernard Shaw the twin nickname of Chesterbelloc. Their England conjures a picture of happy contented villagers, of old men drinking with friends. outside the pub, of the rolling English road, and of a simple unexamined patriotism. And from this view of the world, from his deeply held religious faith, and from his teeming imagination, G. K. Chesterton created a unique amateur detective who has gained an assured place in the canon of mystery writing.

Physically, Father Brown could not be more unlike the conventional romantic, handsome, and confident amateur detectives of the Golden Age of mystery writing. In the story "The Blue Cross," we see him through the eyes of Valentin, described as the head of the Paris police. Admittedly at the time, Father Brown, for purposes of his own, was exaggerating his apparent innocuousness, but we can be sure that what Valentin saw, so did other characters who encountered Father Brown. We are told that in the railway carriage the two were sharing was a very short Roman Catholic priest going up from a small Essex village, who seemed to Valentin to be "the essence of those Eastern flats; he had a face as round and dull as a Norfolk dumpling; he had eyes as empty as the North Sea; he had several brown paper parcels, which he was quite incapable of collecting .... He had a large, shabby umbrella, which constantly fell on the floor. He did not seem to know which was the right end of his return ticket."

Valentin was not the only person to be taken in by this seeming innocence and simplicity. The bumbling exterior hides one of the most acute brains in the history of fictional detection, and those apparently empty eyes miss nothing. Unlike most of the Golden Age heroes of detective fiction, essentially he works alone. He has no professional supporter to do the routine legwork or provide additional police support when required, as has Lord Peter Wimsey in Inspector Parker. He is not bizarrely eccentric, as is Agatha Christie's Poirot. Unlike Sherlock Holmes, he has no Watson to ask questions which the more simple-minded readers might like to put and whose purpose is to demonstrate the great detective's brilliance and superior intellect. Naturally, given the decades in which he operates, he has no scientific advice available, indeed no official person whose help he can readily enlist in moments of crisis. He solves crimes by a mixture of common sense, observation, and deduction, and by his knowledge of the human heart. After years of hearing confessions, he knows the best and worst of which human beings are capable even though those secrets are locked in his heart. As he says to Flambeau, the master thief whom he outwits in "The Blue Cross" and whom he restores to honesty, "Has it never struck you that a man who does next to nothing but hear men's real sins is not likely to be wholly unaware of human evil?" And he has another advantage in being a priest, of never being required precisely to explain his presence since it is assumed he is occupied with his priestly function, and of being a man in whom many might naturally confide.

Although we are told that Father Brown was parish priest in Cobhole in Essex before moving to London, we meet him in other and very different places, in England and overseas and in a variety of settings and company across the whole social and economic spectrum. Nothing and no one is alien to him. We never encounter him in the daily routine of his pastoral duties at Cobhole, never learn where exactly he lives, who housekeeps for him, what kind of church he has or his relationship with his bishop. We are not told his age, whether his parents are still living or even his Christian name. In each of the stories he makes his quiet appearance unannounced, as much at home with the poor and humble as he is with the rich and famous, and applying to all situations his own immutable spirituality. But he is always a rationalist with a dislike of superstition, which he sees as inimical to his faith. Like the other characters in the stories—and like us, the readers—he sees the physical facts of the case, but only he, by a process of deduction, interprets them correctly. We see what is apparently obvious however bizarre; he sees what is true. Chesterton loved paradox and, because we encounter Father Brown often in incongruous or bizarre company and he comes unencumbered by his past, the little priest is himself a paradox, at once mundane and unthreatening, but also mysterious and iconic.

In a book entitled *A Century of Detective Stories*, published by Hutchinson between the wars (the precise date is nowhere mentioned in the volume), G. K. Chesterton wrote the introduction. After paying tribute to Edgar Allan Poe and Sherlock Holmes, he sets out the advantages and disadvantages of the short mystery story as compared with the longer novel. He points out that "the long story is more successful in one not unimportant point: that it is sometimes possible to realise that a man is alive before we realise that he is dead." In the short story "the narrative is so brief that often the living characters may be left at the end looking rather like conventional corpses." But although the police novel can be used for a fuller development of character, Chesterton comments that "it is not always filled with life, but rather padded as something else." His own short stories are always filled with life. In *A Century of Detective Stories* Chesterton included one of his own, "The Secret Garden." We can therefore assume that it is one he himself particularly valued, and it seems right to include it in this new edition.

With such a large output, it would be unreasonable to expect all of the more than fifty Father Brown stories to be equal in quality and readers will have their own favorites. But even if a single story slightly disappoints, the quality of the writing never does. Chesterton never wrote an inelegant or clumsy sentence. The Father Brown stories are brilliantly written in a style richly complex, imaginative, vigorous, poetic, and spiced with paradoxes. He was an artist as well as a writer and he sees life with an artist's eye. He wanted his readers to share that poetic vision, to see the romance and numinousness in commonplace things.

> Men lived among mighty mountains and eternal forests for ages before they realised they were poetical; it may reasonably be inferred that some of our descendants may see the chimney-pots as rich a purple as the mountain-peaks, and find the lamp-posts as old and natural as the trees ("A Defence of the Detective Stories").

His characters are vividly described and stand before us in all their eccentric diversity. He is particularly skilled at evoking the effect of changing light on landscape, its power to transmogrify and beguile, so that the seemingly mundane and familiar become pregnant with mystery:

> Outside, the last edges of the sunset still clung to the corners of the green square but inside a lamp had already been kindled; and in the mingling of the two lights the coloured globe glowed like some monstrous jewel and the fantastic outlines of the fiery fishes seemed to give it indeed something of the mystery of a talisman; like strange shapes seen by a seer in the crystal of doom ("The Song of the Flying Fish").

With so rich a literary feast it has been suggested that the stories are best savoured a few at a time, rather than gulped at a single sitting.

In one respect G. K. Chesterton was ahead of his time. He was one of the first writers of detective fiction to realise that this popular genre could be a vehicle for exploring and exposing the condition of society and of saying something true about human nature. Before he even planned the Father Brown stories, Chesterton wrote that "the only thrill, even of a common thriller, is concerned somehow with the conscience and the will." We read the Father Brown stories for a variety of pleasures, including their ingenuity, their wit and intelligence, and for the brilliance of the writing. But they provide more. Chesterton was concerned with the greatest of all problems, the vagaries of the human heart. It is because of this all-embracing humanity that the Father Brown stories will continue to entrance, entertain, and solace readers inhabiting a world infinitely more complex and dangerous than was the England in which Chesterton wrote. It is not surprising that eminent historians of the mystery genre have for decades agreed that, at their best, the Father Brown stories are among the finest crime stories ever written.

Reindeer Pictures

— The following review of the book by Aidan Nichols, O. P., G. K. Ches-
terton, Theologian (Sophia Institute Press: Manchester, NH, 2010)
written by A. N. Wilson was published in the July 30, 2010 issue of the
Times Literary Supplement.

A recent enjoyable reading of G. K. Chesterton's Father Brown
stories made me aware of a strange discrepancy between the author
and the hero. Chesterton, with his comedic lightness, his painterly
sense of colour, his Dickensian love for the grotesque, patently enjoyed creating this series of extraordinary dramas, in which there
intrudes the shambolic and apparently ineffectual little priest with
his unmemorable features and his umbrella. Yet it is the priest with
one-liners of the theological nature. In the first story, when Flambeau, the great French thinks he has passed himself off successfully
as a priest, Brown delivers a crucial riposte: "You attacked reason.
It's bad theology." It struck that it would be very useful to have a
book by Father Brown about G. K. Chesterton. The point of such
book would be to show whether Brown's view of life—that of the
quiet, reasonable Catholic theologian—and Chesterton's flamboy-
ant, jokey 1890s vision coincided, as Chesterton believed they did.
To put it another way, was Chesterton a theologian?

Aidan Nichols is one of the most well-regarding Christian
thinkers published in English today. As a well-grounded Thomist
theologian, and a Dominican, he seems admirably equipped to supply the perspective my recent reading of Chesterton had called for.
Has he succeeded? Yes and no. He begins his book with the proposition that Chesterton is a theologian. (Later on, we even find the suggestion that Chesterton be made a Doctor of the Church.) Nichols
hopes to find Chesterton the resources to "relaunch the mission of
a Christian intelligentsia in contemporary English society." He further believes that *Orthodoxy* (1908), a book Chesterton wrote four-
teen years before becoming a Roman Catholic, provides "the best
introduction to Gospel religion."

Nichols then gives us two chapters that place Chesterton in his
context. He describes Chesterton's early socialism and his move

away from this towards the Distributism of his later years. In his socialist days he had described William Morris in terms that also apply to himself, as a "prophet of the merrier and wiser life." In the central Chapter of his book, "Chesterton and the Edwardian Cultural Crisis," Nichols expounds how and why Chesterton became the confident Christian apologist who deplored the imperialism of Kipling, the lofty negativism and perspectivism of Nietzsche, and what he saw as the intellectually soggy agnosticism of Huxley. In *The Victorian Age in Literature*, Chesterton identified "a curious cold of emptiness and real subconscious agnosticism such as is extremely unusual in the history on mankind." Insofar as he was a passionate democrat, Chesterton wished to side with the majority of Europeans (the dead) against the new generation of agnostics and the materialist determinists. That he did so with great brio is not in question. But Aidan Nichols is only partially able to persuade the reader that Chesterton's project was successful.

In a chapter titled "The Edwardian Culture Crisis," one might expect some mention of what was happening at this date in the Catholic Church. This was the period when the then Pope, Pius X, was waging war on "modernism." George Tyrell, the renowned Jesuit theologian, was denied a Catholic burial because of his supposed departure from the truth, even though his books when read today seem purely Christian. There is no doubt that Pope Benedict XVI, by writing a book on Jesus Christ which recommends Protestant biblical commentaries, would have been regarded by Pius X as a dangerous modernist. The anti-modernist witch-hunts of the early twentieth century (which compelled some such as the great Abbé Loisy, to leave the Church, and others such as Baron von Hügel, to censor themselves) were troubling episodes, and it is surely a puzzle that so open-minded a man as Chesterton should have risked breaking the heart of his Anglo-Catholic wife by trying to join the Roman catholic Church in such a climate. (Her tears made him delay or a decade.) Nichols sheds no light at all on this puzzle, which is partly biographical, but also, surely, theological.

On Chesterton's theology itself, Nichols is excellent, expounding its essential benignity. Chesterton hated the tone of Nietzsche's "all fountains are poison where the rabble drink." For Chesterton, a philistine was a man who was right but did not know why: he was therefore prepared to listen to the opinions and prejudices of "ordinary people." "Smile at us, pay us, pass us; but do not quite forget; / for we are people of England, that never have spoken yet."

Nichols reminds us of Chesterton's belief that God was an artist, that creation was best understood as "creative" in our popular sense. God was a playwright who had written a good drama messed up by the actors. And in his fifth chapter, Nichols said Chesterton invented a new argument for the existence of God which Nichols calls the "argument from joy." In his study of Dickens, Chesterton introduces the topic of the gratuitously joy-provoking character of existence be describing Dickens as a man who, "if he had learned to whitewash the universe, had done so in a blacking factory." Elsewhere, Nichols writes: "In his life of Francis of Assisi, Chesterton refers to joy in the face of existence—ontologically significant joy —as a sign of our relation to the divine creative act." Nichols goes on to quote P. N. Furbank, who summarised Chesterton's artistic and spiritual goal as being to dig for the "submerged sunrise of wonder."

Nichols's strongest chapters are those in which he (generously) sees Chesterton as a Thomist, and those in which he investigates Chesterton's Christology. The generosity is demonstrated when Nichols refers to Chesterton's reading of Aquinas as rather "cavalier." It is hard to know how much of Aquinas Chesterton read: he is said to have boasted that he had not read him at all before sitting to write his book *St. Thomas Aquinas.* Bu he undoubtedly absorbed the neo-Thomism of the early decades of the twentieth century, and this quickened his appreciation of the uniqueness of human beings. Chesterton imagined an archaeologist who "had dug very deep and found the place where the man had drawn a picture of a reindeer. But he would dig a good deal deeper before he found a place where a reindeer had drawn a picture of a man."

Some of Chesterton's best reflections on the mode are in the *Everlasting Man* (1925), a book that I would rate higher than *Orthodoxy*, in which he argues that humanity is not just the product of ordinary biological growth. The point is made through a redeployment of the painting analogy—"Monkeys did not begin pictures and men finish them. Pithecanthropus did not draw reindeer badly and Homo Sapiens draw it well ... the wild horse was not an Impressionist." In the *Everlasting Man*, Chesterton triumphantly provides a bridge between what Nichols (following Hans Urs von Balthasar) calls the "mythopoeic" (fictional mythology) and the philosophical.

It is all good as far as it goes, and I have never read a better exposition of Chesterton as a thinker. But in Chesterton himself I feel a huge and damaging gap; and I was therefore disappointed that Nichols did not address it—or, more worryingly show due awareness of the need to address it. Chesterton seems like a thinker with no sense of darkness. He fails to grasp the widely held conviction that Christianity, with the cross at its centre, presents a sombre picture of the world, albeit one in which tragedy is ultimately eclipsed by hope. Dietrech Bonhoeffer said he could only worship a God who had suffered—and you can imagine repeating that in Haiti or Rwanda today. I should feel rather queasy reading Chesterton's *Orthodoxy* aloud in a disaster zone.

Setting the World Right, With G. K. Chesterton's Help

— *The following interview with Fr. Ian Boyd, Editor of* The Chesterton Review *was published in the September 15, 2010 issue of* ZENIT *and the November 2010 issue of Challenge magazine. The interview was conducted by Andrea Kirk Assaf.*

MECOSTA, Michigan, SEPT. 14, 2010—This year marks the one-hundredth anniversary of the publication of a collection of essays by the popular English Catholic apologist G. K. Chesterton titled *What's Wrong with the World?* The president of the G. K. Chesterton Institute for Faith and Culture of Seton Hall University in New Jersey, Basilian Fr. Ian Boyd spoke with *ZENIT* about the enduring appeal of Chesterton and the prophetic quality of his book.

ZENIT: What does the Chesterton Institute do?
Fr. Boyd: The institute was founded during the centenary of Chesterton's birth in 1974 to do what T.S. Eliot said should be done in a note at the time of Chesterton's death. Eliot said that we should continue to do in our day what Chesterton began in his; so we took Eliot's advice as the motto for the Chesterton Institute. The basic idea of the institute is, through publishing—such as our own quarterly *The Chesterton Review*—and conferences, to continue the communal work of Chesterton and his remarkable circle of friends into our own day.

ZENIT: Who was in Chesterton's circle?
Fr. Boyd: There is a famous painting by James Gunn called "A Conversation Piece," and in that are Chesterton, Hilaire Belloc, and one who is far less known than he should be, Maurice Baring. These three were friends and represent the breadth of the Chesterton tradition. Baring came from an English liberal family who owned banks. One of his claims to fame is that he introduced Russian literature into the English-speaking world; he spoke Russian, lived in Russia, and attributed his conversion to Christianity to living within a religious culture as Russia was in that day.

ZENIT: Did they think of themselves as having a collective vocation?
Fr. Boyd: There was something of that—Belloc was the teacher to the group, Chesterton's training was as an artist at the Slade

School of Art, and Chesterton looked to Belloc for a theology of history. Baring represented, with his knowledge of half a dozen languages and so on, the breadth of Christian culture.

ZENIT: One hundred years after Chesterton published this book whose centenary you are marking, does this book still contain some of the author's trademark wisdom that can speak to us today?

Fr. Boyd: In all of Chesterton's writings there is a prophetic quality, so you sometimes feel the people Chesterton was writing for were not the people of his day, but rather the people who read him many years later. He was a person who was a very important figure in his own time, particularly the young Chesterton in the period before the First World War. He was simply one of the best-known figures in the English letters. He became a classic writer in the sense that people quoted him who had never read him; his sayings became part of the treasury of English wisdom literature.

Chesterton saw that people in the modern age were like sheep without a shepherd, who were being misled by false shepherds. I think Chesterton saw his mission as being apostolic really, because people didn't realise the treasure that they held in their Christian faith. The notable writers of the day like the Shaws, H.G. Wells, and so on were teaching them to despise the Christian faith. Chesterton became a voice for the faithful.

Charles Williams wrote an essay about Chesterton's poetry in which he said that in the modern age there was no one to speak for God or for the ordinary human being, that God was defenseless, unarmed, and without a voice. One way of understanding Chesterton is that he stood forward to say "I will be your voice, I will be your weapon." He articulated the deepest feelings that the ordinary, mute man or woman was unable to express. He defended them from a host of modern enemies who would deprive them of that treasure [of the Christian faith].

ZENIT: Despite his Catholicism, didn't Chesterton enjoy a broad appeal among English readers?

Fr. Boyd: Chesterton became a Catholic in 1922, so his period as a Roman Catholic was relatively short, but right from the beginning he was a spokesman for Catholic truth. He was a kind of ecumenical figure, beloved by evangelical protestants as well as sacramental Christians. He was also a kind of patron saint of journalists, even agnostic, unbelieving journalists have looked upon him as their hero. His wit and humor shouldn't be underestimated, and he was so evidently a good man. I don't think there's any example of Chesterton losing a friend. H.G. Wells and Chesterton quarreled, and in a series of letters Chesterton brought him back to say, "I don't believe there is a God, but if there is one I hope I will get to heaven because I was your friend." Wells thought Chesterton was a good advertisement for Christian faith.

ZENIT: **What is there about *What's Wrong with the World* that still speaks to us today?**

Fr. Boyd: For one thing, what you find in it is a social theology. Chesterton and his Anglican friends, long before he became a Roman Catholic, were concerned with evangelising the culture itself. They recognised that most ordinary people absorb the thought and the behavior of the culture in which they are immersed, so that a toxic culture wounds the people who are part of it. One good example a priest friend of mine pointed out to me is that of abortion. Fifty years ago or even closer to our time, even unbelievers and agnostic doctors looked upon abortion as something shameful. Now it is accepted by so many people; I don't think people have become worse but it means that a healthy culture has become somewhat toxic.

We must be concerned, as Chesterton was, with the cleansing of the collective mind and imagination. This is what we mean by evangelising the culture that Chesterton and a number of other writers speak of. One thinks of Newman, about to be beatified, who began his work in the 1830s, and Chesterton, who died in the 1930s—there were one hundred years of two remarkable writers, national figures, who led that work of renewal through writing, the power of the word.

ZENIT: **How do you think these great Catholic writers, such as Chesterton and Newman, came to enjoy such a following in a decidedly non-Catholic country as England?**

Fr. Boyd: Christopher Dawson remarked on this just as a sociological fact, that all this remarkable Catholic literature has come out of a non—Catholic culture—very fine writers, and also sacramental writers in the sense that they teach Catholic truth without talking directly about religion. Muriel Spark would be an example of this phenomenon. Chesterton himself is a great religious teacher who is never sectarian, who presents Christian truth by indirection. Doesn't he say somewhere that he believes that in the end truth can only be taught through parable, through allegory—stealth evangelisation, so to speak.

ZENIT: Why is this a good year to pick up *What's Wrong with the World?* What do you think readers will find controversial?

Fr. Boyd: You learn Chesterton's social philosophy through this book, and also some key principles of right thinking. Of course, all books should be read in the context of their time. A countercultural argument runs right throughout the book. The section on women might be particularly provocative in our day. One main point is that it's a cheerful book. Chesterton, as the Russians called him, is a teacher of hope. In one passage he challenges the saying that you can't turn back the hands of time: a clock, Chesterton writes, is a mechanical mechanism, and so you only have to move the hands back with your finger to wherever you like! Human society, he said, is also a construction. Humans have the power, as sub-creators, to transform a society. We are not doomed. If something is wrong with the world, then we set out to make it right.

What's Wrong with the World

— *The following article was published in the June 2010 (Vol. 17, No. 2) issue of* The Defendant, *the newsletter of the Australian Chesterton Society.*

What indeed! The question is as pertinent now as when it was first posed. Exactly one hundred years ago this month one of Chesterton's most significant books appeared under this title and many of the arguments therein have since become Chesterton orthodoxies.

Whether Chesterton's meant the title to be a statement of what was wrong with the world, or whether he was asking a rhetorical question is not clear. Chesterton's original suggestion for a title was What's Wrong? and included the question mark. But when a new title was agreed upon with the publisher, the mark was omitted from both the title page and the chapter pages. An ornate device which may or may not be a query mark is embossed below the name of the author on the first edition cover and the spine, which adds somewhat to the confusion. Characteristically Chesterton makes a joke of the first (rejected) title in his dedication to G.F.G.Masterman and recounts how he astounded a "mild lady visitor" when he told her that he had been doing "What's Wrong" all the morning; and in another instance how, in front of a visiting person, he explained that he had to run upstairs and do "What's Wrong," but would return downstairs shortly. On this evidence alone one can sympathise with the publisher's plea for a change in title.

Although *What's Wrong with the World* ran to nine editions in the first year of publication, and is generally considered part of the Chesterton canon and has been in print, on and off, for a hundred years, it suffered disparaging criticism from practically all the main reviewers of that time. Two examples selected from many reflect the general opinion of the literati: the *Evening Standard* reviewer was the most withering: "Mr. Chesterton's discussions are so dreary and meaningless that nobody but a poor slave of a reviewer could make the attempt to follow them ... page after page of thickest dotted nonsense it was ever our misfortune to read." *The Times* critic was more analytical but no less dismissive: "He is nullified as a political and social critic because he does not realise that the evils of society are the result of conglomerate good intentions, not of individual ill-will. Mr. Chesterton puts it all down to 'the rich' like any man on a chair in Regent's Park." After paragraphs like this the review ends with what one might call a back-handed compliment " alleviating the earlier onslaught." He admits there is more good than bad in the book: "[Chesterton] sees man sanely as an animal living in a coloured world that has sap in its stems and blood in its veins. He hates the nonsense of Christian Scientists and false Buddhists, he praises the freedom of man and the scope of the home ... and all that he says about women, their functions and nature as the preservers, the isolates, the treasure houses of wisdom without specialism, is true and particularly useful at this time." (Evidently *The Times* and its reviewer did not support Women's Sufferage, a contested issue at that time).

One hundred years after its publication, *What's Wrong with the World* continues to exasperate the reader and yet more often inspire him—exasperate because Chesterton's style—judged by today's standards—is overly discursive and his arguments are packed with clever but sometimes tiresome epigrams and paradoxes, We may suspect that an epigram such as, "What is wrong with the world is that we do not ask what is right" is chosen more for effect than for elucidation.

When Chesterton defends female liberty in the home he argues that such liberty is advanced by the act of wearing a skirt rather than trousers because when "men wish to be stately, impressive as judges, priests, or kings, they wear the long trailing robes of female dignity." "The whole world is under petticoat government," he writes, "for even men wear petticoats when they wish to govern." One can understand *The Times* reviewer's impatience with this wobbly line of reasoning.

And yet, *What's Wrong with the World*, like all Chesterton's writings, continually surprises with precious shafts of light and commonsense. We forgive him his mannerisms and his obscure references to people and events long forgotten and his occasional tardiness in getting to the crux of the argument, because of the wisdom that he dispenses on every page—none more so than in this astonishingly percipient paragraph:

> Man has always lost his way. He has been a tramp ever since Eden; but he always knew, or thought he knew, what he was looking for. Every man has a house somewhere in the elaborate cosmos...Man has always been looking for that home which is the subject matter of this book. But in the bleak and blinding hail of scepticism to which he has been now so long subjected, he has begun for the first time to be chilled, not merely in his hopes, but in his desires. For the first time in history he begins really to doubt the object of his wanderings on the earth. He has always lost his way; but now he has lost his address.

And there we have the key: what is wrong with the world is, after all, a religious question, true when the book was published, and even more true today. The peoples of the West have lost their religion their address. Chesterton saw this clearly one hundred years ago and everything he wrote was a warning of the consequences.

(With apologies to Worldsworth) we may well cry out: "O Chesterton, thou shouldst be living at this hour ... we have need of thee."

―――――――――

What's Right with the World

— *The following article by Gerald J. Russello, a Fellow of the Chesterton Institute at Seton Hall University was published in the July 9, 2010 issue of* Inside Catholic. *A version of this essay was presented at a conference on "What's Wrong with the World," sponsored by the Chesterton Institute and the Russell Kirk Center for Cultural Renewal held in Mecosta, Michigan.*

This year marks the centenary of G. K. Chesterton's *What's Wrong with the World*. The book continues to inspire and surprise with its prophetic insights on issues from economics and property, to its bracing defense of the "wildness of domesticity." And what is wrong with the world for Chesterton? "What is wrong with the world is that we do not ask what is right." In other words, the evils are plain, but to solve them we must know what is the good that will correct these evils. As Chesterton put it in his opening chapter, "The Homelessness of Man:"

> We agree about the evil; it is about the good that we should tear each other's eyes out. We all admit that a lazy aristocracy is a bad thing. We should not by any means all admit that an active aristocracy would be a good thing. We all feel angry with an irreligious priesthood; but some of us would go mad with disgust at a really religious one. Everyone is indignant if our army is weak, including the people who would be even more indignant if it were strong. The social case is exactly the opposite of the

medical case. We do not disagree, like doctors, about the precise nature of the illness, while agreeing about the nature of health. On the contrary, we all agree that England is unhealthy, but half of us would not look at her in what the other half would call blooming health.

At a stroke, Chesterton anticipates—and refutes—he proponents of what is sometimes called the neutrality of liberalism. Such a program focuses on means, rather than ends; process, rather than substance: Thus, American political culture is inundated with talk of rights but little discussion of what rights might be *for*. We have built remarkable bureaucracies to solve problems, but without providing a description of what solutions to those problems would look like. Joined to this lack of what may be called (but Chesterton does not) teleology is an ideology of innovation. The reformers in Chesterton's day were convinced that the future held endless possibility, and was to be preferred over the dysfunctional present or the boring past. He writes:

> We often read nowadays of the valor or audacity with which some rebel attacks a hoary tyranny or an antiquated superstition. There is not really any courage at all in attacking hoary or antiquated things, any more than in offering to fight one's grandmother. The really courageous man is he who defies tyrannies young as the morning and superstitions fresh as the first flowers. The only true free-thinker is he whose intellect is as much free from the future as from the past. He cares as little for what will be as for what has been; he cares only for what ought to be.

Chesterton applies his analysis to mistakes modern reformers make about man, woman, and child, and concludes with "the Home of Man." His focus on the family unit is crucial, because for Chesterton the family is the center of human society, and we must understand what the family is before we can help it. He defends the family both against the socialists who would end the family in favor of the state as well as the capitalists who would destroy it in the name of individualism. Indeed, in his incisive parable about Hudge the socialist and Gudge the capitalist, they amount to the same thing in terms of their damage to the family.

Chesterton confronted liberalism in its heyday, when progressives thought they were at the vanguard of a new world. Tradition and religion were hidebound and destined to disappear. The American writer and critic Russell Kirk faced a different world: When Kirk was writing his great books and essays in the 1950s and 1960s, such as T*he Conservative Mind*, he had already begun to discern the end of liberal hegemony and an opportunity to renew enduring norms.

However, Kirk was left to contend with the results of the same mistakes concerning human nature that Chesterton had identified. They both criticised the illusions of social engineers, capitalist economic redistribution, a fetish for technology, and a misplaced reliance on the moral authority of science. But where Chesterton could at least invoke the common history and morals of the West in his debates with progressives, today that kind of common language has almost been lost.

With Chesterton, however, Kirk realised that imagination would be the most important tool in any cultural renewal. Kirk saw coming an Age of Sentiments, spurred by new technologies that rely on image, not on rational argumentation that was characteristic of the age of liberalism. "The immense majority of human beings will feel with the projected images they behold upon the television screen; and in those viewers that screen will rouse sentiments rather than reflections. Waves of emotion will sweep back and forth, so long as the Age of Sentiments endures. And whether those emotions are low or high must depend upon the folk who determine the tone and temper of television programming." And those folk must be infused with the moral imagination, or else the tone of the ever-present images will be low indeed.

Chesterton used his amasing facility for paradox and wordplay, on display in every page of *What's Wrong with the World*, to showcase the flaws in modern ideology. Kirk created an alternative thought-world for those seeking refuge from liberalism's death throes. But each served the same cause of reminding the West that it is as important to know what is right with the world as it is to know what is wrong.

The prophecy of the genius of G. K. Chesterton

— The following article by Michael Coren, writer, broadcaster and speaker, was published in the October 10, 2010 edition of The Catholic Register.

We are generally not well served by journalism today. Catholic journalists in particular sometimes seem more intent on pleasing their secular friends than in defending the Church. Oh for another Gilbert. Who? Please! Gilbert Keith Chesterton, who wrote the truth of permanent things, of first things, of Catholic things. Born in 1874 in London, England, he enjoyed the best in British private education but chose not to go to university, which partly explains his visceral refusal to adopt convention and think and write within partisan definitions. He drifted into journalism but once afloat he sailed perfectly, and often against the wind.

On the fashionable nationalism of the Edwardian age, for example, "My country, right or wrong, is it thing that no patriot would think of saying except in a desperate case. It is like saying, my mother, drunk or sober." On literature, "A good novel tells us the truth about its hero; but a bad novel tells us the truth about its author." On being controversial, "I believe in getting into hot water, it keeps you clean."

Books came early and frequently. *Greybeards at Play* in 1900, *Twelve Types* in 1902, a Biography of Robert Browning the following year. Then in 1904 one of his finest works, *The Napoleon of Notting Hill*. Ostensibly about a London district declaring independence from Great Britain, at heart it explained Chesterton's belief that the state was more often than not a problem rather than a solution and the greater the intervention of government the more profound the damage to the governed.

He married Frances Blogg in 1901 and they had an intensely happy, though childless, life together. She was a steadying influence on his notorious untidiness and lack of organisation. "Am at Market Harborough," he once wrote to her. "Where ought I to be." Her reply? "Home." At a time when H.G. Wells was celebrating infidelity and George Bernard Shaw deconstructing marriage, Chesterton insisted that family was at the epicentre of any civilised society. In 1922 he became a Roman Catholic. "The fight for the family and the free citizen and everything decent must now be waged by the one fighting form of Christianity," he wrote. And, "The Christian ideal has not been tried and found wanting; it has been found difficult and left untried."

Step forward the grand knight of the Church. With his brother Cecil and the journalist and author Hilaire Belloc he embraced Distributism, based on concepts of family autonomy and small-scale production leading to authentic democracy. Neither socialist nor capitalist, and never liberal in the contemporary sense. "A citizen can hardly distinguish between a tax and a fine, except that the fine is generally much lighter," and "Too much capitalism does not mean too many capitalists, but too few capitalists."

He possessed a sparkling ability to hold up a mirror to the addled society around him and show its absurd reflection. "Journalism largely consists of saying Lord Jones is Dead to people who never knew that Lord Jones was alive." And, "The Bible tells us to love our neighbours, and also to love our enemies; probably because they are generally the same people."

There were biographies of St. Francis, St. Thomas Aquinas and Charles Dickens, compilations of columns and journalism, autobiography and works of apologetics and history such as *Orthodoxy, Heretics* and *The Everlasting Man*. There was poetry—"The Ballad of The White Horse" and "Lepanto" and the creation of the priest detective Father Brown.

He was as witty as Wilde, original as Joyce, clever as Kafka. Yet he remains an icon to too few partly because he spoke and wrote as a Catholic. In the final years of his life Chesterton predicted that the absolutes of right and wrong would become blurred, religion publicly condemned and that we would care more for animals than babies and would worship sex while mocking love. We would, he said be governed by whim and fashion. "Tradition means giving votes to the most obscure of all classes: our ancestors. It is the democracy of the dead. Tradition refuses to submit to that arrogant oligarchy who merely happens to be walking around."

He was, quite clearly, not only a genius but a prophet.

Chesterton at Notre Dame

— Rufus William Rauch is Professor Emeritus of English at Notre Dame. He is the author of articles in journals of literary criticism and the history of ideas.

Chesterton came to the University of Notre Dame in the autumn of 1930 as a visiting professor at the invitation of the president, the Rev. Charles L. O'Donnell, C.S.C. By 1930 Chesterton was at the height of his fame and prestige as a brilliant wit and writer on every subject under the sun, master of paradox, defender of the faith and the common sense of the common man. His commitment at Notre Dame was to give two courses of eighteen lectures each, concomitantly, on Victorian literature and Victorian political history. Upper-division students were allowed to register for credit in either one of the two series, but not for both. The lectures were given on weekday evenings in Washington Hall, which was filled to its capacity of about six hundred people.

Unfortunately, no stenographic record was made of the lectures, in those days before tape-recorders, so his chuckles, his sallies, his commentaries on the Victorians and all their works were lost, except in the scribbled notebooks of some of the more perceptive students. He himself spoke from what seemed to be the most fragmentary notes, written on scraps of grocery bags. Even so, he often quoted at great length from the Victorian poets and novelists. The official bookkeepers of credit-hours were hard put to devise suitable examinations at the end of the term. The lectures were a great success, the delight of all who heard them. Almost fifty years later, notes taken on the Victorian literature series by three different attendants were published in *The Chesterton Review.*

By the 1930s Chesterton, of course, was lionised wherever he went, wherever he traveled or lectured or was interviewed; but he was not the kind of literary lion who could easily be domesticated into a kind of *maitre de salon.* At Notre Dame, his kindness, his wit, his interest in people and in ideas, were easily available to all comers. He lived in South Bend during those two months with his wife, Frances, and his secretary, Miss Dorothy Collins. There he received callers from the University, members of the faculty and students, with charming cordiality. He was "lionised," inevitably, by townspeople, on one occasion by a local tycoon, the inventor of the best automobile brake system and the best carburetor of that time. This inventive millionaire's mansion included a beautiful paneled library, but its shelves were but thinly populated. So in anticipation of a great dinner given for Chesterton, a truckload of books was rented from a local bookshop and put in place, including, one supposes, copies of some of Chesterton's books. Chesterton hardly noticed.

The Editor of the Notre Dame student literary magazine, *Scrip* (so-named after the medieval pilgrim's wallet), published a delightful essay on meeting Chesterton in a bookshop:

> I shall always be tremendously pleased to think that I first met Gilbert Keith Chesterton in a book-shop. As the man who introduced me to him said, "You never know who's around the corner." I could just as well have met him in front of a drugstore or a hardware store but, think, afterwards I might have been unable to

disassociate him from soda-fountains and light bulbs, or silver-
ware and pyrex plates... At the time of that first meeting he was
standing in the aisle of this particular book-shop, "browsing,"
he said, "over the books." Finally he caught sight of a volume,
A Short History of Women, I think, and picked it up. An amased
chuckle came from him and then a laugh. He has a unique way
of beginning a chuckle at his feet, and then, body quivering as
the chuckle travels upwards, of ultimately bringing it to a full-
fledged hearty laugh. What he thought can best be described by
what he said after he had read a page of two. "A short history of
women! Fancy that. I never thought anyone would ever attempt
to write a short history of women!" As he turned from book to
book I watched him. He wore a hat that I shall never associate with anyone else except a French *abbé.* About his shoulders
was thrown a fog-cape that I shall never associate with anything
else except a cape some mysterious person might throw about his
shoulders—perhaps Sherlock Holmes. In his hand he carried a
cane, "my *ciupaga"* he called it. "I brought it back with me from
Poland." But he is not a French *abbé,* nor is he mysterious. He is
about the most affable and likeable person I have ever met.

The editor of the Notre Dame student humorous magazine, the
Juggler, asked Chesterton to contribute a cartoon or two. Chesterton
responded with his customary generosity and drew two caricatures-
of himself, in the context of his lectures on the Victorian Age: probably the most amusing of his many drawings and cartoons. They
were published in the December 1930 issue, introduced enthusiasti-
cally by the editor:

This Christmas performance is offered with a just pride because
the guest star, Gilbert Keith Chesterton, is the most distinguished who ever appeared on the Funny Fellow's boards—or,
for that matter, those of any other college humorous publication. The Funny Fellow was tempted to give him the entire stage
because his own efforts seem so trivial. Mr. Chesterton steals the
show, as he should. The foremost man of English letters today
is famous for his humor, and he seems to be able to transcribe
his wit through his pencil. We doubt that Queen Victoria would
banish him as he has her do in this excellent caricature; but after attending his lectures on the Victorian Period we can understand why smug Victorians would snub him, as they did during
his early days in Fleet Street.

After his sojourn in South Bend, Chesterton was interviewed at some length by the *New York Times*. He was asked to comment on Sinclair Lewis' *Main Street* (Lewis had just won the Nobel Prize), and to compare his impressions of South Bend as a Main Street town:

> I really found Main Street a most charming and entertaining thoroughfare, and I was not only entertained by its citizens, but I found them to be a most commendable lot of people .... Of course, there were many points about it that struck me, as an Englishman, as rather peculiar, but I find no fault with them; in fact, in many ways I came to admire them.

He did speak of the "shady side of the street" as well as the sunny side, but his conclusion was typically generous:

> I can enjoy myself walking along its sidewalks, and even if its architecture is not beautiful, even if its people have certain peculiarities, nevertheless I can see that they have admirable qualities and that they have found happiness in their own town. Who am I that I should tell them what to read or what plays to see when they go a big city?

> And you know as I sat at my window in my house in South Bend and saw the leading banker drive along in his motor car, saw the best known lawyer stop and talk to his doctor, saw girls dressed as smartly as those in any big city, saw the laughter, the general good humor, the evident enjoyment; and as I took part in the complete and full life that the professors at the college were leading, I wondered whether these people in that little town are missing anything in life. Are they deprived of any real pleasures, living in a small town? I do not think they are.

A memorable party was given for him on campus by Professor Charles Phillips in his rooms in Sorin Hall. Phillips had published a book on the history and martyrdom of Poland, where he had served during World War I as director of the Knights of Columbus Relief Mission. Their love and admiration of Poland formed a bond of friendship between them. Chesterton's hosts at the party had to use devious and nefarious ways to find a sufficient supply of good ale and real beer for their guest—it was during the dismal period of prohibition. Conversation flowed, and, as Senator John J. Connolly of Canada has recalled,

Chesterton's stein "was never empty for more than a minute." The party went on into the wee hours of the morning, to the considerable concern of those who were responsible for returning him safely to the bosom of his family. In addition to Phillips, his hosts were a group of younger members of the faculty: Messrs. Fenlon, Manion, Rauch, Connolly, O'Grady, Engels, Moran, McCole. On another occasion, Chesterton was taken, by his own request, on a tour of speakeasies in South Bend, to sample the varieties of home-brew available to selected customers.

When Charles Phillips died in 1933, Chesterton sent a warm tribute to his memory tribute to his memory, published in *Scrip:*

> Charles Phillips was a man who could not be mistaken. Charity shone from him like a visible light, and the great work he did on the history of Poland, the most tragic and chivalric of nations, was but one example of a general instinct of generosity for taking a handsome view of human problems, which was obvious in his contact with any student or stranger. I know one stranger at least, who will never forget him.

The University called a special convocation in November 1930 of its faculty and student body to confer an Honourary Degree of Doctor of Letters on Chesterton. In his remarks expressing his appreciation, he recalled that he had received an Honourary Doctorate from the University of Edinburgh. In that ceremony he was tapped on the head with the cap of John Knox. In this ceremony in America he said he was very grateful not to be struck on the head with the hat of Senator J. Thomas Heflin of Alabama—one of the notorious leaders of the Ku Klux Klan!

Autumn is the season of football. Chesterton was duly taken to a Notre Dame game in the new stadium, which seats fifty-eight thousand people. He didn't understand much of what was going on the playing field (so different from cricket or even rugby!), but he was moved by the spectacle of the roaring thousands and especially by the cheers for "Old Notre Dame—Shake down the thunder from the skies!" Whereupon he wrote a poem, "The Arena," dedicated to Notre Dame. A typical Chesterton poem, at his best, somewhat reminiscent of "Lepanto," it is not only a rollicking evocation of the "rah-rah" and controlled violence of college football, but also a vision of the great conflict past, present, and future: the gladiators of Nero's Rome, whose cheering shout is *Te morituri salutant*; the gladiators of Notre Dame whose cheer is "Those about to live salute Thee"; and in its third part a kind of vision of the end of the world. This poem is probably the most "mystical" celebration of football ever written. Its opening lines evoke a familiar scene.

> I have seen, where a strange country
> Opened its secret plains about me,
> One great Golden Dome stand lonely with its golden image, one
> Seen afar, in strange fulfillment,
> Through the sunlit Indian summer
> That Apocalyptic portent that has clothed her with the Sun.

Chesterton was well remembered in subsequent years. When he died in 1936, the student literary magazine, *Scrip,* published a special memorial number. A Chesterton Club had been formed by a group of students, and when Sir Arnold Lunn was brought to the University in 1937 by President John F. O'Hara, C.S.C., to direct a graduate program in apologetics, some of Chesterton's books were prominent in the reading list. Debates were held on such subjects as "Is One Religion as Good as Another?" and "Is There a God?" Lunn offered a Chesterton medal, designed by Eric Gill, for the best student essay in apologetics. But the War brought these activities to an end.

John Bennett Shaw's magnificent collection of Chesterton's books, drawings, and other memorabilia came to the Memorial Library in the 1960s. An exhibition of the Shaw Chesterton Collection was held in 1979 in the Rare Books and Special Collections Department, with an annotated catalog by Anton C. Masin. That brings us to the Chesterton Celebration of 1980.

Drawing by G. K. Chesterton

CHRISTIAN WRITER'S WORK REVIVED

Holy Cross program marks eightieth anniversary
of G. K. Chesterton visit

— *The following article by Borsnislaus B. Kush was published in the March 19, 2010 issue of the* Worcester Telegram & Gazette.

Candace Jaegle gets together with a small group every second Saturday of the month at the Webster House to talk about a pre-selected book, but the works of James Patterson, Danielle Steele, Stephen King and other popular authors, which are usually dissected by book club *aficionados*, are never discussed. In fact, the literature pored over at the Webster Square eatery has never won Oprah Winfrey's seal of approval, nor has it made *The New York Times'* best-seller list, at least not recently. Rather, Ms. Jaegle and her fellow critics minutely and lovingly analyse the prolific writings of Gilbert Keith Chesterton, an Englishman who once was considered a literary "bear" but whose works, for the longest time, gathered considerable dust on library bookshelves throughout the world. Now, there's revived interest in Mr. Chesterton's works, especially among Christians, with study groups cropping up around the country, including the one that meets in Worcester. "I'm hooked on him," said Ms. Jaegle, a fifty-nine year-old legal secretary with the Massachusetts Justice Program. "He's witty and he's right on with his insights."

Mr. Chesterton, who lived from 1874 to 1936, authored more than one-hundred books and was a historian, economist, journalist, theologian, and literary and social critic. In addition to the books, the author, more commonly known as G. K. Chesterton, wrote hundreds of poems, five plays, two hundred short stories, and some fifty or so novels about a priest-detective named Father Brown, who was portrayed by Alec Guinness in a movie and by Kenneth More on PBS' "Mystery" series. A convert to Roman Catholicism, Mr. Chesterton, who was born in London, is frequently referred to as a Christian apologist. His circle of acquaintances included Bertrand Russell, Clarence Darrow, H.G. Wells, and George Bernard Shaw, all of whom he publicly debated.

Monsignor Thomas J. Sullivan, who organised the G. K. Chesterton Society of Worcester, the group in which Ms. Jaegle is a member, said people are attracted to Mr. Chesterton because of the breadth of his work. "He certainly had a lot of interests," said Monsignor Sullivan, who is chancellor for the Diocese of Worcester. Ms. Jaegle said she first learned about Mr. Chesterton while watching the old Mother Angelica program on the *EWTN* network. Curious, she read some of the Father Brown books. "Father Brown is like (Chesterton) baby food," said Ms. Jaegle, a Worcester resident. "Some people aren't going to like it but those that do usually move on." She said she became a fan after reading *The Everlasting Man*, the book that C.S. Lewis said made him rebuke atheism and embrace Catholicism.

Monsignor Sullivan said the local Chesterton group, which has about fifteen members, evolved about eight months ago from another group that met about six times a year to discuss the works of authors who converted to the Catholic faith. He said his favorite Chesterton work is *The Dumb Ox*, a biography of St. Thomas Aquinas. "I really enjoy going to the meetings," said Ms. Jaegle. "It's fun and I learn so much. It's like working on an educational degree but not going to school."

Mr. Chesterton's local admirers said area residents can learn more about their favorite author at a program Thursday that marks the eightieth anniversary of the writer's visit to the College of the Holy Cross. Mr. Chesterton was a friend of the Rev. Michael J. Earls, a priest at Holy Cross, and stopped by the school on Dec. 9, 1930. He was greeted by some students dressed in the attire of past literary figures and later, while reciting Joyce Kilmer's poem "Trees," planted a white cedar in front of O'Kane Hall. The "Chesterton Tree" died about forty years later but a replacement tree still stands on the spot.

The March 25 program, which was be held at the Rehm Library, featured presentations by Fr. Ian Boyd, founder and Editor of *The Chesterton Review* and President of the G. K. Chesterton Institute for Faith & Culture and Dermot Quinn, Associate Editor of *The Chesterton Review*. Additionally, an exhibit of photos of Mr. Chesterton's visit and some rare editions of his book are on display at the Dinand Library. "We're certainly not expecting large crowds, but I think that individuals interested in Mr. Chesterton will find the exhibit interesting," said Mark Savolis, the head of archives and special collections at Holy Cross. A newsreel of Mr. Chesterton's visit can also be viewed on *YouTube*.

G. K. Chesterton "Revival" Week

— *The following article by Msgr. Thomas J. Sullivan, Treasurer of the G. K. Chesterton Society in Worcester, was published in the March 19, 2010 issue of the* Worcester Catholic Free Press.

Two separate events marking the literary contributions and ongoing significance of G. K. Chesterton will take place Worcester in the next week. The first takes place at the DCU center tomorrow. The other evening, will take place at the college of the Holy Cross.

Gilbert Keith Chesterton (1874-1936) was an influential English writer of the early twentieth century, He was known for his prolific and diverse output, writing more than one-hundred books and 4,000 published essays, over fifteen million published words in all. He wrote extensive philosophy, poetry, biography, Christian apologetics, fantasy, and detective fiction, especially the well-known "Father Brown" mystery stories. Dubbed "the prince of paradox,"dozens of his books are still being reprinted. It was his book on Charles Dickens that began the revival of interest in that nearly forgotten nineteenth-century author. His biography of St. Thomas Aquinas, *The Dumb Ox*, is thought by many Thomistic scholars to be the best ever written on the Angelic doctor. Referring to himself as an "orthodox Christian" over a period of years and having written *Orthodoxy* (1908), perhaps his most famous book, he embraced the Catholic faith in 1922, twelve years before his death. He was the most famous twentieth-century convert in the world.

The Catholic Men's Conference will host a talk by the president of the American Chesterton Society, Dale Ahlquist. Traveling from Minnesota, Ahlquist's topic will be Chesterton's *What's Wrong with the World?* on the hundredth anniversary of its publication. He is the creator and host of the Eternal Word Television network series, "G. K. Chesterton: Apostle of Common Sense" and "Common Sense 101: Lessons From G. K. Chesterton."He is also the publisher of *Gilbert Magazine,* author of the Chesterton University Student Handbook, Editor of *The Gift of Wonder: The Many Sides of G. K. Chesterton*, and Associate Editor of the *Collected Works of G. K. Chesterton* (Ignatius Press). He has been called "one of the most respected Christian scholars in the world" and has delighted audiences around the country with his variety of talks on the great English writer. This is his fourth visit to the Worcester area. He spoke at St. Paul's Cathedral in 2005, at the graduation of Lancaster's Trivium School in 2006, and at the 2007 Catholic Men's Conference.

The scene will shift to Holy Cross on Thursday, March 25, for a special presentation titled "Chesterton in America." The event, which is being cosponsored by Holy Cross' Center for Religion, Ethics and Culture and the G. K. Chesterton Society of Worcester, is free and open to the public in the Rehm Library in Smith Hall. The program marks the eighieth anniversary of Chesterton's four-day visit to Worcester in 1936, which was hosted by Holy Cross. In addition to speaking and receiving honours at the college, he spoke at Mechanics Hall opposing "liberal divorce laws." The featured speakers at Holy Cross will be Fr. Ian Boyd, and Professor Dermot Quinn.

An internationally recognised Chesterton scholar, Fr. Boyd is the author of *The Novels of G. K. Chesterton*. For many years he was a Professor of English at St. Thomas More College at the University of Saskatchewan. Currently, he is a member of the Department of English at Seton Hall University in New Jersey. Fr. Boyd also lectures on the subject of sacramental themes in modern literature. Among the Christian authors whose work he discusses are T.S. Eliot, Graham Greene, C.S. Lewis, Flannery O'Connor; Piers Paul Read, Muriel Spark, and Evelyn Waugh. In nineteenth century literature, he is interested in the work of such authors as Charles Dickens, Anthony Trollope and Nathaniel Hawthorne. He is the founder and Editor of *The Chesterton Review* and the president of the G. K. Chesterton Institute for Faith & Culture based at Seton Hall.

Professor Quinn teaches history at Seton Hall, is a member of the board of advisors of the G. K. Chesterton Institute for Faith & Culture and a member of the Editorial Board of *The Chesterton Review*. He was educated at Trinity College, Dublin and New College, Oxford, where he was awarded a doctorate in 1986. Quinn has written extensively on Chestertonian themes and has authored three books including *The Irish in New Jersey: Four Centuries of American Life*, *Patronage and Piety: The Politics of English Roman Catholicism, 1850-1900* and *Understanding Northern Ireland*. He has also written many articles and reviews in the field of British and Irish history. He was Fellow of the James Madison Program at Princeton University, Academic Year 2008-2009.

Chesterton's invitation to visit Holy Cross came at the behest of his friend and admirer, Father Michael J. Earls, S.J., a Professor of English at the College from 1914 to 1937. The priest himself was a productive man of letters, writing poems, plays, novels and essays and maintaining a great deal of correspondence with friends, both famous and unknown. The highlight of Father Earls' public career was bringing Chesterton to Holy Cross in the winter of 1930. The visit attracted national interest. Chesterton enjoyed his time at the college, and spoke of "Father Earls' terrifying hospitality." He wrote that his "visit to Holy Cross was the high point of his second trip to America," He offered many observations on the United States in his first book on America, *Chesterton in America*, written nearly a decade earlier.

College of the Holy Cross, Worcester, MA

221

"DRIVING WITHOUT DESTINATION"
Finds Walsh Gallery

History Professor's essay brings direction to University's newest art exhibit

— *The following article by Ed Millar, Staff Writer about the Chesterton Institute Art Exhibit, "Driving Without Destination," based on an article by the same name by Professor Dermot Quinn, was published in the* Setonian, *the student newspaper of Seton Hall University on September 23, 2010.*

If I were to emerge from the folds of this newspaper and ask you about the current state of affairs within the world, after you had recovered (hopefully) from the initial shock of my appearance, I do not think it would be too bold to say that you would formulate some sort of answer. However, had I asked about events occurring within your own town, how quick would you be able to form an answer? Would you claim that "nothing" was happening?

The Walsh Gallery's new exhibit, "Driving Without Destination," addresses this cultural phenomenon. The exhibit focuses on the world's growing infatuation with standardisation and how it has transformed a society into one focused on convenience and generalities, or the concept of the "big picture." Yet it also questions the cost at which we become "worldly." Curated by Jeanne Brasile and Tony Capparelli, "Driving Without Destination" contains twenty-two works centered around such notions of fading localism, interconnectivity, globalism, consumerism, and their respective implications, both physical and metaphysical. The exhibit is based on an essay by Dermot Quinn, Seton Hall's Professor of History and Graduate Program Director, called "Driving Without Destination: A Distributist Journey in New York State," which is found in the August 2000 issue of *The Chesterton Review*. Within this essay, Professor Quinn connects the reality of diminished localism and increased global standardisation with the notion of a "graying" of modern society: the destruction of distinction and the adoption of homogeneity.

The late nineteenth century English writer G. K. Chesterton, for whom *The Chesterton Review* is named, once stated that the blight of modernity was "standardisation by a low standard." America's obsession with convenience has society down the path easier taken: a culture where consumption, not production, is the standard. As corporate giants like Walmart, Costco, McDonald's, and Starbucks flourish, "Driving Without Destination" shows that there is an insidious homogenisation growing within contemporary American society, or what Professor Quinn calls the "lonely anonymity of modernity." Entering the "Driving Without Destination" exhibit, viewers can witness the overpowering concerns of "lonely anonymity" that are fueled by a global standardisation.

Larry Ross' painting "From Here to There," best epitomises this, depicting a familiar image for many: a drive to a dull city, which is captured in the vehicle's side mirror. The stark rigid lines of the painting emphasise the "lack of character" of the city: it is not attractive, nor does it pretend to be. However, the image in the side-view mirror reveals that this lack of character or distinction has become the norm: the driver is traveling "from here to there," but is also occupying a space that is neither here nor there: "'all driving and no destination." Pages can be written detailing each particular piece, but that may undermine the intended message of the exhibition: it is time to cease consumption and begin production.

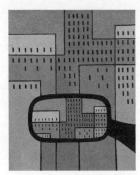

Larry Ross, "From Here to There",
acrylic on canvas, 20" x 16", 2010

223

France Culture public radio discovers Chesterton

— *The following note was prepared by the French journalist and writer Basile de Koch.*

On Saturday, May 8, 2010, Alain Finkielkraut, the philosopher and author, chose to devote his entire France Culture public radio weekly program, *Répliques (Arguments)*, to "The Dazzling G. K. Chesterton."

Such a title was a clue that, departing from Finkielkraut's well-loved program's habitual style, few disagreements were expressed on air. Both guests shared the host's enthusiasm for his subject.

This marked a significant event in a country where G. K. Chesterton is still mostly unknown. Finkielkraut himself confessed he only came across his work early this year, as new translations of *Heretics* and *Orthodoxy* (by Lucien d'Azay) came out.

Most notable is certainly how G. K. Chesterton's "paradoxical Christianity" instantly resonated with one of France's leading philosophers, whose agnosticism is as famous as his intellectual rigor.

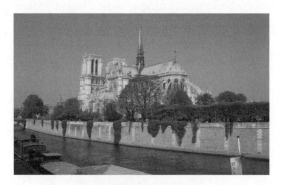

View of Notre Dame Cathedral, Paris

Religion and the Conservative Mind

— *The following article by Dr. Dermot Quinn, Professor of History at Seton Hall University and member of the Editorial Board of* The Chesterton Review *and the Board of Directors of the G. K. Chesterton Institute for Faith & Culture was published in* The Political Reviewer *(Vol. XXXV, 2006).*

To know *The Conservative Mind* is to know the mind of its remarkable author, Russell Kirk. He was an old-fashioned man—courtly, retiring, serene, formal in dress and manner—whose view of the world, proclaimed by every photograph, was traditional, anti-modem, even obscure. Captured in his study, his library, his home, surrounded by pens, books, family, and friends, he looks every bit the paternalist man of letters, a figure unmistakably of the past. To critics, he was a sort of mid-western Evelyn Waugh, tweedy, fustian, fond of a dram, a *contramundum* crank. To friends, he was a man who knew the good life and lived it to the full, preaching domestic joys and practicing them with panache. To the unpersuaded, Kirk's social poise was social pose. By dress and manner, by truculent tory-ism, he mocked a world he did not understand. To the persuaded, he understood the world too well and wanted nothing to do with it. Certainly his conservatism seemed at times compounded of com-plaint and cussedness. Mass production and mass consumption, his-tory forgotten, the old ways of faith at a loss: if this was modernity it was not for him. His home at Piety Hill, with its simpler commerce of family life, seasonal change, sacramental connection to the land, was more to his taste. In one sense, critics who dismiss him as a right-wing type, a persona, get the point yet miss it entirely. He played a role he wrote himself, actor and lines in perfect harmony. As for the part, he was proud to call himself Catholic, gentleman, husband, father, a man of letters, friend. These were badges of honour, not (as the psychologisers would have it) social masks concealing some more authentic self. "Manners maketh man" said William of Wyke-ham in the fourteenth century. The style is the thing itself. Kirk embodied the dictum. Of all men, he was mannerly, courteous, self-consciously gallant. At the heart of that manner, at the core of his private being, was religion. When the pen was laid down and the last letter written, he remained a man of God.

Such was the author. What of the book? Here the story is different. If Kirk the Man and Kirk the Manner were one and the same, *The Conservative Mind* is a volume where appearances deceive. Things are never quite as they seem. It is shot through with irony and surprise, with odd juxtaposition and unexpected insight. In the first place, it is paradoxical: here is a book so old-fashioned as to be positively original. *The Conservative Mind* (perhaps the conservative movement as a whole) is the philosophical equivalent of one of those grandfather shirts that have come into fashion once again: it is so uncool that it is suddenly all the rage. In 1953, even more so today, the book's anti-modernity was sufficiently complete as almost to be itself modern. It mocks conventions, derides received opinion, strikes dissenting attitudes. Its rejection of the current is itself *au courant.* The book was also novel in the confidence of its conservatism. In 1953, after a Hitler, an Auschwitz, a war to end war, it required more than usual self-assurance to bring together Edmund Burke and John Adams, Walter Scott and John Calhoun, Cardinal Newman and William Lecky, and to propose that such superannuated worthies had anything to say to a world whose enormities they could never have imagined. The reaction, he surely knew, would be laughter among the chattering classes. (Another irony, by the way: As they talked and talked, those self-same chatterers undermined their own claim that the point of the death camps was that all chatter must cease. The old moral categories no longer hold, they said. God is dead. The Word made Flesh has been incinerated. Speech falls silent, unable to utter the unutterable, name the unnamable. Never has the inadequacy of language been more articulately urged.) How could Kirk's miscellaneous assembly make sense of Dachau, explain Hiroshima? Yet he persevered with them, offering a new generation old truths. That took *elan,* a dash of intellectual *bella figura.* And notice a final paradox. The very dustiness of Kirk's style marked him as an original. Simply as literature, as mid-twentieth century prose, *The Conservative Mind* has an oddly Victorian feel: it breathes the language of waistcoat and fob in an age of T-shirt and exposed navel. The authorial voice—gnomic, orotund, erudite, vaguely dyspeptic and world-weary—could pass for Froude or Macaulay, Gladstone or Disraeli. Here was not the received pronunciation of Michigan State University, the way a professor is supposed to talk in a state-run college of agriculture.[1] In an age of dry academic prose Kirk had panache; in an era of specialisation, his learning was broad and deep. *The Conservative Mind* was thus more innovative than critics allowed. It was also funnier, livelier, better informed. No wonder he found the modern university, and the modern literary world, unwelcoming. He was too big, they too small; he too protean, they too neat. For all his erudition, Kirk did not fit the standard liberal arts college, a place full of conformist nonconformists, every opinion as standard as a shop-bought loaf of bread. Kirk was *genuinely* nonconformist, a scholarly one-off. Most selection committees would have thrown up their hands and raced for the door.

What, then, to make of this singular man and book? What were his fixed principles, the ideas that make sense of the rest? This symposium examines some of them but let me suggest that, of them all, religion was most important. Faith, specifically the Christian faith, under-girded his conservatism, providing the foundation for other notions—property, order, respect for the law, family life—that filled out the rest of his philosophy. But there was nothing simple or straightforward about it. Religion operates variously throughout the book, sometimes providing a ground for moral confidence, sometimes for doubt, sometimes revealing man's moral mastery, sometimes his depravity, sometimes opening to us the knowability of the world, sometimes locking us more deeply in its mystery. It was Kirk's perfect metaphor, the idea that contained the totality of his mind. Yet this versatility could also be weakness. Sometimes he seems to ask too much of it. Subtle distinctions begin to seem more like discrepancies as Kirk struggled to contain the complexity of his own intellectual impulses. A man of faith, he was not simple-minded. This was as it should be. The perplexities in his piety, finally resolved, make it more persuasive as a philosophical and practical commitment.

The complexity has biographical roots. Religion played an unusual role in Kirk's thought, also in his life. Unbaptised as a child, his growing up was far from churchy. His parents held to a vague, undogmatic spiritualism, the kind of empty numinosity that nowadays finds echo in new age movements but then lay halfway between deism and watered down biblicism. They might have approved of Clement Attlee's clipped response to Christianity: "like the social teaching: no time for the mumbo-jumbo." (At the risk of getting ahead of ourselves, precisely the opposite might be said of Kirk. If by "social teaching" is meant sentimental humanitarianism—doles justified in the name of the *via dolorosa,* the Nicene Creed reduced to a commitment to niceness—he wanted nothing to do with it.) There were plenty of ghost stories when he was young, but not much Holy Ghost. Auto-didacticism saved him. Gradually, then more urgently, he discovered deeper truths in Christianity through extensive read-ing, especially the early fathers of the church. Finally, he em-braced Catholicism, being received into the Church, after desul-tory and *pro forma* instruction, in 1964. As with T.S. Eliot, so with Kirk: "he became a Christian on discovering he already *was* one—a very common type of conversion."[2] The Catho-lic Church remained home for the rest of his life, not without alarms but never with any anxiety that his decision had been wrong. Kirk gave some account of his journey in *The Sword of Imagination,* a quirky memoir of a "half century of literary con-flict" in which revelation and reserve are dispensed in roughly equal measure. Writing in the third person—a device designed to keep unnecessary revelation at a distance yet all the more re-vealing for that—he described a bookish conversion, a scholar's realisation that Catholicism was, simply, *true.* Like Hilaire Bel-loc, his faith owed nothing to enthusiasm or evangelical fervor, to sudden epiphanies, to flashing moments of truth:

> Therefore it was on no road to Damascus that Russell Kirk ... came to believe in the Apostle's Creed. His was an intellectual conversion, if conversion it may be called. After Kirk had read for years about ultimate questions, and reflected upon them, late in 1953 he obtained formal instruction in Catholic doctrine from ... Father Hugh O'Neill. The learned priest was somewhat surprised to learn that Kirk's reason for seeking him out was merely the yearning of intellectual curiosity: Kirk desired to have the principle dogmata explained to him, that he might tru-ly understand...It was the intellectual love of God that worked upon Russell Kirk; he never became an enthusiast, but the doc-

tors of the church persuaded him...Reading the [early] fathers, Augustine and Gregory and Ambrose especially, [he] gave up his previous spiritual individualism ... "The calm judgment of the world is that those men cannot be good who, in any part of the world, cut themselves off from the rest of the world." Therefore the Church had been raised up.[3]

This debt to patristics is suggestive, recalling the experience of converts such as Newman and Christopher Dawson whose discovery of the church was also, at root, historical. "The Fathers made me Catholic," Newman once wrote to John Pusey; and, on another occasion, "To be deep in history is to cease to be Protestant."[4] Kirk could have written the same thing. Likewise, he shared Dawson's sense that, a commitment to Christianity once made, it was either Rome or nothing. Dawson's description of Newman applies neatly to Kirk:

There were but two paths—the way of faith and the way of unbelief, and as the latter led through the halfway house of Liberalism to Atheism, the former led through the half way house of Anglicanism to Catholicism.[5]

The logic of conversion was the logic of the church.

Yet *why* did the fathers lead Kirk to Catholicism? At one level, it was because of the persuasiveness of their case. Religion was a *fact,* a reality, a truth not to be wished away. The Catholic form of it, he came to believe, was vindicated again and again by the calm judgment of the world. Religion formed societies and held them together, it gave shape to man's deepest desires, it remained the one reality through time and space that seemed to express and explain the infinite variety of things. That was a powerful evidence of the truth of *something.* With Newman and Dawson, Kirk was led to Catholicism by the notion that all history, properly understood, points in the direction of the Church. Yet Kirk's *acceptance* of the argument was rooted in something more than its intrinsic merit. At the risk of pyschologising a philosophical commitment, his embrace of the Church had to do with its authoritativeness, its confidence, its splendid finality. When Rome spoke, the matter was over. There was a touch of Bossuet in his enthusiasm for a church that spoke language of unbendable conviction. In a disordered world, it represented order; in an age of chaos

—in the chaos of *every* age—it remained serene. Catholicism for Kirk was not the question, it was the answer. "Jesus Christ will teach you, in His own words and in those of His apostles, all the things that make a state happy," Bossuet proposed in *Politics Drawn from the Very Words of Holy Scripture.* "His gospel makes men all the more fit to be good citizens on this earth in that it teaches them to make themselves thereby worthy to become citizens of Heaven."[6] Kirk admired and envied such certainties. The Rock of Ages was the rock of Peter.

The search for certitude is a reasonable impulse. "You mount to heaven in one flight," says Pierre to ecstatic Violaine in Claudel's *L'Annonce Faite a Marie.* "But I need, just in order to mount a bit, the work of a cathedral and its deep foundation."[7] Most of us are with Pierre: we cannot do it alone. Weak and uncertain, we crave the assurance of doctrine, authority, community, tradition. Kirk certainly did. His admiration for John Henry Newman, for example, owed much to their shared hostility towards private judgment in religion and politics—that is to say, towards liberal individualism.[8] Yet the assurances of certainty come at a price. With Kirk, it sometimes seems, the need for fixed principle introduces a degree of conditionality into his Catholicism, as if certainty itself was the object of his devotion, the church only its secondary instrument. Notice how he tended to admire Rome when it acted as a bulwark against modernism but reproached it when it took the modernist side. Such selectivity is called Protestantism. There was still a bit of the kirk in Kirk. Consider, for example, his defense of papal infallibility. He approached the teaching in an unfussy, practical, non-theological, down-to-earth way. "This doctrine, so much assailed by modernists," he wrote, "was a necessary fiction, like the English legal doctrine that the king can do no wrong, or [the notion that Supreme Court] decisions are final. ... An ultimate power of decision on questions of faith and morals must repose somewhere; church councils cannot be meeting perpetually; so it is simply in the nature of things that papal infallibility must be sustained by the church."[9] "Necessary fiction" sounds more like Tory pragmatism than Petrine ecclesiology. The irony is obvious: here was a reformation defense of a counter-reformation doctrine. And the conditionality continues. Kirk had no patience for Catholics who claimed religious sanction for political revolution, finding the sight of *Marxisant* clerics in battle fatigues especially gruesome. Nor had he any time for liberalism within the Church either as principle or policy. He thought Pope John XXIII foolish when he entertained "hopes of gaining concessions from the masters of Kremlin" and was unsurprised when it resulted in a million votes for the Italian Communists in 1963. By contrast, he admired Paul VI as "by nature and instinct a man of order," a pope to steady the listing barque of Peter.[10] As it turned out, the ship was already holed below the waterline, not even Paul able to bail it out. Kirk thought the Second Vatican Council a disaster that left the Church broken, demoralised, and abandoned. "When a Catholic falls away," he quoted Samuel Johnson as saying, "he falls into nothing," the line reworking Chesterton's remark that a man who ceases to believe in God does not believe in nothing but in everything. That was the fate of American Catholicism by the end of Kirk's life.[11] The note of lamentation for a lost faith, and contempt for a modem stripping of the altars, is plain:

> The typical Catholic layman resented prolonged tampering with the traditional liturgy; he was alarmed by the intrusion of radical doctrines into Catholic homilies; he disliked the awkward English of the new "priest's Bible," so inferior to translations previously employed. A few more years of "renewal," it seemed to the Kirks early in the Seventies, would leave American Catholicism shattered to its foundations.[12]

The insight was prophetic. Mercifully he did not live to see more recent calamities.

It would be easy to make a case, then, that, with Kirk, conservatism came first, Catholicism second. The value of faith—*any* faith—seems instrumental, a way of promoting harmony and discouraging dissent. He seems more interested in the contentments of religion than its contents, as if any transcendent tradition is to be preferred over atheism, agnosticism, or enlightenment rationalism. Perhaps so: but this represents a surprisingly frail and provisional allegiance for one convinced that the Church speaks with absolute authority in matters of divine truth. It prompts ancillary questions. What exactly is being conserved in his conservative Catholicism? What is so powerful about tradition that it requires such vigorous defense? Part of the answer lies in historical imagination. Kirk saw value in tradition precisely because it was traditional. Faith was handed down; it was made precious by the passage of time; it derived wisdom from the murmured prayers of the unforgotten dead. Somehow its very survival sanctified it. This is not a poor argument—quite the opposite—but it needs to be handled with care. A sense of the presence of the past, the dead not departed but at our side, is one of the most important truths of Christianity. Yet is also capable of misleading the unwary. It can bleed into a kind of cultural homesickness, into a too easy requiem for some vanished historical Eden. *The Conservative Mind* is shot through with this kind of regret. Kirk mourned the loss of "everything venerable in England, from open fires to church bells,"[13] almost as if offering not only religion as cultural nostalgia but cultural nostalgia as religion, the past itself fetishised and made an object of worship. To be sure, there were good Christian and Tory grounds for this. Kirk thought one component of conservatism was veneration itself—a spirit of humility, simplicity, trust, modesty, self-restraint; all the things, in fact, missing in modernity. But sometimes the spirit of veneration can become detached from the object of veneration so that religion turns into religiosity, into vague, undogmatic spiritualism—all numinosity and no luminosity. This may serve a number of purposes but it is theologically unpersuasive. It seems to return Kirk to his childhood years, the son of well-meaning social ethicists. Like Claudel's Pierre, we still need the deeper foundations of that cathedral to help us mount to heaven. The spirit of veneration is important but it needs to be materialised. Otherwise it will keep us all in moral nonage.

This difficulty needs to be faced. The charge of religious conditionality is surprisingly hard to shake. Strongly anti-utilitarian, Kirk seems to share the utilitarianism he reprobates in others, reducing religion to sacred glue holding together the secular order. *The Conservative Mind,* critical of the Benthamite view of man as embodied appetite, often presents religion as itself one of those appetites, a hunger whose satisfaction brings important benefits to the individual and the world. Again and again the language is of utility, of social value, of good consequences. One is reminded of those surveys that appear from time to time claiming that people of faith live longer, lead happier lives, fulfill the American dream—as if, somehow, the surest way of postponing the afterlife is to hope for it. Kirk had little time for that kind of blather. Sometimes, though, his praise of religion came uncomfortably close to it. Notice the description he offers of Alexis de Tocqueville in *The Conservative Mind.* Here was a man, he tells us, who "knew that a democratic people with religious faith will respect private rights and the portion of posterity far more reverently than a democratic people who have material success as their goal."[14] Or consider his Tory view of natural law: "the laws of nature, ordained by Divine wisdom, make no provision for sharing goods without regard for individual energies or merits ... the true natural rights of men ... are equal justice, security of labour and property, the amenities of civilised institutions, and the benefits of orderly society."[15] Or think of his belief that only "reverence toward God and toward the prescriptive ways of men" will save us from anarchy.[16] Condemning radicals who treated society "as a simple contraption to be managed on mathematical lines," he, too, tended to see religion as, in part, a form of social management. When the "spirit of veneration" is lost, "so much sinks with it."[17] "In the church I see not the mystery of the incarnation," Napoleon once said, "but the mystery of the social order." Kirk sometimes came uncomfortably close to the same idea.

This complacent theodicy is nowhere more evident than in *The Conservative Mind's* treatment of Edmund Burke. Burke was Kirk's chief inspiration—the book is an extended anthem to him, even when he is not directly under consideration—and the influence was subtle and profound. For all the subtlety, however, Burke's "great melody" was occasionally flattened into something too smug and well-fed, the head-patting paternalism of the Tory squire:

> Poverty, brutality, and misfortune are indeed portions of the eternal order of things; sin is a terribly real and demonstrable fact, the consequence of our depravity, not of erring institutions; religion is the consolation for these ills, which can never be

removed by legislation or revolution. Religious faith makes existence tolerable; ambition without pious restraint must end in failure, often involving in its ruin that beautiful reverence which solaces common men for the obscurity and poverty of their lot.[18]

Of all thinkers, and with obvious irony, this sounds closest to Marx, whose disparagement of religion as the opium of the masses was merely a variation on an earlier Benthamite or Burkean theme. True, there were important differences. Marx deployed a false anthropology (man as a mere materialist, no more than a getter and spender) to sustain a false teleology (history as a class struggle and an eventual proletarian triumph). He also relied on shaky methodology. Arguing that ideas derive intelligibility from the conditions they purport to explain, he fell into a circularity: religion is reducible to economic necessity—he seems to claim—because religion is reducible economic necessity. (Not only circular, the argument was also self-refuting. If systems of thought reflect contingencies of time and chance, ideas commanding no respect as things in themselves, why should Marxism be exempt from its own limitation?) Dismissing religion as the sacralising of mundane necessities, Marx misunderstood those necessities—family, warmth, food, shared life—as constitutive of their own simple holiness. To begin by excluding the sacred was to end by discovering its absence. Kirk knew better. Insisting on religion's integrity, its reality as a thing-in-itself, he saw its deeper truths revealed in the prosaic exigencies of ordinary life. His vision was more authentically human and more historically plausible.

Still, puzzles demand solution and Kirk's religion, in *The Conservative Mind* and elsewhere, remains a riddle. Is it possible to rescue him from a kind of spiritual Benthamism, an unduly instrumental account of faith? To do so requires the construction of a conservatism that upholds utility but not utilitarianism, one that sees usefulness not as a social engineer's calculation but as part of a divinely ordered scheme. That in turn requires some account of Kirk's core religious principles and the way in which they shaped his political thought. What were those principles? And how did he make the transition, philosophically, from soulcraft to statecraft? *The Conservative Mind* offers some clues. Unfortunately, he was not a systematic thinker: quite the opposite. His project was to unsettle systems, to destroy ideology, to show the dangers of theory removed from reality. *The Conservative Mind* conveys that distrust of system in form as well as content, the book being haphazard, quirky, and idiosyncratic: a series of self-contained essays more than a monograph. That said, there is a spine holding the thing together. To be more precise, two central ideas form the backbone and it is to these we should now turn.

II

The first of these ideas is the doctrine of original sin. The second is Kirk's understanding of history. Let us examine each. Human depravity bulks large in *The Conservative Mind.* The book exhibits a very Tory insistence on the reality of evil, the folly of schemes of social and personal perfectibility, the inevitability of disappointment in a world of corruption. Pessimism is never far from the surface, as it was never far from the surface in his own life. (Kirk thought of himself primarily as a Christian stoic. His best writing reflects a conviction that the most perduring of the permanent things is sorrow. We would not be human, he thought, without "the inescapable emotion of grief.")[19] Yet this apprehension of man as an exile of Eden was not as gloomy as it sounds. Indeed Kirk used it to justify a politics not of despair but of hope. After all, to recognise the fall from grace was to recognise grace itself as salvifically necessary. Awareness of human weakness was the beginning of wisdom. No man-made city will last without the foundation of faith. The point was well expressed by G. K. Chesterton, a writer who appears only once in *The Conservative Mind* (even then as a thinker "outside the true line of descent in conservative ideas") but was nonetheless a writer Kirk much admired.[20] In his book *Saint Francis of Assisi,* Chesterton examined two seemingly similar dispositions: Greek nature-worship and delight in the ordered cosmos, and Saint Francis's enchantment with the beauty and bounty of God's world. Between them lay a distinction. The first was, at root, a celebration of the self. To assert the intelligibility of the cosmos was to assert the intelligence of the perceiving participant in it. It was to applaud the human capacity to decode, unaided, the deeper mystery and meaning of order and chaos. The second was a hymn of praise to creation itself and to the generosity of the Creator whose gift, unbidden and undeserved, it is. Chesterton noticed a paradox. The glorification of reason, which is ultimately a form of narcissism, always ends in unreason. It leads ineluctably to reigns of terror, to five year plans, to smashing of statues. Thus Chesterton:

> The Greeks ... started out with the idea of something splendidly obvious and direct: the idea that if a man walked straight ahead on the head road of reason and nature, he could come to no harm; especially if he was, as the Greek was, eminently enlightened and intelligent. And the case of the Greeks themselves is alone enough to illustrate the strange but certain fatality that attends upon this fallacy. ... The wisest men in the world set out to be natural; and the most unnatural thing in the world [the worship of the sun] is the very first thing they did ... The truth is that people who worship health cannot remain healthy. When Man goes straight he goes crooked. When he follows his nose he manages somehow to put his nose out of joint; and that in accordance with something much deeper in human nature than nature-worshippers could ever understand. It was the discovery of that deeper thing ... that constituted the conversion to Christianity. There is a bias in man like the bias in a bowl; and Christianity was the discovery of how to correct the bias and therefore hit the mark. There are many who will smile at the saying, but it is profoundly true to say that the glad good news brought by the Gospel was the news of original sin.[21]

For Kirk, too, to understand the fall was to see it, and not in any antinomian way, as a kind of liberation from self. "Original sin and aspiration toward the good are part of God's design," he wrote, one bound up with the other.[22] Alone of doctrines, it made sense of the rest, replacing rationalist optimism, naive and fatuous, with Christian hope, humbly confident that the old Adam, sin, would be crushed by the new Adam, Christ. This was not to disparage rationality. Unlike Luther, Kirk did not think reason "the devil's whore," a seductive mistress. Reason-worship was the problem, not reason. Kirk resembled Michael Oakeshott (to give one example of many thinkers in the conservative anti-idealist tradition) in his hostility to rationalism untempered by empiricism. Liberal experimentalism unrestrained by history and tradition was doomed to fail. Forgetting flawed human nature, the reason-worshipper becomes a sort of fundamentalist of the mind, convinced that intellect alone holds the key to wisdom. Eager for certitude, for system, for procrustean neatness, he forecloses on the mysterious, the unknowable, the things on heaven and earth undreamt of in Horatio's philosophy. The soul gets a dusty answer when hot for certainty—even religious certainty. To understand man's first disobedience was to understand the boundaries, not the boundlessness, of the human capacity to know.

This paradox—epistemological limitation as liberation—holds the first clue to the importance of religion for Kirk. The second is his understanding of history itself as the stage on which the story of sin and redemption is played out. History has meaning, intelligibility, but—precisely because we are limited in vision and wisdom—its truths do not yield themselves to easy apprehension. This, of course, is the central problem of faith. We look for the finger of God in history, Newman wrote, and we look in vain. How can we be sure to read the signs aright? How can we be sure they *are* signs? Why presume that history has lessons to teach of any kind, let alone Godly ones? These are troublesome questions and Kirk honestly admitted to difficulty in answering them. To read *The Conservative Mind* is to encounter an author in two minds about the prescriptive significance of the past. Indeed his attitude to history reveals a deeper dualism running through his thought, an uneasy balancing of the empirical and the idealist, the physical and the metaphysical. On the one hand, he was committed to history as descriptive of the distinctiveness and multifariousness of human experience. It chronicled the particular, the private, the unique, the unrepeatable, the contingent—in other words, precisely those realities that reveal man's moral agency, his freedom to make and mold his own world. That gave it especial claim to respect, almost veneration. But to recognise uniqueness and unrepeatabilty is to make a dangerous bargain with history. It estops the very possibility of prescriptive and predictive lessons at the very moment when the past seems ready to teach them. If, as L.P. Hartley famously wrote, "the past is a foreign country—they do things differently there," then history's very historicity, its completed action, is the point. Its lesson is that there is no lesson. Kirk resisted such a notion but his belief in historical contingency pointed him, willy-nilly, in that direction. As with original sin, he intuited, history forces us to be humble, to abandon narcissistic presentism, to leave behind the search for novelty, to realise there is nothing new under the sun. A line of W.B. Yeats comes to mind. He, too, saw history as terrain radically different from our own, a closed, scarcely knowable world that demanded almost mystical—certainly non-rational—engagement. Once, looking over the landscape of Ireland, he thought of its peasantry as "a people, a community bound together by imaginative possessions, by stories and poems which have grown out of its own life, and by a past of great passion which can still awaken the heart to imaginative action." Here was the world of mystery, local truth, private memory: the past made present but also closed off to outsiders. Kirk, too, understood history as the language of particular experience. To speak that past-centered language is to resist grand design, easy abstraction, overblown metaphysics. It is to prefer the customary, the conventional, the idiosyncratic—experience itself—as source of wisdom and mode of understanding. Claes Ryn has written recently that "ideological universalism that scorns historically formed societies is a potential source of unending war and great [disaster]."[23] That is as good a summary as any of Kirk's position. Humility is the key, hubris the danger. To know history is to know the limitation of knowledge itself.

Yet this poses a problem. To prefer experience over theory, the real over the ideal, is all very well, but that preference must itself be cloaked in theory to become intelligible or persuasive. Even empiricists must make sense of sense; even they cannot presume it will make sense on its own. To deny abstraction is itself an abstraction; to reject historical laws amounts to historical law. Kirk saw the contradiction. Distrusting *a priorism* was for him an *a priori* position. To disparage ideology was his ideology. This seems to injure his enterprise from the beginning—his own form of original sin, as it were—rendering it incoherent and absurd. He seems to look in two directions, insisting on the pastness of the past—"they do things differently there"—yet also on the permanence of its truths. To propose the latter is to deny that history, precisely as history, has any lessons at all. The past simply becomes an earlier version of a truth already known, an illustration of some insight achieved by philosophy or theology, history as a catalogue of examples, not itself the source of wisdom.

Kirk's answer was to resort to a notion of unchanging human nature, of eternal verities providentially enfolded in the endless particularities of time. For all its suspicion of metaphysics, *The Conservative Mind* is a paean to providence, a song of praise to grand design. The thinkers Kirk admired reasoned their way to reason's limits and sensed that sense alone made little sense. It is not an easy epistemology to carry off. Certainly the language of the book is loftily theodician. "History is the gradual revelation of a supreme design, often shadowy to our unblinking eyes, but subtle, resistless and beneficent ... God makes history through the agency of man;"[24] the "conservation of society [is] based upon the grand design of piety;"[25] the "foundation of human welfare is Divine providence;"[26] society "cures its own maladies, or effects its own adjustments, by a process at once natural and Providential;"[27] a "divine intent rules society as well as conscience, forging an eternal chain of duty of right and wrong which links great and obscure, living and dead ... Political problems at bottom, are religious and moral problems."[28] "Providence is the proper instrument for change, and the test of a statesman is his cognisance of the real tendency of providential social forces;"[29] it "acts through the instincts and intuitions of our feeble flesh, [demonstrating] that religion and politics are inseparable, that the decay of one must produce the decay of the other."[30] Examples need not be multiplied. We are not mere individuals, each assertion seems to claim, but exist, rather, as participants in a set of divinely ordained associations—the family, the community, the nation, the state, the communion of saints itself— that remove us from our baser selves and make us more authentically human. The clamor of history, impossible to hear unless the soul be properly attuned to it, is not a cacophony but harmony, a soul-sweet sound. *The Conservative Mind* takes its stand with both the mess and the music of history.

How does Kirk come to this balance? Recall his mid-western youth and the sources he used to read himself towards conversion. The springs of his faith were the early fathers, Augustine especially. Later he came to Newman. From both, and from others, he derived an understanding of history as theodrama, as a God-play in which the news of original sin was trumped by the greater news of the incarnation of Christ and the redemption of man by His death and resurrection. Augustine was the key. From him, Kirk saw the meaning of history, its central intelligibility, as the relationship between the sacred and profane entangled in human time. Two great cities—the City of God, the City of Man—are perpetually at war and it is this conflict that gives History its foundation and fulfillment. The earthly city "ruled by love of self and contempt of God" cannot live at peace with the heavenly city ruled "by love of God, even to the contempt of self." The world knows these cities not separately but radically entwined. Augustine was no Manichean, of course. His entire project was antimanichean. He saw history as a fusing of the sacred and profane, the pagan and the godly. Salvation history does not exist separately from secular history but is intimately bound up with it. This has important eschatological implications. Since the two cities "have been running their course mingling one with the other through all the changes of times from the beginning of the human race, and shall so move on together until the end of the world, when they are destined to be separated at the last judgment."[31]

It is hard to overstate the importance of this vision in Kirk's thinking. Later Augustinian writers—think of Luther in the sixteenth century or Bossuet in the seventeenth—saw the soul-drama in Augustine's notion of history but missed his subtle account of human, that is to say, historical, agency. Luther fell into the manichean trap Augustine avoided. His dualism is too dark, too dismissive of reason, too rooted in the Fall, too doubtful of the human capacity to build an earthly Jerusalem. Bossuet went in the opposite direction: too confident in his own power to interpret the divine will, too certain that the heavenly city could be identified with precise historical epochs, too indifferent to human agency and historical contingency, too cheerful, too naive, too panglossian. Kirk avoided these dangers by reaching back to the source—Augustine's denial that the heavenly city is linked with any particular era and his corollary assertion that every era, every historical moment, is shot through with divine as well as human significance. God's encounter with Man exists in time and through time and defines time itself. In that sense, the point of the past is that it is *not* past. History is not completed action but living reality. 'There are no dead," Kirk liked to say: there are the merely departed.[32] We are all full of ghosts, he quoted Lafcadio Hearn with approval in *The Sword of Imagination:* "all our emotions and thoughts and wishes, however changing and growing through the various seasons of life, are only compositions and recompositions of the sensations and desires of other folk, most of them dead people."[33] It was an admirably Augustinian insight. From Augustine, he derived the two pillars of his historical and moral imagination. The first was insistence on cosmic harmony, the key notion in Greek thought in the centuries before Christ, that was later appropriated and baptised by the Early Fathers in the centuries after. When Christopher Dawson described "Augustine's profound sense of the aethetic beauty of order and [his] doctrine that even the evil and suffering of the world find their aesthetic justification in the universal harmony of creation" he could have been describing Russell Kirk. The second debt was to Augustine's transformation of that ancient necessitarianism into a radically new commitment to human agency, to historical processes, to the possibility of human freedom within a theodician schema. It is precisely the latter that makes history possible: eternity enters time not to destroy but to transform it, to give it intelligibility, to make it *mean* something. To see the immutable in the mutable, the permanent in the impermanent: this is not to deny but to affirm the very solidity, the here-and-nowness, of history. The novelist Andrew Klavan makes the point well: "to be in this very moment as if it were forever is not to stop the work of life but to begin it afresh in celebration."[34] That gracious intrusion of eternity into time is precisely what time means.

We begin to see, then, the sources and significance of Kirk's vision of the past. He was Burkean but, before Burke, Augustinian. History is more than a passing show, a meaningless succession of empires and kings. It is revelation itself—the unceasing reality of God's life made visible in the lives of His people and in His created order on earth. Hidden in the chaos, visible only when passing clouds no longer obscure the sun, are harmony, stability, and peace; the signs of God's providential presence, the marks of true religion and its greatest gifts. Order was thus not social narcosis, a tyrant's dream of popular sedation. Much more profoundly, it was physical and metaphysical, earthly and heavenly, a meeting of the present and the past, a communion of the living and the dead. Burke understood this. So did Kirk. Interpreting him in *The Conservative Mind,* he painted a beguiling vision of true order:

> Society is immeasurably more than a political device. Knowing this, Burke endeavoured to convince his generation of the immense complexity of existence, the "mysterious incorporation of the human race." If society is treated as a simple contraption to be managed on mathematical lines—the Jacobins and the Benthamites and most other radicals so regarded it—then man will be degraded into something much less than a partner in the immortal contract which unites the dead, the living, and those yet unborn, the bond between God and man. Order in this world is contingent upon order above.[35]

This was not the Napoleonic or Marxist notion of religion as nonsense for the natives. Kirk drew from Burke truths that Burke left unsaid, truths, perhaps, he did not recognise himself. Notice how he teases out incarnational implications from this "immortal contract." Kirk recognised the patrisitic and medieval sources of Burke's intuition that the very particularity of custom and tradition contain glimpses of the divine, that the historical, the local, and the contingent, without losing their uniqueness are part of design, that the natural law is a participation in divine life. Augustine and Aquinas were the true progenitors of Burke's wisdom. Synthesising Aristotle and Augustine, St. Thomas offered a theodicy that respected human freedom and creativity while accommodating them within a scheme that acknowledged structure, design and purpose. The natural and the supernatural are inseparable as experienced truths. In the order of the universe, he wrote in *Summa Contra Gentiles,* natural things tend to participate in divine goodness as their ultimate end according to their proper nature. To discover the proper place which man occupies in the order of nature, to reflect this order in the human soul, to find God's intention in creating the world for man: that is the task of the philosopher, theologian,

historian, of every man.[36] "This, then, is the ultimate perfection
to which, according to philosophers, a human soul can arrive,"
he repeated in *De Veritate,* "namely, that in it the whole order of
the universe can be described with all its causes. In this also all
men find their ultimate end, which will be realised in the vision
of God."[37] Kirk took this as a motto. The scholastic schema
of human freedom within divine order was foundational to his
philosophy of history, his Christian Toryism, his understanding
of society as communion of the living, the dead, the still to be
born. He admired Burke but only because he was a Thomist.

This has a crucial consequence. The permanent things of
which Kirk so often spoke—order, harmony, even, for that matter, sorrow and grief—are, first and foremost, *things.* The gifts
of the Creator—those "bond[s] between God and Man" he calls
them—come to us as lived, experienced, sacramental realities.
They are incarnated in persons, cultures, traditions, ways of
life. God participates in our life, and we in the mysterious life
of God, in the ordinary and extraordinary dailyness of living.
Eternity is not simply more time: it is *all* time. The alpha and
omega, the beginning and end, are made visible in history and
through history in Christ and in His mystical body which is the
Church. Here, to give the point practical expression, is Kirk's
description of Burke's notion of rights:

> Burke's natural right is the Ciceronian *jus naturale,* reinforced
> by Christian dogma and English common law ... [For him],
> natural right is human custom conforming to Divine intent.
> He dislikes having to define it closely; natural right is an Idea
> comprehended only by the Divine intellect; precisely where
> it commences and terminates, we are no fit judges. To think
> that divine law could not operate without the sanction of
> our human legislation would be presumptuous. But so far
> as we can delineate the features of natural justice, it is the
> experience of mankind which supplies our knowledge of the
> Divine; and the experience of the species is taught to us not
> only through history, but through myth and fable, custom
> and prejudice.... Natural law can enter our cognition only so
> far as it is embodied in social prescription or charter. The rest
> remains a sealed book to us.[38]

The source is Augustine through Aquinas. Eternity enters time and transforms it. God is manifest in the material, the sacramental, the down-to-earth. He is not *outside* history, directing its ends as an omnicompetent conductor. He is *inside* history as its very action and source.

This is a key turn in the argument. As we have seen, the strongest objection to Kirk is that his veneration of the past, his respect for the prescriptive claims of tradition, is a kind of moral and cultural particularism, an elegant situation ethics that somehow tips the balance in favor of gentlemanly behavior. "What may be right on one occasion and for one man may be unjust folly for another man at a different time," he has Burke claim, evidently approving the idea. On the face of it, this seems an alarming return to that self-limiting historicism that understands behavior solely by reference to time and place and thus explaining good and evil also explains it away. It seems to empty history of moral moment precisely by emphasising the moment, not the morality. In fact, the argument does no such thing. To propose that "natural rights do not exist independent of circumstances" is not to provide sanctuary for the relativist: quite the contrary. To urge prudence in moral judgment is not to assert the plasticity of moral standards themselves. (Indeed it is to claim that prudence itself is one of those moral standards.) But Kirk's point is not so much about natural rights as about the way we grasp them circumstantially. Circumstance is the tangible way we grasp intangible truth. We know goodness by doing good; we know joy by being joyful. The metaphysical, in other words, is not anti-physical, a denial of here-and-nowness. It is what the physical *means.* To understand incarnation is to understand that history, experience, and culture derive worth not because Christ empties them but because, emptying himself, he embraces them, revealing their true meaning by revealing himself through them and with them and in them. The Word was made flesh and dwelt amongst us. He is amongst us still. History is not over. It has hardly begun.

Seen in this way, Kirk's Toryism is radically deeper than a desire to hold on to the best of the past, some kind of nostalgia for a world rapidly passing from sight. Rather, its attachment to *things*

—solid, tangible, sensible realities—is a commitment to other-worldly truths made present in the world as we know and grasp it today. Incarnation was at the heart of it. The conservative mind resisted system but it held fast to certain principles—the notion of divine providence, the importance of tradition and order, distrust of "sophisters and calculators," the inseparability of property and freedom, hostility to rapid change, the belief that political problems were at bottom religious and moral problems—and these, for all their seeming grandeur, could only be grasped in modest, prosaic, quotidian ways.[39] Material things matter. They matter because they speak spiritual truth. Tangible goods enshrine the intangible Good: property honestly earned and happily handed down; family life nurtured in shared sorrows and joys; trust bestowed in the shaking of hands; people hardy and independent while honourably reliant on others—parents, children, friends; local communities solving local problems, with the state not as a first but a last resort; history cherished in landscapes, churches, objects of beauty. All of society, all the doings of man, have sacramental significance. Kirk's project was to bring that significance to bear on a generation who had either forgotten or never known it.

Sacramentality—spiritual truth made known in material things, material things newly understood as spiritually significant—demands a radical re-ordering of mental categories. If Kirk's first debt was to Augustine, his second to Aquinas, his third to Burke, his last was to Newman. Throughout *The Conservative Mind,* as we have seen, an epistemology is a work, a way of knowing, a crafting of experience into intelligibility, a shaping of multifariousness into unity. Much of that epistemology derives from what Newman called the "Illative Sense." We have begun to realise, I hope, that Kirk's skepticism about rationalism was not irrational. His prejudice in favor of prejudice was not prejudicial. His defense of dogma was a form of humility, recognition of the limitation of pure reason in the face of the deepest longings of man. Some words from Newman, and Kirk's understanding of them, constitute the epistemological center of the book. They provide a bridge between the various oppositions that define his project—between the physical and metaphysical, the particular and universal, the mutable and immutable. They repay quotation:

If, then, we do not form our lives, or even our sciences, upon a logic of words or a museum of specimens, what exactly is the source of our first principles, of our governing motives? "It is the mind that reasons, and that controls its own reasonings [Newman writes in *The Grammar of Assent*], not any technical apparatus of words and propositions. This power of judging and concluding, when in its perfection, I call the Illative Sense." It is [Kirk exegesises] the combined product of intuition, instinct, imagination, and long and intricate experience. Yet [it] is not infallible in any man ... We must correct our own particular Illative Sense by reference to Authority; for Authority, which is a sort of filtered collective Illative Sense, provides the purgation of individual error. As Newman wrote in his essay on John Keble (1846), "Conscience is an authority; the Bible is an authority; such is the Church; such is Antiquity; such are the words of the wise, such are hereditary lessons; such are ethical truths; such are historical memories, such are legal saws and state maxims; such are proverbs; such are sentiments, presages, and prepossessions."[40]

Thus through a hundred winding ways, we emerge from shadows and types to reality. Long experience, intricate reasoning, even a false start or two, will build us our cathedral. A man who is wise will use it to mount to heaven.

The debt to Newman transforms the book. No longer simply an expositor of patristic or scholastic thought, Kirk is now involved in an encounter with ideas that have shaped modernity—even postmodernity—in the last century or so. Consider the context. Newman wrote as nineteenth century science began to claim for itself an epistemological high-ground that excluded, as a matter of course, the subjectivity of the perceiver in favor of the objectivity of the world. Radically empirical, committed to verifiability, convinced that absolute reality may be made known to those who seek it, the scientist sought the extinction of the subject and, as one recent theologian has well described it, "the emergence of the objective world in its full splendor."[41] That agenda—more philosophical than scientific—was given heft in the early twentieth century by the likes of Carnap, Russell, Ayer and Wittgenstein, zealous positivists all. For the early Wittgenstein, a recent biographer has written, "as the self withdraws, the world in itself emerges. When subjectivity ... vanishes into absolute privacy, reality remains in splendid objectivity."[42] But this quest for splendid objectivity did not last long. Logical positivism held only brief sway, soon to be challenged by thinkers such as Martin Heidegger who proposed that the subject remained a legitimate locus of philosophical inquiry. By mid-century, Heideggerian phenomenology offered a very different account of knowing, the perceiver now restored to something like centrality, perception itself understood as freighted with cultural, historical, personal significance. Objectivity, newly problematic, began to seem unattainable, even undesirable. To be sure, the epistemological naiveté of scientism—hard fact as alone worthy of consideration—was sometimes replaced by historicism equally naive, with writers such as Thomas Kuhn (for example) discovering, but then overemphasising, non-scientific elements in scientific change. Still, Kuhn was typical of many in drawing attention to the multiple social and personal commitments embedded in scientific (and all other) accounts of the world. Of course, this was not without hazard. This legitimate and necessary return to subjectivity ran the danger of anti-rationalism—the possibility of any objective truth dismissed—and of solipsism—the perceiving self incapable of perceiving anything other than self-created worlds. That was a risk most mid-twentieth century phenomenologists were prepared to embrace.

Perhaps this is too bald a summary of nineteenth and twentieth century philosophy. Still, it surely has a place in Kirk's story. Newman was a strikingly modern thinker and, understanding him, Kirk was able to offer a newly persuasive account of history that appealed beyond the usual denominational or philosophical categories. History's emphasis on the local, the finite, the culturally unique could now be seen as part of this new phenomenology of man. All our ways of knowing, caught up as they are in the complexity of the personal and the particular, the inescapable here-and-nowness of our lives, are not to be seen as forms of limitation but as radical apprehension of the variety, indeed of the infinitude, of things. It was a creative response to created order; a new way of perceiving the intelligibility of the world.

III

Thus we approach the heart of the matter. William F. Buckley, Jr. has observed that Kirk disliked the term "conservative," preferring to describe himself a "realist." It was a good instinct, one that other conservatives should take to heart. But, realist or conservative, he was also curiously modern-modern enough to speak a language of signs and symbols, of culture and cult, of intuition and imagination, of reason's power and reason's limits. With him, an intellectual man of parts, Edmund Burke seems not so very far from Edmund Husserl, Froude closer than might be thought to Freud. Such versatility should silence his critics for a time. All the same, the modernism should not obliterate a deeper realism. He was a realist, yes, but what was the reality he claimed to know? It was partly—only partly—a Johnsonian insistence on the solidity of things. Realism has its small satisfactions—refuting Berkeley by stubbing at a stone, kicking at Kantians by refusing to penetrate their impenetrabilities. We should not willingly give up these pleasures. Nor, however, should we become addicted to them. Honest empiricism may keep our feet on the ground but without idealism, without some metaphysical principle, we would deny ourselves the sky above and the sun beyond. If Kirk held to solid things, he also held, more firmly, to the solidity of their meaning. Their deeper intelligibility had to do with order and freedom, without which conservative schemes—any human scheme, for that matter—may not survive. "Order, in society, is the harmonious arrangement of classes and functions which guards justice and obtains willing consent to law and ensures that we all shall be safe together," he wrote in *Redeeming the Time.* Likewise, to assert "freedom as an absolute, somehow divorced from order, [is to] repudiate our heritage of practical liberty and expose ourselves to the peril of absolutism." This was well said but it was not, for all that, very different from Bentham or Mill. The difference came from the source. Order was a thing altogether more compelling than harmonious social arrangements. "In the moral realm," he wrote, "it is the realising of a body of transcendent norms—indeed a hierarchy of norms and standards—which give purpose to existence and motive to conduct."[43] This existential purpose, to summon Aquinas once again, is to discern the place man occupies in the order of nature, to reflect this reality in the human soul, to find God's intention in creating the world for man, and to live in accord with the divine will. Order and freedom were nothing less than manifestations of the life of God in the earthly life of man.

This does not make God a Tory any more than it made non-Tories ungodly. Crude schemas of that sort are more Bossuet than Kirk. It is, however, to place his stout, sensible, empirical, system-resisting conservatism into a metaphysical mold without which it might have collapsed into cultural nostalgia or social snobbery. In manner and appearance Kirk was patrician but his head and heart were humble. So, too, *The Conservative Mind.* The book's confident erudition is at the service of a more modest piety. Kirk's theme is what happens when men *try* to do what they cannot do—what happens to them and their world when they come to believe themselves masters of a destiny they cannot control. That said, his own project could not have been more ambitious. Not a moral philosopher, still less a theologian, he attempted nevertheless a kind of theology of history in which he sought to explore, in time and through time, the meaning of time itself. That meaning—call it the purpose or the end of time—will become clear only at the end of time. In the meantime, we may discern, in ways obscure but not wholly invisible, the hidden hand of God.

History, in this sense, does not have utility. We do not learn from it, the better (as Santayana has it) to avoid its mistakes. That is to forget another truth—the reality of original sin. Yet the past is a place of discovery precisely because it represents not finished or completed action but action awaiting completion, human striving groaning for its last perfection at the end of time. History is the *memory* of the continuing presence of permanent things in a world fallen but redeemed. To forget it is to forget ourselves. To abandon *memory* is to abandon spiritual truths made manifest in material things. Words of the poet Wendell Berry come to mind. Describing a country funeral where the old gather one more time to say farewell to one of their own, then return, diminished, to fields themselves soon to pass from

view, he ponders the meaning of "memories doomed to die."[44]
What does keeping faith mean? Where should our loyalty lie—
with an unrecoverable past or a world still to come? The two, he
realised, were not separable, one somehow existing at the expense
of the other. What we owe the future, he says

> is not a new start, for we can only begin
> with what has happened. We owe the future
> the past, the long knowledge
> that is the potency of time to come.
> That makes of a man's grave a rich furrow.
> The community of knowing in common is the seed
> of our life in this place. There is not only
> no better possibility, there is
> no other, except for chaos and darkness,
> the terrible ground of the only possible
> new start. And so as the old die and the young
> depart, where shall a man go who keeps
> the memories of the dead, except home
> again, as one would go back after a burial,
> faithful to the fields, lest the dead die
> a second and more final death.

Kirk, too, feared that second and more final death. He pre-
sumed, however, to offer an answer to it. The answer to death, of
course, is life: life here, life now, life in the world to come; the life of
the mind, the life of the heart, the life of the spirit; the corporate
life of the living, the dead, the yet-to-be-born. For Kirk himself, it
was a life richly lived—in Piety Hill, among books and family and
the laughter of friends, fields and hills leading the eye to horizons
beyond and histories behind. It was the life, in other words, of a
man of faith and a man of God. For those who never knew him but
who wish to have some share in it, and for those who seek participation in that greater life of which any man's life is only a portion, *The
Conservative Mind* is a good place to start.

[1] Delightfully, Kirk called his first university president a "chickenologist."

[2] Russell Kirk, *The Sword of Imagination: Memoirs of a Half century of Literary Conflict* (Grand Rapids, Ml: Eerdmans, 1995) p. 233.

[3] Ibid., p. 230-231.

[4] Quoted in Christina Scott, A *Historian and his World:* A *Life of Christopher Dawson* (Transaction Publishers: New Brunswick, 1999) p. 63.

[5] Quoted, Ibid.

[6] Jacques Bossuet, "Politics Drawn from the Very Words of Holy Scripture," in *Introduction to Contemporary Civilisation in the West* (Columbia University Press: New York, 1960) p. 874.

[7] Paul Claudel, *The Tidings Brought to Mary: L'Annonce Faite a Marie,* trans. Wallace Fowlie (Gateway Press: Chicago, 1960) p. 17.

[8] Russell Kirk, *The Conservative Mind: From Burke to Eliot* (Regnery: Chicago, 1953) p. 251.

[9] Kirk, *The Sword of Imagination,* p. 275.

[10] Ibid., p. 274.

[11] Ibid., p. 425.

[12] Ibid.

[13] Kirk, *The Conservative Mind,* p. 335.

[14] Ibid., p. 191.

[15] Ibid., p. 49. This is Kirk's reading of his hero, Edmund Burke.

[16] Ibid., p. 58.

[17] Ibid., p. 59.

[18] Ibid., p. 31.

[19] Ibid., p. 81.

[20] Ibid., p. 359.

[21] G. K. Chesterton, *Saint Francis of Assisi* (St. Hugh's Press: London, 1944) p. 27-29.

[22] Kirk, *The Conservative Mind,* p. 30.

[23] Claes Ryn, *America the Virtuous: Crisis of Democracy and the Quest for Empire* (New Brunswick: Transaction, 2003) quoted in Paul Roberts, "A Recipe for Tyranny," *Times Literary Supplement,* (January 2, 2004) p. 10.

[24] Kirk, *The Conservative Mind,* p. 36.

[25] Ibid., p. 25.

[26] Ibid., p. 27.

[27] Ibid., p. 105.

[28] Ibid., p. 7.

[29] Ibid., p. 8.

[30] Ibid., p. 118-119

[31] Augustine of Hippo, quoted in Christopher Dawson, "St. Augustine and the City of God," in Dawson, *Dynamics of World History* (ISI Books: Wilmington, DE, 2002), p. 325.

[32] Kirk, *The Sword of Imagination,* p. *114.*

[33] Ibid., p. 19

[34] "Two Lessons in why it is a wonderful life," *The Star-Ledger,* (Newark, NJ: December 24, 2003).

[35] Kirk, *The Conservative Mind,* p. *60.*

[36] See Andrew Woznicki, "The Christian Humanism and Adequate Personalism of Karol Wojtyla" in *Pope John Paul II Lecture Series,* College of St. Thomas Centennial 1885-1985 (College of St. Thomas: St. Paul, MN, 1985) p. 38.

[37] Ibid.

[38] Kirk, *The Conservative Mind,* p. *44.*

[39] Ibid., p. 7.

[40] Ibid., p. 249.

[41] Thomas Guarino, "Contemporary Theology and Scientific Rationality" in *Studies in Religion/Sciences Religieuses 22/3* (1993) p. 312.

[42] Fergus Kerr, quoted ibid.

[43] Russell Kirk, *Redeeming the Time* (Wilmington, DE: ISI Books, 1998) p. 33.

[44] Wendell Berry, "At a Country Funeral" in *Collected Poems (*1957-1982), (New York: North Point Press, 1987) p. 159.

Russell Kirk

Chesterton's Educational Vision

— *The following is an excerpt from the paper delivered by Dr. Karl Schmude at the G. K. Chesterton Institute Conference in Buenos Aires, October 2006, published in* The Defendant, *December 2006.*

The true realist is the true romantic, for he has not mistaken fantasy or fashion for fact—for what is perennially true and important and life-giving. He has recognised actual things, and actual people, as they are, and seen them as freshly created and radiantly real. This is notably evident, I think, in Chesterton's work of social philosophy, *What's Wrong with the World,* which is where he offers, perhaps, his most extended reflection on education and its broader effects.

I would like to focus on one chapter from that book, the chapter entitled "The Broken Rainbow," in which Chesterton deals with the subject of colour. He was an artist as well as a writer, having studied at an art school in London in his early years and producing sketches and cartoons and chalk drawings throughout his life. And so he readily looked at colour as a sign and reflection of a deeper condition—in this case, what he sees as wrong with education. He compares what he calls the present "chaos of colour" to a "shattered rainbow," and he suggests that this disorder of colour derives from a lack of philosophy or right intellectual order. By contrast, says Chesterton, the miniature pictures painted by medieval artists communicated the objective importance and value of colour. The old artist, he notes, "contrived to convey an impression that colours really were significant and precious things, like jewels and talismanic stones. The colour was often arbitrary; but it was always authoritative." As a result, it was treated with a respect that is not accorded by the contemporary artist. What educators now need to do, suggested Chesterton, is "to teach people to relish colours like liqueurs. They have the heavy business of turning drunkards into wine tasters. If ever the twentieth century succeeds in doing this, it will almost catch up with the twelfth." (Chesterton loved to turn the notion of "progress" on its head and, with good humour, throw it into the face of his contemporaries!) His conclusion is that the sheer abundance of colours in our time, combined with the loss of a colour scheme, is "a pretty perfect parable of all that is wrong with am modern ideals and especially with our modern education. It is the same with ethical education, economic education, every sort of education." We are, said Chesterton, "like children who have mixed all the colours in the paint-box together and lost the paper of instructions." Or, as he put it in another chapter of *What's Wrong with the World,* the problem for modern man is not that he's lost his way. Man has always lost his way. The problem for modern man is that now he has lost his address.

When we come to the question of how Chesterton's affirmation of objective reality shaped his attitude to education, we find something of a paradox. On the one hand, he exalted the importance of education—as being nothing less than "the soul of a society as it passes from one generation to another." On the other hand, he held a dim view of formal education, and was especially dismissive of intellectuals as a class." In his autobiography, he described "education" as the "period during which I was being instructed by somebody 1 did not know, about something I did not want to know." The basis of his view seemed to be that modern schemes of education dealt far too much with theories rather than things, and that it was therefore too divorced from reality to be of any practical value. No doubt he would have readily echoed the comment of Mark Twain, that he never let his schooling interfere with his education. On his first tour of the United States, Chesterton gave a lecture in Detroit on "The Ignorance of the Educated." His thesis, according to a newspaper report at the time, was that "the besetting evil of all educated people is that they tend to substitute theories for things." The uneducated man never makes this mistake. He states the simple fact that he sees a German drinking beer: he does not say "there is a Teuton consuming alcohol." For this reason, Chesterton saw that a chief task of education is not to learn things, but to unlearn them— "to unlearn all the weariness and wickedness of the world and to get back into that state of exhilaration we all instinctively celebrate when we write by preference of children and of boys."

Unlike many of his school friends (at St. Paul's in London), Chesterton did not attend university but went to art school. He did not regret this choice, not least because the experience of art school fostered his visual imagination and creativity, which proved such a bonus when he became a writer. (We have already seen his deep sensitivity to colour, and his awareness of its importance not only in art but more broadly, and his writings are full of the most graphic pieces of description.) Yet his avoidance of university also spared him from mingling with the Intelligentsia, of whom he said in his autobiography that, while it thought a great deal about thinking, it did not actually think. Thus, to spell out the paradox I have been seeking to outline, Chesterton was in favour of education, but not the prevailing modes or schemes of education. He valued "education" as the transmission of "the soul of a society," or, as he put it in one essay, "the realisation of a permanent simplicity that abides behind all civilisations,..." and equips a person to resist the "latest fads of culture, the latest sophistries of anarchism [that] will carry us away if we are uneducated: we shall not know how very old are all new ideas." We will fail to appreciate so many things that are "not at all new as an idea; ...only new as an idolatry."

THE TEST OF LITERATURE
John Henry Newman's holy imagings

— The following commentary by Bernard Manzo was published in the July 30, 2010 issue of the Times *Literary Supplement.*

John Henry Newman once remarked that he had "no tendency to be a saint .... Saints are not literary men, they do not love the classics, they do not write tales." Yet he did not see the telling of "tales" as a merely "literary" matter, and his efforts to imagine the holiness of the saints sustained his spiritual life. He could describe the Roman Catholic Church as "the poet of her children; full of music to soothe the sad and control the wayward—wonderful in story for the imagination of the romantic; rich in symbol and imagery...her very being is poetry."

In 1833, not long before the Oxford Movement began in earnest, Newman composed a poem relating a "dream" in which he "envied those who had the presence bright / Of gifted Prophet and strong-

hearted Saint, / Whom my heart loves, and Fancy strives to paint."
He encounters a stranger who, despite being "so meek in mien, / It
seemed untrue," speaks on occasion with a "stern force," provok-
ing suspicions of "deep craft" or "hidden pride"; but "Then came a
voice, St. Paul is at thy side." The poem suggests that what his "Fancy
strives to paint" is not adequate to the reality (he does not recognise
the saint), even as it attempts to realise the presence of a saint. With
its echoes of George Herbert (the corrective "voice" at the close, the
revelation of holiness in something unexpectedly plain), the poem
locates itself in the Anglican tradition, yet it prefigures some of the
conflicts that Newman would have with the English Church.

His visions of the saints and Fathers of the a early Church—in
his polemical accounts of the lives of the Fathers for the *British
Magazine*, and in the series of *Lives of the English Saints* brought
out under his aegis—were an affirmation of ideals of holiness radically contrary to some of the presuppositions of his culture. Newman saw himself as recovering the Catholic heritage of the English
Church; his opponents saw him as virtually a traitor. The notion of
a saint "so meek" as to be suspected of "craft" resembles that which
Newman would present in his sermon on "*Wisdom and Innocence*"
(1843)—a sermon that Charles Kingsley, accusing Newman himself
of craftiness, would attack as a license to dishonesty.

Newman responded to the attack by attempting to portray his
own mind, "that living intelligence, by which I write, and argue, and
act," and by recapitulating the development of his religious opinions. In his *Apologia pro Vita Sua* (1864), he employed the utmost
rhetorical skill to dispel an impression created, in part, by that skill:
to dissipate the prevalent view of him as a cunning rhetorician
who made use of specious arguments to support the falsehoods of
"Romish" religion, and to explain, by conveying his vision of the
Catholic Church, how he came to accept its claims, and to join its
communion in 1845. He sought to provide an image of his mind
that would be a master interpretation of his works; reactions to that
image varied, and still vary.

He had greater success (though not complete success) in persuad-
ing his contemporaries of his own honesty than of the credibility of

his Church or the credibility of his reasons for submitting to it ("He maybe an honest man, but his system is dishonest," wrote Sir James Fitzjames Stephen in *Fraser's Magazine*.) For those more sympathetic to Newman, however, the *Apologia* told the story of someone willing to abandon everything for the truth. He strictly limited himself to a discussion of his "religious opinions," avoiding any mention of his conduct, or of his spiritual life, yet his single-minded pursuit of the truth could itself be seen as an exhibition of heroic virtue.

The *Apologia* has, in many ways, determined how the writings and the life of Newman have been interpreted—not least for those prepared to see him as a saint. It portrayed the "living intelligence," showing the gradual movement of the mind towards certain beliefs, and how that movement was felt and experienced. Newman declared that he had a "preference of the Personal to the Abstract" as a mode of explanation. He saw ethos and doctrine as correlative, and, when examining a body of thought, he sought always to discern the spirit that animated it. He saw acts of thought as personal acts, reflecting the "moral temperament" of the thinker, and he considered "paper logic" to be a crude representation of the living mind, doubting whether acts of faith could be fully analysed: "no analysis is subtle and delicate enough to represent adequately the state of mind under which we believe, or the subjects of belief as they are presented to our thoughts." To represent this activity of mind, Newman turned to fiction, with both of his novels, *Loss and Gain* (1848) and *Callista* (1855), portraying characters coming gradually to faith. That these individuals do so in circumstances likely only to impede such a movement brings out the connection of belief to the "moral temperament."

Newman distinguished between "real" and "unreal" ways of looking at the world, and the distinction had to do not only with the content of ideas, but with the way in which they could be held. For an idea to be "real" it had to be possible to live by it. To be real as a person, one had to live in accordance with what one professed. It was possible to tell what people really believed by what they did; and people did not always explicitly recognise the ideas that actuated them: "while all men have a reason ... not all men can give a reason." In his own efforts to be "real," Newman sought, again and again, to give adequate expression to his ideas, to say what it was he really thought; his concern for "reality" was the concern of someone preoccupied with problems of expression. To look at the world in a real way was to discern which ideas were really operative in the world.

Newman saw Christianity as ultimately expressive of a single living idea, "integral view." The Scriptures were a record of an idea that lived in the fullness in the minds of the Apostles , whose writings, though inspired by God, were comparable to the other forms of literature ("St. Paul's epistles then, I consider to be literature in a real and true sense, as personal, as rich in reflection and emotion, as Demosthenes or Euripides.") As a collection of occasional writings, the Scriptures could not be taken to express definitively the idea at the core of Christianity ("a man of genius cannot go about with his genius in his hand: in an Apostle's mind a great part of his knowledge is from the nature of the case latent or implicit.") The idea, in any case, was so complex as to transcend definitive expression. It was the inexhaustible fullness of this idea that justified the search for mystical senses of the Scriptures, the use of all the devices of interpretation: one could go beyond the "letter" because no mere letter could contain the fullness of the truth.

The progress of the Church in history—its slow accumulation of dogmas—was a process of development that brought out what was implicit in the original vision. That vision—the revelation of God at the core of Christianity—was "not enlarged, if propositions are added, nor impaired if they are withdrawn"; for if they should be added, this would be with "a view of conveying that one integral view, not of amplifying it," and that view "does not consist in them; they are but specimens and indications of it." The idea transcends all its "indications." "One thing alone has to be impressed on us by Scripture, the Catholic idea, and in it they are all included." To consider these "indications" to be complete would be a form of bigotry, for the dogmas are "after all, but symbols of a Divine fact, which far from being compassed by those very propositions would not be exhausted, nor fathomed, by a thousand." Those propositions might be correct, but they could not be adequate.

For Newman, ideas became influential when apprehended by the imagination. "The heart is commonly reached not through reason; but through the imagination." To realise holiness, one had to imagine it first and to live by faith was, to some extent, to live by the imagination, to see oneself "in an immense unbounded system with a height above and a depth beneath." To reflect on the Scriptures, one had to invent. "If we would meditate on any passage of the gospel history, we must insert details indefinitely many, in order, to meditate at all; we must fancy motives, feelings, meanings, words, acts, as our connecting links between fact and fact as recorded." By providing clear images of holiness, even legends of the saints could be beneficial. "By the sympathy of many minds, and the concert of many voices, and the lapse of many years, a certain whole figure is developed with words and actions, a history and a character, which is indeed but the portrait of the original ... in its particulars more or less the, work of the imagination."

Legends of this kind were among the less reputable works of the imagination (Newman scandalised some of his contemporaries by his qualified defence of them), and they invited questions about how (or whether) the imagination could be controlled and how one could be sure it was in conformity with reality. Newman was well aware of the peril of becoming besotted with figments. In his *Lectures on Certain Difficulties felt by Anglicans in CatholicTeaching* (1850), he spoke of Anglo-Catholics as inhabiting an imaginary world: "as in fairy tales, the magic castle vanishes when the spell is broken, and nothing is seen but the wild heath, the barren rock, and the forlorn sheep-walk." In his *Lectures on the Present Position of Catholics in England* (1851) he described the popular English tradition of anti-Catholicism as a mishmash of legends. So when could the imagination be trusted?

Newman was willing to make high claims for the capacity of the imagination to reveal ultimate realities. In an essay on "Poetry, with reference to Aristotle's Poetics" written for the *London Review* in 1829, he maintains that "the poetical mind ... full of the eternal forms of beauty" reveals "that perfection ... to which as a limit the present system of Divine Providence actually tends" and that "Revealed Religion" is "especially poetical"—so much so that "with

Christians, a poetical view of things is a duty." Yet he insists that this capacity is conditional on a "right moral state of heart." Newman presents much the same idea in a poem on "Angelic Guidance" written a few years afterwards, in which, wondering whether he has received intimations from an "unearthly Friend," he hesitates about crediting the vision. "Were I Christ's own, then fitly might call / That vision real; for to the thoughtful mind / That walks with Him, he half unveils his face"; yet such assurance is not for "earth stain'd souls."

The poetry of Newman can be faulted with being too little responsive to the visionary. Seeking to propagate correct doctrine, Newman subjects his visions to strict control; and his verses observe a strict metrical regularity which can, on occasion, become jingling. "The Dream of Gerontius" is something of an exception: in that poem, squaring dogma with Scripture, he calls on his powers of interpretative imagination. Newman was at his most inventive when working with received, sacred images. Yet he could perceive religious impulses in imaginative literature that did not have patent religious designs. In an essay written for the *British Critic* in 1839, in which he sought to make sense of the Oxford Movement as a cultural phenomenon, he referred to Scott and Coleridge as "indications of what was secretly going on in the minds of men": individuals who gave partial expression to what would be more perfectly expressed by the Tractarians. (Stephen Prickett has claimed that the "Oxford Movement was a religious flowering of the English Romantic movement.")

Newman went on—thinking probably more of Keble than of Scott or Coleridge—to suggest that "the taste for poetry of a religious kind has in modern times in a certain sense taken the place of the deep contemplative spirit of the early Church," so that poetry "is our mysticism": "so far as any two characters of mind tend to penetrate below the surface of things and to draw men away from the material to the invisible world, so far they may certainly be said to answer the same end." In an essay on "The Mission of Saint Benedict" in 1856, he remarked on how Benedictine spirituality exhibited a "poetical frame of mind" wholly distinct from a "scientific" consciousness whereas "the aim of science is to get a hold of things ... to master them, or to be superior to them," the "poetical frame of mind" requires:

as its primary condition, that we should not put ourselves above
the objects in which it resides, but at their feet; that we should
feel them to be above and beyond us, that we should look up to
them, and that, instead of fancying that we can comprehend
then, we should take for granted that we are surrounded and
comprehended by them ourselves.

If "poetical" experience resembles contemplation, then does
contemplation supersede poetry? Not long after becoming a Catholic (and with something of the zeal of a convert) Newman would
claim that "poetry is the refuge of those who have not the Catholic
Church, for the church herself is the most sacred and august of poets." By conceiving of the "literary" as an image of the personal, he
could see it as a substitute for something that existed more fully elsewhere, or even as a usurpation. In a sermon preached at St Mary's,
Oxford, on the "Danger of Accomplishments," he claimed that responses to imaginative literature separate "feeling and acting," because in responding "we have nothing to do; we read, are affected,
softened or roused, and that is all"; yet "God has made us feel in
order that we may go on to act in consequence of feeling; if then we
allow our feelings to be excited without acting upon them, we do
mischief to the moral system within us." In a sermon on "Unreal
Words," he claimed that "literature is almost in its essence unreal,
for it is the exhibition of thought disjoined from practice." In *The
Idea of a University* (1852), Newman affirmed that the cultivation
of the intellect was an intrinsic good, an end in itself, but he warned
against a religion of "imagination and sentiment" in which us experience could be referred only to the "constitution of our nature,"
rather than to its transcendent nature. Where "conscience, which
our intimates a Lawgiver"—referring to God—comes to be interpreted merely as a "moral taste or sentiment, which has not sanction beyond the constitution of our nature," there arises the danger
of discarding from Christianity "the theological, the mysterious,
the spiritual" and of retaining only "the morally or esthetically
beautiful," to produce a condition of "intense self-contemplation"
in which "conscience" becomes merely "self-respect." Literary pur-
suits were to be regarded as an innocent diversion, connected to the
perfection of nature; but nature was not grace.

The Parochial and Plain Sermons of Newman were very much a chastening of the imagination and an affirmation of the supremacy of the conscience in the religious life. Ian Ker, Newman's biographer, has commented on the "ruthlessly realistic spirituality" of these sermons, which present faith as a form of obedience, and as sustaining, and sustained by, a form of life. They insist that the life of grace is a matter of acquiring a discipline of seeing the supernatural in and through the ordinary, carrying out everyday duties, with grace becoming present in humdrum efforts. The "ruthless" aspect of the sermons is in their exploration of the ways in which these efforts can be evaded; and they attempt to interpret various attitudes towards the world—ranging from a comfortable worldliness, to a rigid scrupulosity about lesser duties, to a highly emotional sense of being liberated from the "law" by "faith"—precisely as evasions of the requirements of the conscience. The sermons explore how the way one thinks relates to the way one lives; faith, for Newman, implies decorum, as it belongs to a way of living.

Newman was concerned with how ideas lived in the mind and with how they were lived out, but he did not feel that one could explain belief reductively by referring it solely to the character of the believer, and he considered ideas to possess an intrinsic force and a capacity for development such that "doctrine may be rather said to use the minds of Christians, than be used by them." In controversy, one of his most frequent ploys was to show that his opponents argued in a manner determined by principles of which they were not aware; and in his *Apologia* he interpreted the development of his own views in much the same way, attempting to identify the principles that had ruled his thinking throughout his changes of religious allegiance. His ability to trace implications, coupled with his keen satirical sense (an almost irritable sensitivity to incongruity), made him a formidable controversialist. Yet his sense of ideas as "using" minds limited, him as a novelist.

While he is concerned, in his novels, with the ways in which beliefs are acquired and lived out, his characters do not feel fully individuated. They exist not as independent centres of life, but as illustrations. This matters less in *Loss and Gain*—taken up as it is mostly with conversation, in which the inconsistencies of various religious views are exposed—than in *Callista*, which, working up early Christian stories of the martyrs into a historical romance, seeks to present more visceral emotional states, greater extremes of sanctity and wickedness. In his *Apologia*, Newman recognised in himself a tendency to "rest in the thought of two and two only absolute and luminously self-evident beings, myself and my Creator." For Newman, the religious life seemed often a matter of trying to reconcile a sense of the presence of God, conferred by interior experience, with an experience of the world that seemed "simply to give the lie to that great truth, of which my whole being is for fun." The truth had to be discovered in himself, and protected. "If I looked into a mirror, and did not see my face, I should have the sort of feeling which actually comes upon me, when I look into this living busy world, and see no reflexion of its Creator .... Were it not for this voice, speaking so clearly in my conscience and my heart, I should be an atheist, or a pantheist, or a polytheist when I looked into the world." The imagination had to be subordinated to the conscience, for the conscience was the sole "reflexion" of God in the world; and the imagination, working with the conscience, had to be asserted against a world that obscured the truth.

Newman saw in the Catholic Church a collective life to which he wished to entrust himself wholly, though this desire for surrender coexisted in him with great strength of will, force of character, and with a consciousness (sometimes anguished) of isolation. His awareness of the difficulties of communication, and his loneliness, made friendship all the more important to him—to the extent that he could envisage, as a feature of life in heaven, an "eternal and direct communion ... with our friends around us, whom at present we know only through the medium of sense, by precarious and partial channels, which give us little insight into their hearts." His friendships were frequently centred on the ideal, the "Catholic idea," and he consistently sought a quasi-monastic form of life. Some commentators have seen something questionable or excessive in his friendships: Geoffrey Faber wondered whether they might have had "a homosexual root," and Frank M. Turner suggested that Newman "pursued Catholicism" to "legitimate a monastic life" dwelling "among other celibate males and outside the company of women." More recently, though, John Cornwell, in *Newman's Unquiet Grave* has seen in Newman's friendships a rejection of the "isolation and inner reserve that went with the culture of Catholic clericalism," and has claimed that his life affords a "lesson in the scope for mature, intimate friendship within a life of priestly celibacy." Yet Newman saw the spiritual life as a lonely one. In the winter of 1835, staying with his closest friend, Richard Hurrell Froude, who was then near death, Newman prepared for publication a sermon in which he spoke of how those who seek to devote themselves to Christ "now and then, as they walk their way ... see glimpses of God's work in others; they take hold of them awhile in the dark, but soon lose them; they hear their voices, but cannot find them." In the public pronouncement, one can detect a private mourning.

Newman went on to suggest that the memory of the saints could be a remedy for loneliness. "Who are to sympathise with us in our joys and sorrows? who are to spur us on by the example of their own success? St. Paul answers us—the cloud of witnesses of former days." The beatification of Newman is a principal object of Pope Benedict's visit to Britain in September. The ceremony will underwrite the confidence shared by many Christians that Newman has joined that "cloud of witnesses," though opinions on the nature and meaning of his witness continue to vary. He remains—for all his efforts to portray his "living intelligence"—a somewhat elusive, enigmatic figure. As he himself once said, "Hid are the Saints of God."

Blessed John Henry Newman

UK Hearts Opened to Message of Faith and Reason

— *The following articles appeared in the November 2010 issue of* Challenge *magazine on the occasion of Pope Benedict XVI to England for the beatification of Cardinal Newman.*

UK Jubilant Over Cardinal Newman's Beatification

— *The following account of Pope Benedict's Beatification Mass by Edward Pentin first appeared in* ZENIT.

A rainbow appeared over Cofton Park as Pope Benedict arrived for the beatification mass of Cardinal John Henry Newman, the nineteenth century English theologian who has had a significant influence on the Holy Father's own life. Large numbers of faithful from all over the country and further afield had braved the rain and made their way from the very early hours of the morning the venue near Birmingham, not far from Cardinal Newman's resting place in Rednal. This was a particularly special beatification mass: not only was it the only such Mass celebrated by Pope Benedict XVI, but it was also the first beatification of an Englishman for centuries.

The Holy Father arrived in the popemobile and, as in Glasgow, was driven through a crowd of around 70,000 jubilant pilgrims. On either side of the purpose-built altar were the world "Heart Speaks to heart," the theme chose by the Pope for the papal visit, and taken from the crest of Cardinal Newman. As well as bishops of England, Wales and Scotland, members of the royal family and government figures were also in attendance. So, too, were relatives of Cardinal Newman—descendents of his cousin—and Deacon Jack Sullivan whose miraculous healing of a back problem was last year attributed to Cardinal Newman's intercession. The ruling led to today's beatification, ending a cause which has been investigated since 1958.

In his homily, the Holy Father praised the theologian's spirituality and holiness. He singled out his vision for education that was "firmly opposed to any reductive or utilitarian approach" and highlighted Blessed John Henry's famous appeal for an intelligent and well-instructed laity. But he also reflected on his life as a priest, recalling his "profoundly human vision of priestly ministry" that manifested itself in the oratory he founded, his visits to the sick, his comfort of the bereaved and care for those in prison. "'Heart speaks to Heart' gives us an insight into his understanding of the Christian life as a call to holiness, as experienced as the profound desire of the human heart to enter into intimate communion with the Heart of God," the Holy Father said. "He reminds us that faithfulness to prayer gradually transforms us into the divine likeness." The Pope began his homily be recalling that today the country was commemorating the seventieth anniversary of the Battle of Britain when, against the odds, the Royal Air Force won a famous air battle against the Nazis. "For me as one who lived and suffered through the dark days of the Nazi regime in Germany, it is deeply moving to be here with you on this occasion, and to recall how many of your fellow citizens sacrificed their lives, courageously resisting the forces of that evil ideology," Pope Benedict said. "Seventy years later, we recall shame and horror the dreadful tool of death and destruction that war bring in its wake, and we renew our resolve to work for peace and reconciliation wherever the threat of conflict looms."

Father Richard Duffield, provost of the Birmingham Oratory who also read the Declaration of Beatification during the morning Mass, said the beatification was "beautiful" and went "extremely well." He said that the Holy Father's decision to dwell on the "pastoral and the spiritual" aspects of Blessed John Henry's life "struck exactly the right note."

After the Mass, the Holy Father was taken to the Birmingham Oratory where he saw where Cardinal Newman lived and visited the library where he studied.

Pope Benedict XVI

Pope Praises Newman's Holiness

— *The following note was reported by* ZENIT.

While acknowledging the contribution of Cardinal John Henry Newman's keen insight into the most "pressing subjects" of his day, Benedict XVI affirmed at the cardinal's beatification Mass that he was also a holy pastor of souls. The Pope presided at an open-air beatification Mass of Cardinal Newman, which took place in Birmingham's Cofton Park on the culminating day of the Pope's state visit to the United Kingdom.

Newman, who was an influential and well-known Anglican scholar and priest, and a founder of the Oxford Movement, entered the Catholic Church in 1845. He studied for the priesthood in Rome and joined the Oratory of St. Phillip Neri in 1847. Upon moving back to England, Father Newman founded the first English Oratory in 1948, which was initially located in Maryvale, near Birmingham. In 1851, he was asked by the bishops of Ireland to found a Catholic university there, which is known today as University College, Dublin. Father Newman was known mostly as a scholar and author, noted most prominently for his popular autobiography *Apologia Pro Vita Sua* (1865-66). He was made a cardinal when he was seventy-eight years old, and he died at the age of eighty-nine in Birmingham.

At his beatification Mass, Pope Benedict XVI said, "In Blessed John Henry, that tradition of gentle scholarship, deep human wisdom and profound love for the Lord has borne rich fruit, as a sign of the abiding presence of the Holy Spirit deep within the heart of God's people, bringing forth abundant gifts of holiness."

The Pope Routed Enemies

— The article that follows was written by William Oddie and first published in the Catholic Herald.

The papal visit began in anxiety which quickly turned to relief and ended finally in euphoria. In the words of Dr. George Carey, Archbishop of Canterbury until 2002, in the *News of the World:* "he came, he saw, he conquered."

Perhaps the first thing that needs to be said is that this was above all a personal triumph for the Holy Father himself. What came over consistently was the huge warmth, the seemingly inexhaustible loving kindness of the Pope's gentle but nevertheless powerful personality. Despite his intellectual impressiveness, which was evident throughout, everyone now knows that this is no withdrawn, scholarly rigorist, incapable of relating to people or understanding their lives: this alleged coldness, it was widely claimed, was what explained the supposed lack of enthusiasm about the visit, even among Catholics. Well, we will hear no more now about his purported lack of charisma, an assessment invariably followed with a comparison, to Pope Benedict's disadvantage, with John Paul II. Pope Benedict is, we have now all seen, hugely charismatic: but his charisma is of a different kind, less dramatic, less forcefully energetic than that of Pope John Paul.

They were always very different men: but Pope Benedict has all the charisma he needs, and in both the senses given by the Oxford Dictionary: 1) "a compelling attractiveness or charm that can inspire devotion in others" and 2) "a divinely conferred power or talent." For, in the end, let us never forget that what we have witnessed has come from God, whose presence has been very close throughout not only to the Pope himself but also to all who were praying for his success— protecting, inspiring, allaying our fears and in the end fulfilling all our hopes.

Interview by Genevieve Pollock of *ZENIT,*
with Newman Scholar Joseph Pearce

— *Joseph Pearce, an Englishman and a Catholic convert who has studied and written about Cardinal John Henry Newman, spoke with* ZENIT *about the Pope's visit to the United Kingdom and the beatification ceremony. Pearce, currently serving as writer-in-residence and Associate Professor of Literature at Ave Maria University, has published numerous books on the great Christian intellectuals including* Literary Converts, Tolkien: Man and Myth, C.S. Lewis and the Catholic Church *and* The Unmasking of Oscar Wilde, *all available from Ignatius press.*

ZENIT: Benedict XVI had never presided over a beatification ceremony until that of Blessed John Henry Newman on Sunday. Why do you think the Pope chose Cardinal Newman in particular to single out with this gesture?

Pearce: The Holy Father was certainly paying a special tribute to Blessed John Henry Newman in his decision to preside personally over the beatification ceremony. As such, I think that the Pope's decision to beatify Newman personally was also connected to the fact that the beatification would take place in England, thereby facilitating the papal visit.

During the four days of engagements, millions of people in England and Scotland truly opened their hearts to the Pope and his message of faith and reason amid the quagmire of a decaying culture; the Holy Father's words shone forth as a beacon of sanity and sanctity.

ZENIT: In his homily at the beatification ceremony, the Pope specifically mentioned Blessed John Henry Newman's appeal for an "intelligent, well-instructed laity." Could you say something more about this?

Pearce: In his work on the needs and nature of Catholic education, much of which was published in his important work, *The Idea of a University*, Newman emerges as one of the finest and most eloquent advocates of an integrated liberal arts education for the laity. The underlying and underpinning principle of such an education is that the Catholic laity must be well versed in theology, philosophy, literature, and history, and that they must be able to see how each of these intellectual disciplines informs the other.

ZENIT: The Pope also spoke about Blessed John Henry Newman's example of priestly life and ministry. In your opinion, what aspects of his priestly testimony are most noteworthy?

Pearce: A major aspect of Newman's philosophy was that a living faith must be lived faithfully. Newman's own life as a priest was exemplary, serving to illustrate the power of the priestly ministry if lived in accordance with the call to holiness implicit to the ministry itself.

ZENIT: Could you say something about your own reflections— as one who has spent significant time studying Newman—regarding the beatification ceremony?

Pearce: As an admirer of Newman, as an Englishman, and, more to the point, as an English Catholic convert, I was simply overjoyed by his beatification. Newman is rightly considered to be the father of the Catholic revival and the seismic power of his conversion continues to reverberate throughout the English-speaking world.

ZENIT: What do you see as Blessed John Henry Newman's most important message to Catholics today?

Pearce: Newman's most important message to today's Catholics is conveyed in the many works in which he affirms and elucidates the inextricable bond between faith and reason.

In *The Idea of a University* he affirms the efficacy of an integrated liberal arts education in which faith and reason (*fides et ratio*) elucidate the splendour of truth (*veritatis splendor*). His *Apologia pro Vita Sua* is perhaps the greatest autobiographical spiritual aeneid ever written, with the obvious exception of St. Augustine's incomparable *Confessions*. In the *Apologia*, as in his semi-autobiographical novel, *Loss and Gain*, he illuminates how the path to faith is lit by the light of reason.

Joseph Pearce

Caritas in Veritate in Gold and Red
The revenge of Justice and Peace (or so they may think).

— *The following piece by George Weigel was published in* the National Review Online *on July 7, 2009.*

In the often unpredictable world of the Vatican, it was as certain as anything could be in mid-1990 that there would be a 1991 papal encyclical to commemorate the centenary of *Rerum Novarum* —the 1891 letter of Leo XIII that is rightly regarded as the *Magna Carta* of modern Catholic social doctrine. The Pontifical Council for Justice and Peace, which imagines itself the curial keeper of the flame of authentic Catholic social teaching, prepared a draft, which was duly sent to Pope John Paul II—who had already had a bad experience with the conventionally *gauchiste* and not-very-original thinking at Justice and Peace during the preparation of the 1987 social encyclical, *Sollicitudo Rei Socialis*. John Paul shared the proposed draft with colleagues in whose judgment he reposed trust; one prominent intellectual who had long been in conversation with the Pope told him that the draft was unacceptable, in that it simply did not reflect the way the global economy of the post-Cold War world worked.

So John Paul dumped the Justice and Peace draft and crafted an encyclical that was a fitting commemoration of *Rerum Novarum*. For *Centesimus Annus* not only summarised deftly the intellectual structure of Catholic social doctrine since Leo XIII; it proposed a bold trajectory for the further development of this unique body of thought, emphasising the priority of culture in the threefold free society (free economy, democratic polity, vibrant public moral culture). By stressing human creativity as the source of the wealth of nations, *Centesimus Annus* also displayed a far more empirically acute reading of the economic signs of the times than was evident in the default positions at Justice and Peace. Moreover, *Centesimus Annus* jettisoned the idea of a "Catholic third way" that was somehow "between" or "beyond" or "above" capitalism and socialism —a favorite dream of Catholics ranging from G. K. Chesterton to John A. Ryan and Ivan Illich.

It was, in a word, a rout—the Waterloo for Justice and Peace. Ever since, Justice and Peace—which may forgive but certainly does not forget—has been pining for revenge.

It didn't get it during the last years of the pontificate of John Paul II, despite efforts to persuade the Pope to mark the thirtieth anniversary of Paul VI's 1967 social encyclical, *Populorum Progressio*, with a major statement—or, when that stratagem failed, to mark *Populorum Progressio*'s 35th anniversary. Evidently incapable of taking "No" for an answer, Justice and Peace kept beavering away, with an eye toward *Populorum Progressio*'s fortieth-anniversary in 2007. It is one of the worst-kept secrets in Rome that at least two drafts of such an encyclical, and perhaps three, were rejected by Pope Benedict XVI.

That Justice and Peace should imagine a *Populorum Progressio* anniversary encyclical as the vehicle for its counterattack against *Centesimus Annus* is itself instructive. For in the long line of papal social teaching running from *Rerum Novarum* to *Centesimus Annus*, *Populorum Progressio* is manifestly the odd duck, both in its intellectual structure (which is barely recognisable as in continuity with the framework for Catholic social thought established by Leo XIII and extended by Pius XI in *Quadragesimo Anno*) and in its misreading of the economic and political signs of the times (which was clouded by then-popular leftist and progressive conceptions about the problem of Third World poverty, its causes, and its remedies). *Centesimus Annus* implicitly recognised these defects, not least by arguing that poverty in the Third World and within developed countries today is a matter of exclusion from global networks of exchange in a dynamic economy (which put the moral emphasis on strategies of wealth creation, empowerment of the poor, and inclusion), rather than a matter of First World greed in a static economy (which would put the moral emphasis on redistribution of wealth). Interestingly enough, Paul VI himself had recognised that *Populorum Progressio* had misfired in certain respects, being misread in some quarters as a tacit papal endorsement of violent revolution in the name of social justice. Pope Paul tried a course correction in the 1971 apostolic letter, *Octogesima Adveniens*, another *Rerum Novarum* anniversary document.

Now comes *Caritas in Veritate* (Charity in Truth), Benedict XVI's long-awaited and much-delayed social encyclical. It seems to be a hybrid, blending the pope's own insightful thinking on the social order with elements of the Justice and Peace approach to Catholic social doctrine, which imagines that doctrine beginning anew at *Populorum Progressio*. Indeed, those with advanced degrees in Vaticanology could easily go through the text of *Caritas in Veritate*, highlighting those passages that are obviously Benedictine with a gold marker and those that reflect current Justice and Peace default positions with a red marker. The net result is, with respect, an encyclical that resembles a duck-billed platypus.

The clearly Benedictine passages in *Caritas in Veritate* follow and develop the line of John Paul II, particularly in the new encyclical's strong emphasis on the life issues (abortion, euthanasia, embryo-destructive stem-cell research) as social-justice issues—which Benedict cleverly extends to the discussion of environmental questions, suggesting as he does that people who don't care much about unborn children are unlikely to make serious contributions to a human ecology that takes care of the natural world. The Benedictine sections in *Caritas in Veritate* are also—and predictably—strong and compelling on the inherent linkage between charity and truth, arguing that care for others untethered from the moral truth about the human person inevitably lapses into mere sentimentality.

The encyclical rightly, if gingerly, suggests that thug-governments in the Third World have more to do with poverty and hunger than a lack of international development aid; recognises that catastrophically low birth rates are creating serious global economic problems (although this point may not be as well developed as it was in previous essays from Joseph Ratzinger); sharply criticises international aid programs tied to mandatory contraception and the provision of "reproductive health services" (the U.N. euphemism for abortion-on-demand); and neatly ties religious freedom to economic development. All of this is welcome, and all of it is manifestly Benedict XVI, in continuity with John Paul II and his extension of the line of papal argument inspired by *Rerum Novarum* in *Centesimus Annus*, *Evangelium Vitae* (the 1995 encyclical on the life issues), and *Ecclesia in Europa* (the 2003 apostolic exhortation on the future of Europe).

But then there are those passages to be marked in red—the passages that reflect Justice and Peace ideas and approaches that Benedict evidently believed he had to try and accommodate. Some of these are simply incomprehensible, as when the encyclical states that defeating Third World poverty and underdevelopment requires a "necessary openness, in a world context, to forms of economic activity marked by quotas of gratuitousness and communion." This may mean something interesting; it may mean something naïve or dumb. But, on its face, it is virtually impossible to know *what* it means.

The Casket

— The Casket *is a weekly paper published in Antigonish, Nova Scotia, Canada by the Casket Printing and Publishing Company. It was first published on June 24, 1852 by John Boyd. Its first edition consisted of four pages, two in English and two in Gaelic. Mr. Boyd established the paper a "Guardian of Liberty" and his masthead bore the motto: Liberty: choicest gem of the Old World and fairest gem of the new. The name of the paper was suggested by a local doctor, William Currie. The word, casket, at that time meant a treasure box, a container of precious things. The newspaper is still being published. Its founder, John Boyd was the great-uncle of Fr. Ian Boyd, Editor of this journal.*

For family history I have a family photo of grandpa Boyd and above the photo it is printed—Proprietor 1860-1888—and beside this photo there is one of Mr. Justice Chisholm and he was the Editor of *The Casket* from 1888-1890. I was thinking that because I think grandpa Boyd's birthdate is 1835 and then he took over the ownership of the Casket from his half-brother John in 1860 or in the article it said "after the disastrous fire in the winter of 1861." Dad's father would have been twenty-five years old and in other sources it stated that grandpa had worked from an early age with his half-brother. The end of the article reads:

Later that year he disposed of his interest in *The Casket* to his half-brother, Angus Boyd, who ran it until 1888. Moderately at least the wish of John Boyd has been fulfilled, it can be said. The Casket has continued. Today after a hundred years, it finds it necessary to address itself with renewed seriousness to that early motto. With this issue, the line appears again upon our title page. Great mechanical and industrial progress has been made since John Boyd first placed it there, but liberty is threatened even more than ever: at that time liberty was young and the new world full of hope: today liberty is despaired of the cult of scientific despotism spreads its evil course across the world. We must address ourselves particularly, along with other myriad small voices of the free world, to strengthening that vital moral tradition—belief in God and observance of His laws—from which liberty springs and without which civil and economic rights and the dignity of man soon become fraudulent myths.

Antigonish, N.S., June 26, 1952.

Flannery O'Connor: Grace without Limit

— *The following article by Amy Sapenoff was published in* Traces *magazine (Volume 12,* No. 7, 2010, pp 15-17) *as an Exhibit Preview feature to the 2010 Rimini Meeting.*

Our path to the Meeting in Rimini actually began in the fall of 2008. A group of friends at the Catholic University of America and the John Paul II institute for Studies on Marriage and Family began to promote cultural initiatives through a small club on campus, Radius. What was initially slow to gain momentum became a real education into what culture is and how we look at it, as we learned what it was to start with a mall question or desire and follow it to its depth.

275

A year later, Fr. Pietro Rossotti, FSCB, a student at the John Paul II Institute and one of the initial members of Radius, suggested that we submit a proposal to the Meeting as a way to continue this education.

From the very beginning, we could see that the work would be bigger than ourselves; accordingly, we invited some of our other friends from the CLU community in Washington to help. Our small team was comprised of Fr. Pietro, Annie Devlin, and James Sternberg, all founding members of Radius and students at the Institute. It also included Abby Holtz and Chiara Tanzi of the University of Maryland and John Martino, Nick Kraus, and myself from the School of Community at Catholic University of America. Our goal was simple: to present something beautiful and distinctly American. At the time, roommate Annie had begun read *The Habit of Being*, a book of Flannery O'Connor's letters during her short career. Flannery, an American short story writer from Georgia who wrote primarily in the 1950s and early 1960s, within the initial pages of her correspondence, had already managed to make what would be a lasting impact on Annie.

The Fifth Roommate—In fact, Flannery became something akin to the fifth roommate in our house! Nearly every exchange at the dinner table struck a chord and Annie would ask, "Well, do you know what Flannery has to say about that?" It seemed Flannery's genius was appropriate for any situation. As it turns out Flannery's genius was even appropriate for a meager proposal to the organisers of the Meeting. However simple the proposal, they agreed to let us prepare one of the eight major exhibits for the 2010 edition. The next step was to begin reading Flannery together, starting with several of her letters. We were immediately compelled by the circumstances of her life. As an adult, Flannery was confined to her small family farm in Milledgeville, Georgia, due to her struggle with lupus, the disease that would eventually take her life at the young age of thirty-nine. There, she would write in the morning and, in the afternoon, accept visitors, write letters, and tend to her beloved flow of peafowl. From the outside, it is easy to perceive her life as provincial and isolated, However, even given these circumstances, what became evident to us through reading her letters was that she lived the limitations given to her with such a profound intensity that her life became dominated by the Mystery at work within her reality. Moreover, what was true for her life was true for her life was also true for her art. she herself stated, "He [the artist] must first of all be aware of his limitations as an artist—for art transcends its limitations only by staying with them" (*Mystery and Manners*, p.171).

It was from this concept that the title and theme of our exhibit: "Flannery O'Connor: A Limit with Infinite Measure." It was at that point that the real work began. To our little group of O'Connorites, we added the expertise of Stephen Lewis, a Professor of the Literature at the Franciscan university in Steubenville, Ohio, and Dino D'Agata, a high school teacher in Washington, DC. In addition to her non-fiction, we started reading some of Flannery's more well-known short stories and discussing them over conference calls every few weeks.

Inspiration and Friendship—What immediately became interesting in her stories was the fact that there were no barriers or limits to the grace that is always offered to her characters, a confirmation of what we had learned from Flannery in terms of her own life and deep Catholic faith. Our work progressed from conference calls to sometimes tedious eight-hour work days. Even though these days often seemed to be "infinite discussion with no limit," the exhibit began to take shape. Within a large space of four rooms at Rimini, we would introduce Flannery's biography and the social and cultural context she was writing within, present her understanding of what it was to be a writer, showcase several of her short stories, and then culminate with the way in which her final short stories and the end of her life coincided.

The work of putting together the content of the exhibit spanned from October to May. It was evident during that time that "Flannery O'Connor: A Limit with Infinite Measure" is the fruit of something much larger than those of us working on it. A number of new friendships were born from this work, including with Fiorenza, the architect in New York who, without previously knowing us or Flannery O'Connor, threw herself into the immense task of designing our 1,000-square-meter exhibit.

Then there is Michael Fitzgerald. Over Christmas break, we decided to get together to watch the film adaptation of Flannery O'Connor's first novel, *Wise Blood*. The film was produced by Michael Fitzgerald, the son of two of Flannery's best friends, Sally and Robert Fitzgerald. At the conclusion of the film, we listened to Michael's commentary. It was evident that he held profound respect for Flannery and her work, expressing a real love for the characters in *Wise Blood*. We mused that it would be great to invite him to join us at the Meeting, speaking on the panel presentation of our exhibit. A few months and several phone calls later, James, Fr. Pietro, Annie, and I found ourselves surprised to be driving up to New York to meet him for dinner.

While dining in a small Italian restaurant in Manhattan, Fr. Pietro and I were able to explain what we had experienced of the Meeting. Michael found the fact that the Meeting is nearly entirely run by young volunteers from all over the world to be particularly remarkable. At the end of the dinner, we invited him to attend the Meeting and speak alongside Stephen Lewis and Davide Rondoni, an Italian poet, about our exhibit. After only a moment's thought, he agreed. It was clear to us sitting at the table that we were not simply inviting Michael to go to Rimini—we were inviting him to see something of our life, of our companionship together which had generated something even more incredible than we could have imagined.

Down South—Once the text of the exhibit was finished, the arrangement of the physical space presented an entirely new set of challenges. Among the most pressing concerns was the gathering of photos to be used. So, Chiara and I rook trip down South, making a "Flannery O' Connor pilgrimage" of sorts. The last stop was Savannah, Georgia, the birthplace of Flannery and where she spent the majority of her childhood. Her house, situated across the street from the Cathedral of Saint John the Baptist where she was baptised, has been turned into a museum open to the public. Our tour guide seemed to have endless anecdotes that helped lo paint the picture of Flannery as a person, the type of person capable of the witty and dark humor she is known for. For examples, her penchant for Grimm's Fairy Tales and the fact that she started referring to her parents by their first names at age six simply seemed in character.

From Savannah, we traveled about two hours north to Milledgeville, Georgia, to visit the family farm, Andalusia, where Flannery lived with her mother in adult years until she died. Seeing the living room that was converted into her bedroom, with a type-writer and her crutches on display, emphasised what we had been working on all along. Flannery's life from the outside seemed to be utterly determined by the limitations imposed by her circumstances. However, it is abundantly clear to us that Flannery only became a great writer by staying within those limitations and accepting them as the very contours of her vocation.

A measure that astounds—Now that the very elements of the exhibit are complete, the dominating sense that we all share, however, is that we are still at the beginning of something—which, even still, we do not fully comprehend, The path that opened up for us in the fall of 2008 shows no signs of simply winding to an end after the Meeting in Rimini this coming August.

What opened up for us has become an experience life-shared by the entire community. I continue to receive interesting input from friends around the country and Annie and I were able to share what we have learned in these past months with our friends all the CLU vacation. Fr. Pietro has been helped with translating by our friend Donatella, and some others from the CLU in Washington, in the awareness that they, too, belong to what is happening, are organising a fundraising event to make the trip to Rimini possible for those of us involved in the exhibit. Within the friendship flourishing in this common work, and the compelling world that Flannery O'Connor's art and witness of life have opened up to us, that which has been most beautifully in evidence is the growing clarity that none of this has its origin only in us. Instead, in simply responding to what was happening in our lives, we have found precisely there—within the apparent limits of reality—and inexhaustibly fruitful depth, the measure of which continues to astound us.

Programmes

Chesterton and Christmas: A Serious Affair

The following report, by David Galalis, of the programme "Chesterton and Christmas: A Serious Affair" co-sponsored by Crossroads Cultural Center, was held on December 16, 2009 at Pope Auditorium, Fordham University, New York City.

On perhaps one of the coldest nights to visit New York City this winter, friends of Crossroads Cultural Center gathered together in a warm room full of poetry, music, and discourse, all aimed at exploring the mystery of the incarnation and birth of Christ through the lens of G. K. Chesterton's works. A few minutes before the start of the evening, the Communion and Liberation Choir burst through the din of the crowd, recalling the participants to the reason of their being there that night—to increase their awareness of their humanity in preparation for Christmas.

Writer Tony Hendra then took the stage and recited a selection of Chesterton's Christmas poetry, as he would do throughout the evening. *The House of Christmas, The Nativity*, and *The Wise Men* were the featured works. A casual conversation between Chesterton scholars Fr. Ian Boyd, Editor of *The Chesterton Review* and President of the G. K. Chesterton Institute for Faith & Culture, and Prof. Dermot Quinn, Professor of History at Seton Hall University, then ensued, ranging from the theological significance of the incarnation, to the contemporary cultural meaning of Santa Claus.

The evening was a celebration of Christmas and Chesterton, said Prof. Quinn. Christmas is the celebration of the Mystery of

---

View towards Piazza della Signoria, Florence, Italy

the universe made flesh, he continued. And, more paradoxically, it is the remembrance of the event by which God made an act of faith by placing Himself helpless in his own creation's arms. And who better to introduce us to some of these mysteries than Chesterton, who, Quinn remarked, was also in love with, and awestruck in front of, the fact of the incarnation.

Fr. Boyd recalled that Chesterton once remarked that all disorder stems from the fear of the phrase, "the word was made flesh." This is why, Fr. Boyd said, it is accurate to say that the work of God is material (God entered history as a human being like ourselves), while the work of the devil is spiritual (the devil makes us fear or doubt the truth of this claim).

Chesterton himself suffered a spiritual crisis at London's Slade School of Art, where he began to entertain the possibility that nothing existed outside his own mind, and that the entire world was a projection of his mind. This idea eventually gripped him entirely, until he was helped back outside himself by his devoutly Christian fiancée. The experience, however, had a permanent effect on him, causing him to distrust the lonely mind in favor of the collective wisdom of the community.

This is the context, Fr. Boyd said, in which we ought to try to understand Chesterton's preoccupation with the incarnation. Upon his eventual conversion to Catholicism from agnosticism, he wrote that his mind was moved to its foundation simply by thinking upon the incarnation—the idea that the creator of the universe should become a human being. Always, in writing about the incarnation, Fr. Boyd observed, Chesterton insisted upon "the fundamental importance of materiality for a correct understanding of what Christmas means." He does so even to the level of the seemingly banal— arguing that Christmas presents are essentially Christian, because they recall the material gift of God to his creation.

Reflecting on these remarks, Prof. Quinn noted that it is impossible to read Chesterton seriously without being overwhelmed by wonder. Fr. Boyd responded that Chesterton himself had said that his purpose as a writer was to awaken the imagination of his readers—to create a sense of wonder about what they already knew. And the greatest object of wonder, continued Prof. Quinn, was existence itself. This is the "supreme adventure of being born" of which Chesterton had written.

The materiality of existence was central to Chesterton's thought, with the incarnation representing a triumphant validation of the flesh. Fr. Boyd said that this was very much in keeping with the understanding of Chesterton as a "sacramental Christian"—that is, Chesterton saw the real presence and action of Christ in material objects and events. To illustrate this, Fr. Boyd told a story of how Chesterton's church put on a nativity play, with a real baby in the crib. At the end of the play, Chesterton approached the boy's mother and asked "may I hold the Christ child?" Thus, for Chesterton, every human life was a reenactment of the Gospel story.

Balancing Chesterton's wonder at existence was his gratitude for it. Prof. Quinn stated that Chesterton once remarked that "[t]he chief idea of my life is taking things with gratitude and not taking things for granted." This gratitude for all things was exhibited in his sacramental life, Fr. Boyd added. When he became Catholic, he had great difficulty with receiving communion, because of how he perceived his fellow Catholics were receiving it casually. As for himself, Chesterton trembled in front of the Holy Eucharistic—in front of the fact of the creator of the universe coming to him under the appearance of bread.

Chesterton's sacramental life permeated even the mundane. Both speakers remarked upon how Chesterton was constantly making the sign of the cross—even before having a cigar—and had even introduced tiny crosses into his signature. These "tiny things" formed a big part of Chesterton's faith and social philosophy. As he wrote in *The Everlasting Man*, referring to the incarnation, "all the eyes of wonder and worship which had been turned outwards to the largest thing were now turned inward to the smallest." Correspondingly, Chesterton's social philosophy, according to Prof. Quinn, was based upon the family—the smallest social unit of society.

If the first two words to describe Chesterton's spirituality are wonder and gratitude, remarked Prof. Quinn, the next is celebration. The whole point of Christmas, that is to say the feast of the incarnation, is that the incarnation ought to be celebrated. In this vein, Chesterton was a close ally with Dickens in rescuing Christmas from puritanical influences. Both Dickens and Chesterton emphasised in their writing the "earthy side" of Christmas. Chesterton, like Dickens, believed that Christmas should be celebrated with carols and food and drink, because if we are celebrating the incarnation, we ought to do it in an incarnational way.

How appropriate, then, that this evening of Christmas discourse was ended by a recitation of Chesterton's *The Wise Men*, which contains this very simple yet crucial "incarnational" passage, summing-up the fact of the Mystery become flesh:

> The Child that was ere worlds begun
> (. . . We need but walk a little way,
> We need but see a latch undone . . .)
> The Child that played with moon and sun
> Is playing with a little hay.

Prof. Dermot Quinn and Fr. Ian Boyd

*   *   *

What's Wrong With the World
Report from Mecosta

The following account of the conference What's Wrong With the World *held at the Russell Kirk Center for a Cultural Renewal was sent by Mrs. Marcia Xavier de Brito, member of the Editorial Board of the Portuguese edition of* The Chesterton Review.

It was a great pleasure and a privilege to be invited to the conference to celebrate the centenary of G. K. Chesterton's *What's Wrong With the World*, organised by the Russell Kirk Center for a Cultural Renewal and the G. K. Chesterton Institute for Faith & Culture which was held on June 11 & 12 in Mecosta, Michigan. The speakers and lectures enjoyed over two days of intellectual camaraderie and conversation. After the welcoming remarks of Mrs. Annette Kirk and Jeffrey Nelson, Fr. Ian Boyd lecture gave the attendees an overview of *What's Wrong With the World*, one of Chesterton's most social focused works, noting the sacramental aspect of his writing and his strong incarnational belief that can be found in all of Chesterton's books and articles.

Gerald Russello's remarks focused on the similarities between Chesterton and Russell Kirk's sociological points of view as not only two of the great thinkers of the twentieth century but also their capacity to foresee problems in our societies. The cult of empires and big conglomerates, criticised both by Chesterton and Kirk, the love for the organic, the local, the familiar were also remembered. During the afternoon, Professor Vigen Guroian talked about *The Cultural Crisis of Our Time: Restoring a Compelling Vision of the Permanent Things*, updating the errors and vices of our contemporary age and the pervasive uses of imagination, too much indebted to the errors Chesterton pointed out in the beginning of last century.

Gerald Russello, Fr. Ian Boyd, Mrs. Annette Kirk,
Prof. Vigen Guroian, Jeff Nelson

Driving Without Destination: an Art Exhibit

The following account on how the Chesterton Institute exhibit "Driving Without Destination" was conceived was written by Tony Capparelli. This exhibit which was held from September 7 to October 2 at the Walsh Gallery at Seton Hall University was curated by Jeanne Brasile, Director of the Walsh Gallery and Prof. Tony Capparelli; and was judged by Jean Brasile, Fr. Ian Boyd, Tony Capparelli, Gloria Garafulich-Grabois and Dr. Dermot Quinn.

I was on a break from my teaching duties in New York City, when I came across an essay, which seemed to strike a chord within me. I already had discussions with others concerning a nagging uneasiness with what seemed to be a homogenisation being pressed upon us from every corner of societal thinking and life. One seemed hard-pressed to know whom he or she was actually addressing, either in business, politics or in everyday life. It seems to me when this occurs we are looking over each other shoulders, and not looking each other in the eye. A societal frost can occur, infecting the human spirit. Though I have read about this in other societies, it seems to me, in scale, a new phenomenon in American daily life.

In 1926, Chesterton's, *The Next Heresy* began for me a quest to have some of this uneasiness expressed through art. Having read this on break from classes, I asked Gloria Garafulich-Grabois to suggest an essay from the *Chesterton Review* which could be the topic for a University Art Exhibit. Mrs. Grabois immediately pulled from the shelf, a past Review, which contained an article by Seton Hall Professor Dr. Dermot Quinn. The essay titled: "Driving Without Destination" proved to be a perfect metaphor for this artistic exploration. An open call to international artists was set in motion from an enthusiastic Seton Hall, Walsh Gallery Director, Jeanne Brasile, who was invaluable, making this show a reality. Jeanne became my co-curator, and helped to make this Fall's exhibit a success.

The following is the curator' statement from this year's exhibit. It is my hope that this topical conversation will continue.

An exhibition of art exploring a Chestertonian theme was pressed upon the curators by today's events. Whether in the United States or abroad, people are being asked to conform their communities, tastes, habits and thinking in ways seemingly at odds with basic human freedom and dignity, or in ways incrementally gravitating towards the same. Our historic American distaste for oppressive, overbearing government however, may be tone deaf to the more subtle ways this homogenisation imposes itself through the softer voice of modern consumer culture.

What will be lost? And who will fall through the cracks? It is here we are confronted through the eyes of the artist. Here, several media explorations comprise this exhibit—a testimony to both Chesterton and the amasingly prescient imagery expressed by Dermot Quinn's essay "Driving without Destination." It is here the curators offer an opportunity for artistic reflection of the same.

Tony Capparelli
Art Department
Seton Hall University, So. Orange, NJ

Larry Ross, "From Here to Here,"
acrylic on artboard, 20" x 30", 2010.

*   *   *

The Pride of Having My Own Business
a Distributist Video

The G. K. Chesterton Institute for Faith & Culture is specially grateful to Mr. Mohamad Almojahed, proprietor of Ayman Upholstery, Inc. in Orange, N.J. for having graciously agreed to participate in the Chesterton Institute's movie project "The Pride of Having My Own Business." *This video, produced and directed by Mrs. Gloria Garafulich-Grabois, was the Chesterton Institute's contribution to the exhibit.*

This short video about Mr. Almojahed and his business gives us some idea of the distributist vision of the good life. As Dr. Quinn states, independent business owners are free people—people who provide for their families, free to build morally decent communities for themselves, free to make provision for their sickness and old age—because they have property. Property enshrines all sorts of notions of privacy, independence, self-reliance, freedom and dignity. Mr. Almojahed has discovered this for himself and hopes that those who come to the exhibition will leave it with a similar sense of the importance of ownership.

Mr. Mohamad Almojahed

*　　　*　　　*

Chesterton in San Sebastián, Spain

Dr. Angel Rubio of Colegio Mayor Ayete in San Sebastián, Spain, sends the following report of the Chesterton Institute conference held on September 23, 2010.

On September 23, 2010 Colegio Mayor Ayete held a conference entitled "What's Wrong With the World." The keynote speaker was Fr. Ian Boyd, who focused on the social thought of G. K. Chesterton which in current times seem to be prophetic. This is how Fr. Boyd referred to Chesterton, as he in his writings, from *Orthodoxy*—considered to be his masterpiece—to the Father Brown Stories, you can identify his views on the problems in society and how his thoughts are relevant today. At the time Chesterton wrote them, his contemporaries view his criticism as unreal or just as complaints of an older British man towards the society he lived in. Now we can prove his critics wrong.

Why do we feel so certain when we speak of Chesterton? We can say that it is because he had great knowledge of human nature, he spoke in plain but daring words with a great sense of humor. The combination of these factors made the reader enter into a process of deep thought and personal renewal. Fr. Boyd mentioned what John Ruskin said: "for every one thousand persons that listen, there is one that think, and for every one hundred persons that think, there is one that can see ... and Chesterton was this one person."

Fr. Boyd also had the opportunity to speak to the students and expressed his admiration for the work of the University of Navarra.

Colegio Mayor Ayete, San Sebastián

*   *   *

Chesterton in Madrid

*The following account of the Chesterton Institute conference at Cole-
gio Mayor Moncloa in Madrid, on September 23, 2010, was written by
its Director, Ricardo Calleja Rovira.*

On September 23, the conference "What's Wrong With the
World, a Hundred Years later" was held at Colegio Mayor Moncloa of the Universidad Complutense de Madrid. Colegio Mayor
Moncloa was founded in 1943 as an initiative of San Josemaría
Escrivá de Balaguer as and educational institution for students
in a home-like setting conducive to serious studies, and open to
culture and good humour. Some authors have recently noted the
parallels between certain aspects the teachings of the founder of
Opus Dei and of the English writer G. K. Chesterton, such as their
expressions "to love the world passionately," "be worldly without
being mundane."

Fr. Ian Boyd's lecture was the first one of Colegio Mayor' lecture series "Surprised by the Truth: Intellectuals and Christians," as
a way to open a debate about fundamental issues around the university life in Madrid through the lectures of Christian intellectuals and writers. The series is also part of the preparation for the
2011 World Youth Day which will take place in Madrid. Fr. Boyd's
lecture was attended by residents of Colegio Mayor, students and
faculty from other universities in Madrid as well as the members of
the group "Friends of Chesterton" in Madrid.

Since the conference, Chesterton has been frequently quoted
in other lectures and colloquiums of our institution including
quotes and anecdotes mentioned by Fr. Boyd at the conference as
well as the clever Chesterton humour that he knows so well and
that he kindly shared with us at a dinner with the members of
Colegio Mayor.

As a result, Colegio Mayor Moncloa has also formed a library
"Surprised by the Truth" which offers a selection of G. K. Chesterton's works as well as works by others such as Joseph Pearce's
biography of Chesterton, *Wisdom and Innocence*. We have indeed

included *The Innocence of Fr. Brown*—Chesterton's detective stories—which were recommended by Fr. Boyd "as a good initiation for those who have not yet read Chesterton." The students started to read the books just a few days after their arrival.

Fr. Ian Boyd & Dr. Ricardo Calleja

*   *   *

Chesterton at the University of Notre Dame:
Eighty Years Later

The following account of the October 4 Chesterton Institute lecture at the University of Notre Dame was written by Professor David Fager-berg of the Department of Theology of the University of Notre Dame, and a member of the Editorial Board of The Chesterton Review.

In October of 1930 G. K. Chesterton came to the University of Notre Dame to give a series of lectures over a six week period. He gave eighteen lectures on Victorian literature on Monday, Wednesday and Friday evening, and eighteen lectures on the history of the Victorian period on Tuesday, Thursday, and Friday afternoon. Total enrollment was limited to six hundred and fifty students, who then received credit after taking an oral examination with professors of the university. Chesterton remarked later that although he gave speeches and conducted debates on a regular basis, his engagement at Notre Dame was the only time he served as a teacher, and that he found the experience quite enjoyable. The same could be said by the students.

In October of 2010, to commemorate the eightieth anniversary of that visit, two lectures were held on the campus of Notre Dame, one by Fr. Ian Boyd on October 4—the day that Chesterton arrived—, and one by Dale Ahlquist on October 11. This visit was co-sponsored by four Centers at the University: Notre Dame Center for Liturgy, the Center for Ethics and Culture, Notre Dame Vision, and the Cushwa Center for the Study of American Catholicism. There were about seventy persons in attendance at each lecture, drawing from both the campus and the community.

Fr. Boyd spoke of Chesterton's two visits to America, drawing on the contrast Chesterton himself described between his first and his second. Fr Boyd added details of the Notre Dame visit at the end.

In Chesterton's remarks upon receiving the honourary doctorate from Notre Dame, he said America had seemed "strangely alien" in his first visit even though he "quickly discovered what kind and generous people the Americans are." But the second visit was quite different. "I did not feel at all like that when I came to America for the second time. If you want to know why I felt different, the reason is in the name of your University. That name was quite sufficient as far as I was concerned. It would not have mattered if it had been in the mountains of the moon. Wherever She has erected Her pillars, all man are at home, and I knew that I should not find strangers."

*   *   *

A Second Conference in Paris

The following note about the Chesterton Institute's second conference in Paris, held on October 14, 2010 was published in the blog of Les Amis de Chesterton, Un nommé Chesterton, *on October 16, 2010.*

For the second year, the G. K. Chesterton Institute for Faith & Culture and *les Amis de Chesterton* held a conference on the figure of the great Catholic writer. This year's theme was "Chesterton and Péguy: The Urgency of Conversion." Over eighty people attended the conference and were attentive during the presentations that evoked Chesterton and Péguy, their social ideas and the establishment of a connection between these two writers.

Dr. Dermot Quinn, Professor of History and member of the Editorial Board of *The Chesterton Review* was the key note speaker. His lecture presented a parallel between Chesterton and Péguy. Father Laurent-Marie Pocquet du Haut-Jussé, author of *Péguy and Modernity*, spoke on the theme of Charles Péguy as a radical critic of modernity. On this same theme, Alain Lanavère, former lecturer at the Sorbonne, focused on several aspects of Péguy's social thought and its connection to that of Chesterton.

The conference also celebrated the centenary of the publication of Chesterton's book, *What's Wrong With the World*. Fr. Ian Boyd, President of the Chesterton Institute for Faith & Culture and Editor of ***The Chesterton Review***, gave a lecture on the ten basic points of the book as well as the social philosophy of Chesterton. Philippe Maxence, Editor of *L'Homme Nouveau* and President of *les Amis de Chesterton* spoke on English Distributism and French Social Catholicsm.

View of Notre Dame Cathedral

* * *

The Chesterton Review en Français

As the interest in Chesterton continues to grow around the world, especially in France with the publication of new translations of his works and their discovery by a new generation of readers, *The Chesterton Review* grows as well.

It was for this reason that during this conference the Chesterton Institute presented the first issue of *The Chesterton Review* in French. This issue contains such Chesterton writings as "Understanding France," "The Claudel Affair" as well as articles by Ian Boyd, Dermot Quinn, Philippe Maxence and others. As in our English language issue, the French edition also contains Book Reviews and News & Comments items.

The Editorial Board of the French language edition is as follows:

Editor in-Chief   Fr. Ian Boyd
Co-Editors   Gloria Garafulich-Grabois and Philippe Maxence

Managing Editor & Translations   Daniel Hamiche
Editorial Board   Dr. Al Kessler
                                    Mrs. Charlotte Kessler
                                    Dr. Brian Sudlow

For more information or to purchase a copy please contact our Editorial Office.

*   *   *

What's Wrong With the World
Conference Series in Chile

Ms. Magdalena Merbilhaa, Director of Red Cultural of Gabriela Mistral University in Santiago, Chile sends the following note about the Chesterton Institute's Conference Series in Chile.

It was with great success that the visit of the delegation of the G. K. Chesterton Institute for Faith & Culture at Seton Hall University; came to a close. During this visit the visitors had the opportunity to visit different cities in this vast and beautiful country. The 2010 lecture series included conferences in Santiago, the capital of Chile; Valparaíso, Chile's most important port city, and Puerto Varas located in the Southern Lake Region.

Fr. Ian Boyd, Editor of *The Chesterton Review*; Dr. Dermot Quinn, Professor of History at Seton Hall University and Gloria Garafulich-Grabois, Managing Editor of *The Chesterton Review* were invited by Red Cultural of Gabriela Mistral University. Since it was established, Red Cultural has had a special interest in the thought and work of G. K. Chesterton and it has gradually increased the level of cooperation with the Chesterton Institute.

Through Red Cultural a conference series was organised which included, first a conference at the Chilean Naval Academy Arturo Prat in the city of Valparaiso, where they were received with the highest honours which included a "Changing of the Guard," a lunch hosted by the Vice-Director of the Academy, a visit to the Naval Museum culminating the visit with a conference on the theme of "Chesterton: the Man and his Times." The conference was well attended by the members of the Naval Academy and as well as public in general.

The following day, Professor Quinn gave a talk on the theme of "Chesterton and his relevance today" to students of Cardenal Silva Henriquez School which is part of Belen Educates Foundation.

In the evening the major conference and round table were held at Universidad Gabriela Mistral on the theme of *What's Wrong With the World.* They key note speaker was Prof. Quinn who spoke about the book and its relevance and importance one-hundred years later and also invited the Chilean members of the panel to participate and speak on the different aspects of the book. The panel participants were:

- Mrs. Alicia Romo Román, Founder and Rector of Universidad Gabriela Mistral on the "Role of the Woman";
- Dr. Joaquín García-Huidobro, Professor of Philosophy of the Universidad de Los Andes on "Imperialism";
- Professor Gonzalo Larios Mongotti, Dean of the School of Humanities and Social Sciences of the Universidad Gabriela Mistral on "Distributism";
- Mrs. Magdalena Merbilhaa Romo, Director of Red Cultural of the Universidad Gabriela Mistral on a "Education";
- Jaime Antúnez Aldunate, Editor of *Humanitas* on a "Philosophical Reflection of *What's Wrong With the World*"

Fr. Ian Boyd closed the programme with a talk about the conclusions and relevance of Chesterton's book one hundred years later.

The Chestertonian visit continued at the campus of Universidad Gabriela Mistral in the southern city of Puerto Varas, where the visitors were hosted by its Director Mr. Enrique Romo who organised a series of lectures during the visit, including Colegio Puerto Varas, American School in Puerto Montt. The main event in Puerto Varas was a conference on the theme of "Chesterton: the man and his times" held at Hotel Patagónico which very well attended by members of the University and the public at large.

*   *   *

The Chesterton Review Spanish Edition

During the Chesterton Institute's November 2010 Chile Conference series, Mrs. Gloria Garafulich-Grabois, Managing Editor of *The Chesterton Review* visited the La Moneda, the Presidential Palace of Chile, where she met Ms. Daniela Godoy, the Chief of Staff of Mrs. Cecilia Morel, First Lady of Chile and delivered a copy of the latest issue of the Spanish edition. Also present were the members of the International Committee of the Chilean Commission for Culture and the Arts.

Mariana Sanfuentes, Constanza Guel de Andraca of the Chilean Commission for Culture and the Arts; Gloria Garafulich-Grabois and Daniela Godoy, Chief of Staff, Office of the First Lady.

* * *

G. K. Chesterton Institute for Faith & Culture
2011 Upcoming Programmes
Celebrating the Centenary of the *Fr. Brown Stories* on the theme of:
Fr. Brown: Moral & Social Parables of our time— a centenary appraisal

January 21, 22, 28 & 29	**Program Series:** *Saints & Sleuths V* Catholic Life in Literature @ Seton Hall University
March 25	**Lecture:** *Chesterton's Fr. Brown* co-sponsored by Crossroads Cultural Center @ John Paul II Cultural Center in Washington D.C.
May 12 & 13	**Conference:** *Chesterton: The Global Economic Crisis* @ University of Zadar, Croatia
June 26-July 9	**Summer Study Abroad Oxford, UK** *The Foundations of Christianity: England* co-sponsored with the Center for Catholic Studies @ St. Benet's Hall, Oxford
July	**Conference:** *Celebrating the Centenary of* The Ballad of the White Horse Oxford, England — *Date: TBA*
August 7-21	**Summer Study Abroad & World Youth Day, Spain** *The Foundations of Christianity: Spain* co-sponsored with the Center for Catholic Studies Pamplona & Madrid
Fall 2011	**Conference:** *Chesterton & Fr Brown* Spain—*Date: TBA*
	Conference: *Chesterton & Fr. Brown* Latin America: Brazil, Argentina, Chile, Uruguay—*Date: TBA*
	Conference: *Chesterton's Fr. Brown* @ the Bernanos Centre, Paris, France — *Date: TBA*

2011 Publications of
The Chesterton Review

English Edition
Vol. XXXVII, Nos. 1 & 2 , Spring Summer 2011— June 2011
Vol. XXXVII, Nos. 3 & 4, Fall Winter 2011 — December 2011

Spanish Edition
Vol. V, No. 1 — Fall 2011

French Edition
Vol. II, No. 1 — Spring 2011

Portuguese Edition
Vol. III, No. 1 — Fall 2011

The
CHESTERTON REVIEW

Vol. XXXVI, Nos. 3 & 4
Fall Winter
2010

Seton Hall University

presents

SAINTS AND SLEUTHS V

Catholic Life in Literature:

G. K. **Chesterton**, Myles **Connolly**, Canon **Sheehan** & François **Mauriac**

G. K. Chesterton

François Mauriac

PERFORMANCE SCHEDULE

Friday, January 21 — 8pm
The Observations of Father Brown
by G. K. Chesterton—radio play adapted by John Dandola
Commentary by *Fr. Ian Boyd, C.S.B.* and *Dr. Dermot Quinn*

Saturday, January 22 — 8pm
Mr. Blue
by Myles Connolly—adapted by Dr. James McGlone
Commentary by *Fr. Gabriel Costa*

Friday, January 28 — 8pm
Trabolgan Abbey
by Rev. P. A. Sheehan—radio play in one act adapted by John Dandola
Commentary by *Dr. Maura Harrington*

Saturday, January 29 — 8pm
Viper's Tangle
by François Mauriac—reading adaptation by John Dandola
Commentary by *Fr. Ian Boyd* and *Dr. Dermot Quinn*

OPEN TO THE PUBLIC — FREE ADMISSION

Sponsored by Seton Hall University's *G. K. Chesterton Institute for Faith & Culture,*
Center for Catholic Studies and *The Celtic Theatre Company*

Myles Connolly

Canon Sheehan

For more information call: 973. 275. 2431
Location: Seton Hall University, Bishop Dougherty Student Center,
Theatre-In-The-Round, South Orange, NJ 07079

SETON HALL UNIVERSITY
1 8 5 6

THE FOUNDATIONS OF CHRISTIAN CULTURE: ENGLAND

CAST 3994; HIST 4218P; ENGL 3413SP; CORE 3748

The Foundations of Christian Culture: ENGLAND
History, Literature and Philosophy

A 3-Credit course in two parts: Spring 2011 lectures at Seton Hall and Summer Study Abroad at Oxford University

Earn credits for Signature 3 (CORE), Catholic Studies, History or English

"This Oxford, I have no doubt, is the finest City in the world."
– John Keats

Seton Hall: April 2011 &
Oxford: June 26–July 9, 2011

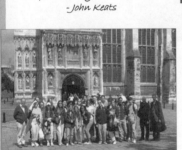

Sponsored by the Center for Catholic Studies and the G.K. Chesterton Institute for Faith & Culture

- Course requirements: Attend 4 lectures at Seton Hall in Spring 2011 and spend 2 weeks at St. Benet's Hall in the summer, examining the origins of Christian culture, visiting sites of historic importance, and reading and reflecting upon the Christian life.
- Enrollment is limited (20). Partial scholarship support is available.
- Trip costs $3600, include airfare, accommodations and full board; tuition included in Spring 2011 fees.
- Enroll by January 25, 2011. Deposit due February 15, 2011.

"One particularly impressive and satisfying aspect of this trip has been the physical, material access we've had to the ancient Christian tradition. It's one thing to sit at one's desk back home and study Christian philosophy and theology, and history, to try to apprehend Christian truths through an intellectual approach. It's quite another to walk around Oxford, to marvel at Canterbury Cathedral, and to experience, to physically enter into, the living history of the Church, the Christian culture." – *Seton Hall student*

For more information or to apply, please contact:

The Center for Catholic Studies
Seton Hall University
400 South Orange Avenue
South Orange, NJ 07079

Phone: 973.275.2525
E-mail: danute.nourse@shu.edu
Website: www.shu.edu/academics/
artsci/catholic-studies/index.cfm

SETON HALL UNIVERSITY

1 8 5 6

The Foundations of Christian Culture: SPAIN

A Spring 2011 Course Trip Sponsored by
The Center for Catholic Studies &
The G.K. Chesterton Institute for Faith & Culture

Includes Spring 2011 lectures, Summer Study Abroad and World Youth Day in Spain

A Specialized Spring 2011 Course coordinated with Study Abroad and World Youth Day, 2011:

Four Spring 2011 lectures at Seton Hall & August 7 – 21, 2011 *In Pamplona & Madrid Spain*

COST $3600
Includes:
Course trip fees
Accommodations
Breakfast & Dinner
Transfers
Some Excursions
World Youth Day
Airfare Included

AN INFORMATION SESSION WILL BE ANNOUNCED

For general information contact:

Phone: 973.275.2525
Fax: 973.275.2594
E-mail:
catholicstudies@shu.edu or chestertoninsti-tute@shu.edu

The Foundations of Christian Culture: SPAIN
CAST 4290; LALS 4290 SP TP; CORE 3748

This 3-credit course will be given in Spring and Summer 2011 at Seton Hall University and *Colegio Mayor Olarain* of the *University of Navarra*.
Lecturers:
Spring 2011: Prof. Caroyn Nadeau; Msgr. Richard Liddy; Fr. Jack Russell; Rev. Sean Cunneen
Summer 2011: Professor Isabel Warleta
The course also includes participation in World Youth Day 2011, Madrid.
Excursions include: San Sebastian, Zaragoza, Loyola, Burgos, Madrid. Discover a wonderful country and have a truly once in a lifetime experience.
+++
Space is limited. Enroll by January 25, 2011 and deposit due February 15, 2011. To apply, please contact catholicstudies@shu.edu or chestertoninsitute@shu.edu.

CENTER FOR CATHOLIC STUDIES
SETON HALL UNIVERSITY

Support for the G. K. Chesterton Institute for Faith & Culture
and *The Chesterton Review*

We acknowledge and thank our major supporters and recent donors: Sean & Marjorie Flanagan, Rosetta & Samuel Giuliano, Ken & Irene Hickman, Fred Hill, John Gregory Odom, Lady Blanka Rosensteil, and many others whose support is greatly appreciated.

Donations from our supporters allowed the Institute to award scholarships to students to attend the Summer Study Abroad programmes in England and Australia in 2005, 2007 and 2009.

Summer Study Abroad Opportunities for 2011

Students from Seton Hall University will participate in the 2011 Summer Study Abroad Programmes:

Foundations of Christian Culture, Oxford, England
Foundations of Christian Culture and World Youth Day, Spain

Students reside, study at and take a two week, 3 credit intensive course. The course surveys history, literature and philosophy relevant to English and Spanish Catholic and Christian culture, with co-curricular programs and excursions to major sights. This program is open to all university students and is sponsored by Seton Hall's *Center for Catholic Studies*, the *G. K. Chesterton Institute for Faith & Culture*. Sponsorship for this past year's program was generously provided by the *Center for Vocation and Servant Leadership* at Seton Hall, a *Lilly Endowment* funded program and the *Fr. Walter Debold Scholarship Fund.*

Announcement

The G. K. Chesterton Institute for Faith & Culture is pleased to announce that as of January 1, 2011 The Chesterton Review has entered into a distribution agreement in Latin America with:

Periodicals Brazil, Sao Paulo, Brazil
Will distribute the Portuguese language issue as well as all language editions in Brazil
For more information please contact: info@periodicals.com.br

Distribuidora Buen Combate
Will distribute the Spanish language issue as well as all language editions in Argentina, Bolivia, Chile, Paraguay and Uruguay.
For more information please contact: ventas@buencombate.com

Letters

Chesterton at Holy Cross Eighty Years Later

"Chesterton in America" was a wonderful event. I attended with my mother, Betty Reidy, whose uncle was Fr. Earls. It was great to hear about Chesterton but it was truly delightful to hear about Fr. Earls. My mother's mother—my grandmother—was Fr. Earls' youngest sister. Her name was Elizabeth Earls (her married name was Shaughnessy). As we left the lecture last evening, my mother recalled the days in the 1930s when Fr. Earls would bring his fellow priests—including several of the colorful characters that Dr. Quinn mentioned—to my grand-mother's home for dinners. (I recall my grandmother saying that several of the Jesuits had creative interpretations on what types of food could be eaten on Fridays in Lent). Although twenty one years apart in age (Fr. Earls was the eldest and my grandmother the youngest of eleven children), the two were close even within a close-knit family. Appar-ently my grandmother—who was an excellent musician—collaborated with Fr. Earls on the piece "Linden Lane."

I never knew Fr. Earls as he died thirty years before I was born. But my grandmother often spoke of him, had his portrait on the wall, and had his many books in her home. I recall a small photograph of Ches-terton on one of her book shelves; I believe it was inscribed to Fr. Earls. The picture stands out in my memory because I remember wondering who such an oddly dressed person could be (in my eyes he was wearing what looked like a sort of cowboy hat, plus cape and cane).

It was quite an experience to hear Dr. Quinn describe the writ-ings of Fr. Earls, someone that I had some familiarity with but did not know well at all. My mother and I actually were pouring through some of Fr. Earls' works recently. We went up to the Special Collections room of the Holy Cross library and looked through his books. While

Water and trees along the path which leads to the cave of Twm-Shon-Catti we were there, we took a look at the directory of alumnae and saw that the name Earls took up quite a bit of space. It turns out that the "singular man with the plural name" eventually had a plurality of relatives who attended the College. In fact, one of his descendants, my cousin Ellen Ryder, is currently the Director of Public Affairs and Editor of *Holy Cross Magazine.*

As each of the speakers last night illustrated, many of the issues that Chesterton addressed eighty years ago are still relevant (particularly in my case the ongoing themes of family and literature). It was a good reminder that history is very much with us. Thanks again for putting on such a terrific event.

Matthew Reidy
Massachusetts

*   *   *

View of a lake in Massachusetts

Chesterton Institute at the University of Notre Dame

On October 4, 2010, before a group of more than seventy students and other members of the community of the University of Notre Dame, Fr. Ian Boyd introduced a man who "seems so happy, one can almost believe he has found God." This same man who once evoked such a response from none other than Franz Kafka is the same one who speaks to men and women in the modern age with a voice as relevant and as deeply joyful as ever. The man Fr. Boyd presented to his captive audience is one who discovered the God who captured his imagination and offers all people an earthly life with heavenly meaning. This discovery was achieved in the midst of the accelerating prevalence of rationalism and secularism at the turn of the twentieth century and has only waxed from then to the present day. On the occasion of the eightieth anniversary of this man's historic visit to Notre Dame, Fr. Boyd introduced again, as if for the first time, G. K. Chesterton, who, when he was grasped by the Catholic faith, found that "instinct after instinct was answered by doctrine after doctrine."

Fr. Boyd's learned lecture, replete with Chestertonian insights and witticisms, was met with approval and a great deal of interest. Chesterton is experiencing something of a resurgence at Notre Dame with the commencement of a theology course devoted to Chesterton, academic conferences that include his thought, and the newfound curiosity of students and faculty alike. As Fr. Boyd unfurled his own observations about Chesterton's visit to Notre Dame and his two-fold "discovery of America," those listening to the lecture were caught up in a discovery or rediscovery of Chesterton as one whose understanding of Catholicism and intellectual inquiry provide a compelling path for the modern day Catholic intellectual. Chesterton is a prophetic figure who recognises and elucidates the Catholic novelty of wedding mystery with evidence: divine revelation with human inquiry. This remarkable paradox was the source of Chesterton's deep joy—an invitation to this same joy is what Chesterton offers to those who read him. Fr. Boyd did much to encourage the Notre Dame community to continue its engagement with the man who, beyond a shadow of a doubt, found God.

Leonard DeLorenzo
Director, Notre Dame Vision
University of Notre Dame

*   *   *

Driving Without Destination:
The making of from "Here to Here"

When I read Dr. Dermot Quinn's excellent article entitled, "Driving Without Destination," I immediately knew I wanted to express my reaction to it with my artwork and to participate in the art exhibit at Seton Hall University's Walsh Gallery. The article touched on similar thoughts that I have had over the years concerning travel and dealing with the worldwide spread of sameness. Corporations, governments and mass communications have joined together, extending into the far reaches of the world, to encourage a oneness. Much of the individual character of countries and regions has been lost and sacrificed for corporate profits and has been aided by the "flattening" of the world through the universal use of the internet. Dr. Quinn's article describes a road trip driving through the countryside.

Since it is my natural inclination, after years of being a professional illustrator, to form visual images in my mind relating to what I read, I immediately had the image of a couple driving a car while unwittingly on a treadmill. I did a small pencil sketch of the idea and put it aside for a few days. When I looked back at it, I still liked it so I did a little research on the car, hair styles and clothing and started in drawing it out on the art board. I did not draw everything with pencil. As I went along I painted things directly in with a brush. To give their "drive" a more artificial, futile quality, I place them and the car inside painted flats. The flats create for them the illusion of a beautiful countryside and the road painted on the flats, which they are "traveling on," has an identical beginning and end. I gave the picture a retro quality by making the car a roadster from the Twenties or Thirties and putting the people in fashions from that era since that was the era that G. K. Chesterton—whose thoughts had inspired Dr. Quinn—had lived in. I wanted a feeling of nostalgia and warmth that would give the painting more universality. A contemporary couple and car would tend to limit the viewer's response to "now." I gave the couple a cheerful, delighted quality to emphasise their innocent obliviousness and to add humor to the piece. They look like the happy model American couple one might have seen in a car advertisement years ago. They are having a wonderful time while unbeknownst to them, they are going nowhere. I put the in raccoon tail in for two reasons. First, having it horizontal gives the feeling of motion at the same time that I realised the people's hair or attire should not look like they are blowing in the wind since they are not really moving through the air; and second, it adds period-related fun. I did not want the picture to look futile.

The theme of the show deals with a serious problem, but there is hope, if we realise the situation expressed in the article. There is hope for the couple in the picture … and for us.

The art exhibit itself was a wonderful and I was extremely pleased to be part of it. I am grateful to the curators and judges: Fr. Ian Boyd, Jean Brasile, Tony Capparelli, Gloria Garafulich-Grabois, Dr. Dermot Quinn and the G. K. Chesterton Institute.

Larry Ross
Madison, N.J.

*　　　*　　　*

Inn and Post Office - Coloured engraving by Eugene Lami

Chesterton in Madrid

I was very pleased to be present at the conference that Fr. Ian Boyd, President of the G. K. Chesterton Institute, gave in Madrid on September 23 at Colegio Mayor Moncloa. It was a very good occasion for the young people that attended the conference to learn more about Chesterton, whose message of faith, joy, gratitude and respect for ordinary citizens, family and small communities is very much needed in the twenty-first century.

As Philip Yancey says in his introduction to G. K. Chesterton's *Orthodoxy*, "he managed to propound the Christian faith with as much wit, good humor and sheer intellectual force as anyone in recent times."

Luis Peral
Senator for Madrid Region
Senate of Spain

*   *   *

Chesterton Around the World

It was hard to imagine that in 2005, after the Chesterton Institute's first conference in Buenos Aires, Argentina that Chesterton would also reach Chile, Spain, France and Brazil. Four countries and three different languages. If we were to also consider the new translations that have just been published we can feel happy to know how mistaken Chesterton was when he doubted the permanence of his literary and journalistic writings.

We are very happy to be part of this Chesterton revival and also to be able to prove him wrong.

Daniel Vergara del Carril
Buenos Aires, Argentina

*   *   *

G. K. CHESTERTON INSTITUTE FOR FAITH & CULTURE
Photo Gallery: WHAT'S WRONG WITH THE WORLD
RUSSELL KIRK CENTER FOR CULTURAL RENEWAL, MECOSTA, MI
JUNE 11 & 12, 2010

1

2

3

4

1. *Fr. Ian Boyd, C.S.B., President of the G. K. Chesterton Institute for Faith & Culture*
2. *Gerald Russello, Fellow of the G. K. Chesterton Institute for Faith & Culture*
3. *Mrs. Annette Kirk*
4. *Attendees*

G. K. CHESTERTON INSTITUTE FOR FAITH & CULTURE
Photo Gallery: DRIVING WITHOUT DESTINATION, An Art Exhibit
WALSH GALLERY AT SETON HALL UNIVERSITY
SEPTEMBER 7 — OCTOBER 2, 2010

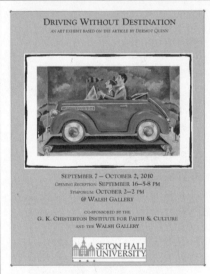

1. Tony Capparelli, curator and juror; Jeanne Brasile, curator and juror; Fr. Ian Boyd, President of the G. K. Chesterton Institute for Faith & Culture and juror; Dr. Dermot Quinn, author of article "Driving Without Destination" and juror; Gloria Garafulich-Grabois, juror.
2. Attendees to the opening
3. Attendees to the opening
4. Fr. Ian Boyd and Tony Caparelli viewing a video submission

G. K. CHESTERTON INSTITUTE FOR FAITH & CULTURE

Photo Gallery: WHAT'S WRONG WITH THE WORLD

COLEGIO MAYOR AYETE, SAN SEBASTIAN, SPAIN

SEPTEMBER 21, 2010

1

2

3

4

1. Fr. Ian Boyd, C.S.B., President of the G. K. Chesterton Institute for Faith & Culture
2. Attendees
3. Tomas Gomez Acebo, Assistant Director Colegio Mayor Ayete; Fr. Ian Boyd, C.S.B.; Juan de Santiago, Director Colegio Mayor Ayete.
4. Attendees

G. K. CHESTERTON INSTITUTE FOR FAITH & CULTURE
Photo Gallery: WHAT'S WRONG WITH THE WORLD
UNIVERSIDAD DE NAVARRA, PAMPLONA, SPAIN
SEPTEMBER 22, 2010

1

2

3

1. Fr. Ian Boyd, C.S.B., President of the G. K. Chesterton Institute for Faith & Culture and Dr. Cesar Izquierdo, Associate Dean, School of Theology.
2. Dr. Jesus Tango Lerga, Institutional Relations; Dr. Cesar Izquierdo ; Fr. Ian Boyd, C.S.B.; Dr. Jose Luis Gutierrez, Professor of Sacramental Theology.
3. Attendees

G. K. CHESTERTON INSTITUTE FOR FAITH & CULTURE
Photo Gallery: WHAT'S WRONG WITH THE WORLD
COLEGIO MAYOR MONCLOA, MADRID, SPAIN
SEPTEMBER 23, 2010

1. *Fr. Ian Boyd, C.S.B., President of the G. K. Chesterton Institute for Faith & Culture and Ricardo Callejas. Director Colegio Mayor Moncloa*
2. *Attendees*
3. *Fr. Ian Boyd and guests*
4. *Fr. Ian Boyd and Salvador Antuñano, member of the Editorial Board of The Chesterton Review Spanish issue with guests.*

G. K. Chesterton Institute for Faith & Culture

Galerie de Photo : CHESTERTON AND PEGUY: THE URGENCY OF CONVERSION

Institut Catholique de Paris, France

October 14, 2010

1 & 2

3

4

1. Daniel Hamiche; Dr. Dermot Quinn; Fr. Ian Boyd; Basile de Koch; Philippe Maxence
2. Fr. Ian Boyd
3. Dr. Dermot Quinn
4. Fr. Ian Boyd; Philippe Maxence and Daniel Hamiche

1

2

3

4

The Chesterton Review
La première édition en français
Vol. I, No. 1 — 2010

Pour information: chestertoninstitute@shu.edu

THE G.K. CHESTERTON INSTITUTE
FOR FAITH & CULTURE
SETON HALL UNIVERSITY

6

1. *Dr. Dermot Quinn and Alain Lanavère*
2. *Philippe Maxence*
3. *Philippe Maxence and Daniel Hamiche*
4. *Jeanne Duchasne and Dr. Dermot Quinn*
5. *Attendee with first edition of* The Chesterton Review *in French*

G. K. Chesterton Institute for Faith & Culture

Photo Gallery: ST. THOMAS AQUINAS & G. K. CHESTERTON

Niteroi Seminary, Rio de Janeiro, Brazil

November 5, 2010

1

2

3 & 4

5

6

1. *Dr. Dermot Quinn and Fr. Ian Boyd*
2. *Fr. Demetrio, Spiritual Director, Niteroi Seminary*
3. *Fr. Ian Boyd with Seminarian*
4. *Attendees*
5. *Attendees*
6. *Fr. Ian Boyd and Dr. Dermot Quinn with organisers and attendees.*

G. K. CHESTERTON INSTITUTE FOR FAITH & CULTURE
Photo Gallery: VISIT TO THE SISTERS OF CHARITY
RIO DE JANEIRO, BRAZIL
NOVEMBER 5, 2010

1

2

3

4

5

1. *Fr. Ian Boyd, C. S. B ., celebrates mass at the House of the Sisters of Charity in Rio de Janeiro.*
2. *Fr. Ian Boyd, C. S. B., blesses medals next to a relic of Mother Teresa*
3. *Blessing over the relic*
4. *Fr. Ian Boyd, C. S. B., Dr. Dermot Quinn, Gloria Garafulich-Grabois, Fr. Leonardo Holtz, Fr. Ligio Torres with the sisters .*
5. *Mother Teresa's medal.*

G. K. CHESTERTON INSTITUTE FOR FAITH & CULTURE

Photo Gallery: WHAT'S WRONG WITH THE WORLD

SAN BENTO MONASTERY, RIO DE JANEIRO, BRAZIL

NOVEMBER 6, 2010

1

2

3

4

5

1. Fr. Ian Boyd, C.S.B., President of the G. K. Chesterton Institute for Faith & Culture, Marcia Xavier de Brito and Dr. Dermot Quinn
2. Fr. Ian Boyd, C.S.B., Dr. Dermot Quinn and Jeffrey Baldez
3. Attendees
4. Dr. Dermot Quinn with attendees
5. Fr. Ian Boyd, C.S.B. with attendees

G. K. Chesterton Institute for Faith & Culture
Photo Gallery: CONFERENCE SERIES in CHILE
Co-Sponsored with Gabriela Mistral University
November 7–12, 2010

UNIVERSIDAD GABRIELA MISTRAL

JORNADAS CHESTERTONIANAS

CELEBRANDO LOS
100 AÑOS DEL LIBRO:
"LO QUE ESTÁ MAL
EN EL MUNDO"

8, 9 y 11
NOVIEMBRE
2010

INFORMACIONES
arodriguez@ugm.cl
414 4562 · 414 4109 · 414 4545

G. K. CHESTERTON INSTITUTE FOR FAITH & CULTURE
Photo Gallery: CHESTERTON: THE MAN AND HIS TIME
CHILEAN NAVAL ACADEMY ARTURO PRAT, VALPARAISO
NOVEMBER 8, 2010

1

2

3 & 4

5, 6 & 7

1. *Fr. Ian Boyd, C.S.B and Claudio Yañez, Vice-Director of the Chilean Naval Academy*
2. *Attendees*
3. *Fr. Ian Boyd, C. S. B. and Dr. Dermot Quinn with guests*
4. *Mrs. Magdalena Merbilhaa, Mrs. Carmen Jaureguiberry, Dr. Dermot Quinn and Mrs. Gloria Garafulich-Grabois at the Naval Museum*
5. *Attendees*
6. *Banner of the Naval Academy of Chile*
7. *Parade*

G. K. Chesterton Institute for Faith & Culture
Photo Gallery: CHESTERTON: HIS RELEVANCE TODAY
Colegio Puente Alto at Universidad Gabriela Mistral
November 9, 2010

1

2

6

1. *Dr. Dermot Quinn*
2. *Dr. Dermot Quinn and Professor of Colegio Puente Alto*
3. *Students of Colegio Puente Alto at Universidad Gabriela Mistral*

G. K. Chesterton Institute for Faith & Culture
Photo Gallery: WHAT'S WRONG WITH THE WORLD
Universidad Gabriela Mistral
November 9, 2010

1

2

3

4

5

6

1. *Dr. Dermot Quinn, Mrs. Alicia Romo Roman, Dr. Joaquin Garcia-Huidobro, Fr. Ian Boyd, C.S.B.*
2. *Dr. Gonzalo Larios, Fr. Ian Boyd, C.S.B., Mrs. Magdalena Merbilhaa, Mrs. Alicia Romo Roman, Gloria Garafulich-Grabois, Dr. Juan Cerda, Mrs. Carmen Jauriguiberry.*
3. *Fr. Ian Boyd, C.S.B.*
4. *Dr. Dermot Quinn*
5. *Attendees*
6. *Mrs. Carmen Jauriguiberry, Dr. Dermot Quinn, Fr. Ian Boyd, C.S.B., Mrs. Alicia Romo Roman, Mr. Jaime Antunez Aldunate, Mrs. Gloria Garafulich-Grabois, Mrs. Magdalena Merbilhaa, Dr. Gonzalo Larios, Dr. Joaquin Garcia-Huidobro.*

G. K. CHESTERTON INSTITUTE FOR FAITH & CULTURE
Photo Gallery: CHESTERTON: THE MAN AND HIS TIME
COLEGIO PUERTO VARAS, PUERTO VARAS — NOVEMBER 11, 2010
AMERICAN SCHOOL, PUERTO MONTT—NOVEMBER 12, 2010

1

2

3

4

5

1. ***COLEGIO PUERTO VARAS;*** *Mr. Ezequias Alliende, Founder; Dr. Dermot Quinn, Mrs. Gloria Gara-fulich-Grabois, Fr. Ian Boyd, C.S.B., Mr. Enrique Romo, Director, Universidad Gabriela Mistral, Puerto Varas and Gabriel Jordan, Director Colegio Puerto Varas.*
2. *Andres Madariaga , classical guitarist and alumni of Colegio Puerto Varas*
3. ***AMERICAN SCHOOL, PUERTO MONTT****: Prof. Jose Sarmiento; Mr. Enrique Romo, Director, Universidad Gabriela Mistral, Puerto Varas; Gloria Garafulich-Grabois; Mrs. Maria del Carmen Urquhart, Director American School;, Dr. Dermot Quinn, and Professor Juan Carlos Cardenas.*
4. *Mrs. Maria del Carmen Urquhart and Dr. Dermot Quinn*
5. *View of the grounds of Colegio Puerto Varas.*

G. K. CHESTERTON INSTITUTE FOR FAITH & CULTURE
Photo Gallery: CHESTERTON: THE MAN AND HIS TIME
UNIVERSIDAD GABRIELA MISTRAL—PUERTO VARAS, CHILE
NOVEMBER 11, 2010

1

2

3

4

5

1. *Fr. Ian Boyd, C. S. B .,*
2. *Conference*
3. *Dr. Dermot Quinn and conference attendees*
4. *Fr. Ian Boyd and Marcela Perez*
5. *Fr. Ian Boyd, C. S. B. concelebrates Mass at Puerto Varas Parish on November 14, 2010*

Make a gift to
The G.K. Chesterton Institute
for Faith & Culture at
Seton Hall University
and receive income for life.

As we confront the challenges of the future, we know that the generosity of those who assist us will make all the difference in our success. That is why we seek your support.

Today, you can make a gift to The G.K. Chesterton Institute for Faith & Culture at Seton Hall University that will provide income to you and a loved one for the rest of your lives — *and* that offers several additional financial benefits:

- ✓ You can claim an income tax charitable deduction for a portion of your gift;
- ✓ If you make a gift of cash, some of the income may be tax-free;
- ✓ If you make a gift of securities, you may reduce or completely avoid capital gains tax on the appreciation; and
- ✓ You can choose a life income plan with a fixed, guaranteed interest rate or one with a variable rate to help you keep up with inflation.

Most importantly, you will have the satisfaction of making a gift to The G.K. Chesterton Institute for Faith & Culture at Seton Hall University that will contribute to the advancement of civilized thought through writing, journalism, debate and public conversation.

To learn more, or for a no-obligation personalized calculation, please complete the form on the following page and return it to the Office of Planned Giving Division of University Advancement at Seton Hall University today.

Yes! I would like to learn more about helping to secure the future of The G.K. Chesterton Institute for Faith & Culture at Seton Hall University.

Please send me information about the following:

❑ Gifts of Appreciated Property   ❑ Life Income Gifts

❑ Gifts of Real Estate   ❑ Estate Planning

❑ I have included The G.K. Chesterton Institute for Faith & Culture at Seton Hall University in my estate plans.

❑ I would consider including The G.K. Chesterton Institute for Faith & Culture at Seton Hall University in my estate plans.

Name: _____

Address: _____

City: _____ State: _____ zip: _____

Telephone: (_____)_____

E-mail: _____

Best day and time to call: _____

Send to:

Director of Planned Giving
Seton Hall University
457 Centre Street
South Orange, New Jersey 07079-2691
Telephone: (973) 378-9850   Fax: (973) 378-2671
E-mail: *guascojo@shu.edu*

ORTHODOXY
Special Centenary Edition

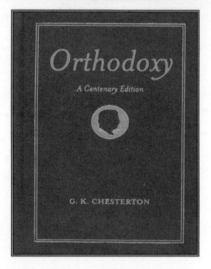

I would like to order _____copy(ies)

Name:_____

Mailing Address: _____

_____

City: _____ Zip Code:_____

Country:_____

Is this a gift: Yes   No

If yes, would you like it gift wrapped?: Yes   No

The Chesterton Review
in Portuguese

Edição Especial em Português

The
CHESTERTON REVIEW

CHESTERTON E OS CONTOS DE FADAS

ISSN 0317-0500   Volume I, Número 1 – janeiro / junho de 2009

The Chesterton Review
Is the journal of the
G. K. Chesterton Institute
For Faith & Culture

Founded in 1974

Fr. Ian Boyd, C.S.B.
President,
G. K. Chesterton Institute
For Faith & Culture
Editor
The Chesterton Review

For more information
contact our Editorial Office
at
chestertoninstitute@shu.e

The Chesterton Review Portuguese Language Supplement

Vol. I, No. 1— October 2009
Chesterton and Fairy Tales

Vol. II, No. 1 — October 2010
St. Thomas Aquinas and Chesterton

Editorial Board

Editor in Chief
Fr. Ian Boyd, C.S. B.
Managing Editor
Gloria Garafulich-Grabois
Editorial Board
Alex Catharino & Marcia Xavier de Brito

The Chesterton Review
in French

The Chesterton Review
Is the journal of the
G. K. Chesterton Institute
For Faith & Culture

Founded in 1974

Fr. Ian Boyd, C.S.B.
President,
G. K. Chesterton Institute
For Faith & Culture
Editor
The Chesterton Review

For more information
contact our Editorial Office
at
chestertoninstitute@shu.e

The Chesterton Review announces the publication of its

first French Language issue

Catholic Literary Revival in England and France in the 20th. Century

Vol. I, No. 1 — Fall 2010

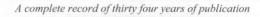

The Chesterton Review
En Español

The Chesterton Review
is the journal of the
G. K. Chesterton Institute
For Faith & Culture

Founded in 1974

Fr. Ian Boyd, C.S.B.
President,
G. K. Chesterton Institute
For Faith & Culture
Editor
The Chesterton Review

Cost:
US$15
Includes air mail shipping

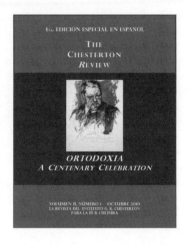

4th. EDICIÓN ESPECIAL EN ESPAÑOL

THE
CHESTERTON
REVIEW

ORTODOXIA
A CENTENARY CELEBRATION

VOLUMEN II, NÚMERO 1 - OCTUBRE 2010
LA REVISTA DEL INSTITUTO G. K. CHESTERTON
PARA LA FÉ & CULTURA

The Chesterton Review
announces the publication of the
fourth Spanish language issue.

Vol. IV
Orthodoxy
A Centenary Celebration

September 2010

Editorial Office:

400 South Orange Avenue
South Orange, N.J. 07079

Tel.: 973 275 2431
chestertoninstitute@shu.edu

Edición Especial en Español

The
CHESTERTON
REVIEW

Primera Conferencia Internacional Ibero-Americana

Segunda Edición Especial en Español
Argentina & Chile

The
CHESTERTON
REVIEW

Tercera Edición Especial en Español

The
CHESTERTON
REVIEW

Tercera Conferencia Internacional
Santo Tomás, Chesterton y
la civilización del amor

Seton Hall University
Center for Catholic Studies

Celebrating its 10th Anniversary

Faith for the Journey, Wisdom for a Lifetime

Featuring:

B.A. Degree Program
Major, minor and certificate programs available

Foreign Study Opportunities
Study Abroad at Oxford, Summer 2009

Bernard J. Lonergan Institute

G.K. Chesterton Institute for Faith & Culture
Featuring The Chesterton Review

Micah Senior Executive Project

Institute on Work

Monsignor Richard M. Liddy, Director

For more information, please contact:
(973) 275-2525 or *nourseda@shu.edu*

Please visit our Web site at *academic.shu.edu/ccs*

Subscribe to **Gilbert Magazine** and Join the
American Chesterton Society for One Low Price: **$42**

Former *Scientific American* magazine columnist Martin Gardner describes *Gilbert Magazine* as "one of the great delights of my life." You will be delighted, too. It's The Magazine About Everything! From current events in the eye of history to pop culture, from family economics to religion, art, and the life of the mind, *Gilbert Magazine* sheds light on the *what is* of human experience.

Each issue features original Chesterton essays, poems, quotations, drawings, and the ever-popular "Chesterton's Mailbag." Regular columnists include James V. Schall, David Beresford, and Dale Ahlquist. Illustrations by popular artists such as Ben Hatke and Ted Schluenderfritz grace its pages. Reviews of the best in books and film, surprising interviews, and original short stories make for cover-to-cover reading. And, as always, the lively exchange of ideas from readers that makes Gilbert Magazine a standout from the crowd.

Join the American Chesterton Society and receive a 20 percent discount on books from its ever-expanding catalog. You will be supporting the efforts of the ACS to get Chesterton's words and ideas back into our classrooms and into the public arena. Be part of the Chesterton revival.

AMERICAN CHESTERTON SOCIETY

❑ Yes, sign me up for an annual membership in the ACS and send me *Gilbert Magazine* for $42.00.

❑ 3 years of Membership and the Magazine for $105.00.

Please make check or money order payable to the **American Chesterton Society** Or provide the following credit card information:

(VISA, MC, AM EX,DIS) _____   Exp. Date _____

_____
NAME

_____

_____
ADDRESS

_____
PHONE NUMBER

4117 Pebblebrook Circle, Minneapolis, MN 55437 phone 952-831-3096 fax 952-831-0387 email info@chesterton.org
Visit our web page at www.chesterton.org for our complete catalog

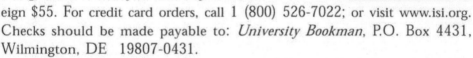

THE
LONERGAN
REVIEW

The Bernard J. Lonergan Institute

proudly announces the publication of *The Lonergan Review*

Edited by Richard M. Liddy

Vol. I, No. 1 of *The Lonergan Review*

General Empirical Method: Perspectives from Bernard Lonergan

Vol. II, No. 1 of *The Lonergan Review*

Forging a New Economic Paradigm

Publication date: January 2009

Publication date: January 2010

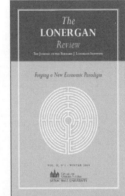

Editorial Office
Bernard J. Lonergan Institute, Seton Hall University, 400 South Orange Avenue, South Orange, N.J. 07079
Tel.: 973.275.2431—email: lonerganinstitute@shu.edu

☐ I would like to purchase _____ copies at US$20.00 each of *The Lonergan Review*

Payment enclosed: _____   Vol.I:_____ Vol. II:_____

Name:._____

Address:_____

City, State & Zip: _____

Telephone: _____

Email: _____

The Chesterton Review

The Chesterton Review *is the journal of the G.K. Chesterton Institute for Faith & Culture*

Editorial Office
400 South Orange Avenue
South Orange, N.J.

Phone: 973.275.2431
Fax: 973.275.2594

Dear Subscriber,

Have you experienced any difficulties with the delivery of the Review?

Have any issues for which you have subscribed failed to reach you?

Has your address changed recently?

For help with these difficulties or for any other enquiries, please contact our Editorial Office:

by e.mail: chestertoninstitute@shu.edu

by fax: 973.275.2594

by phone: 973.275.2431

We shall look into your query and get back to you promptly.

Thank you for your continued interest in *The Chesterton Review* and happy reading!